FAME AND INFAMY

FAME AND INFAMY

BLITZ EDITIONS

Copyright © Bookmart Ltd 1994

All rights reserved. No part of this publication may be reproduced,
stored in a retrieval system, or transmitted in any form or by any
means, electronic, mechanical, photocopying, recording or otherwise,
without prior written permission from the publishers.

Published by Blitz Editions
an imprint of Bookmart Ltd
Registered Number 2372865
Trading as Bookmart Ltd, Desford Road, Enderby
Leicester LE9 5AD

This book was produced
by Amazon Publishing Ltd

Cover design: Peter Dolton
Text design: Jim Reader
Production Manager: Sue Gray
Editorial Manager: Roz Williams

Printed in the Slovak Republic
51738

ISBN 1 85605 198 6

This material has previously appeared in *Fated Destiny*.

Every effort has been made to contact the copyright holders for the pictures.
In some cases they have been untraceable, for which we offer our apologies.
Thanks to the following: Ancient Art & Architecture Collection, Associated Press, Brooke Bond Oxo Ltd,
Bruce Coleman Ltd, Fortean Picture Library, Frank Spooner, Hulton Deutsch Collection Ltd,
Illustrated London News Picture Library, Library of Congress, Midsummer Books,
Peter Newark's American, Historical, Military and Western Americana Pictures, Popperfoto,
National Film Institute/Portfolio, Rex Features, Ian Drury, Jeff Spall, Syndication International,
Liba Taylor, Topham Picture Source.

` Cover: The top two and bottom right pictures supplied by the Hulton Deutsch Collection Ltd.
The bottom left by Popperfoto. Back cover picture supplied by the Hulton Deutsch Collection Ltd.

The Authors
Karen Farrington is a journalist who has worked for both national newspapers, and as a freelance, for the best
selling weekly women's magazines. Her broad experience has brought her into contact with some of the most
intriguing mysteries, compelling crimes and moving animal stories of recent times.

Nick Constable, also a journalist, has spent many years working in Fleet Street and covered top stories including
the famine of Ethiopia, the government-backed assassinations of street children in Brazil and the Gulf War.
He has also worked extensively to expose cruelty to animals in Britain and around the world.

Contents

FAME AND INFAMY

W e all have our dreams – we dream of winning a fortune, of being famous, or of simply living happily ever after. Fortunately for most of us, our dreams don't come true, for dreams have a nasty habit of turning into nightmares.

This book delves into the 'dream-world' of the rich and famous and exposes the tragedies that money can too often buy: the poor little rich boy who thought his fortune could purchase the right to kill; the Hollywood stars who find that their world of make-believe is no protection against the brutal demands of real life; and the ordinary people who find that the money they thought would buy them happiness brings nothing but misery.

Even the innocent creatures who share our world cannot escape the suffering which fame can inflict on them: the dolphin who committed suicide when she could no longer bear to be a performing clown, and the magnificent racehorse who died a bloody and ignominious death, are just two examples of the way that animals too, may be caught up in the vicious and seductive spiral of the search for power and glory.

As you read about the roller-coaster ride that is life, you will learn about the cruelly thin line that separates success and failure, and the terrible price that has to be paid by those who chase their own – or other people's – dreams.

RAGS AND RICHES

DREW BARRYMORE
A bright and burning star

Drew Barrymore's amazing performance in *E.T.* proved she was a true Barrymore – tragically so, since she was unable to escape the sordid destiny that had cursed America's greatest acting dynasty.

When she leant forward to kiss the alien from outer space on the tip of its pug nose, it seemed Drew Barrymore had the world in the palm of her innocent, baby-soft hand.

Cute and charismatic, the six-year-old was starring in one of cinema's biggest blockbusters, *E.T.* No heart could fail to melt at the tender tale of a bug-eyed creature from the stars who was stranded on Earth and fell into the arms of an American family.

And no one could resist the fair-skinned, wispy sensation who played Gertie, one of the three youngsters involved in the unearthly adventure to get E.T. safely home.

On-screen Drew made a bigger impact even than the endearing E.T. Director Steven Spielberg gently coaxed and cajoled an extraordinary performance from the youngster. She grasped the role with an instinctive talent and made it her own.

Pundits forecast a brilliant future for the starlet: surely she would be the Greta Garbo or Meryl Streep of her generation? But as the critical acclaim poured in, no one could foretell the personal hell that fate held in store for Drew.

At 6 she was on top of the world. By 9 she was a heavy drinker; a year later she smoked cannabis for the first time and before she was 13 she was a cocaine addict.

The world watched in horror as the girl with so much promise was sucked into the twilight world of alcohol and drugs at an age when she should have been playing in the park or doing homework.

It would take every ounce of courage she could muster to haul herself out of the mire. Hers was a shocking story in which history played an eerie part.

THE BURDEN OF THE BARRYMORES

Drew was a Barrymore, perhaps the greatest acting dynasty of America, and too many members of that highly talented family had fallen foul of drink or drugs or

both, and marched down a path to self-destruction. Along with success came a hopeless taste for excess.

A little older and Drew herself could have looked back at her ancestors to see how they had wreaked havoc living life in the fast lane. Perhaps she'd have summoned the strength of character which has since become one of her hallmarks, and side-stepped the road to hell. But she was much too young to understand what her father and grandfather before her had undergone. She was destined to take the rocky route they had trodden.

'Drew has always been overwhelmed by being part of such a glorious heritage and wanted to continue the tradition,' says a friend. 'She is a sweet girl and I think that

Opposite: Despite her problems Drew blossomed into one of Hollywood's most beautiful women. Perhaps success just came a little too soon.

Above: Aged 4, Drew was pleading to be allowed to audition for film roles. Two years later she was, for a while, the world's biggest child star.

A BRILLIANT FUTURE BECKONED – BUT DREW WANTED TO LIVE LIFE IN THE FAST LANE THAT LED TO HELL.

Above: *Drew was the fourth generation of an acting dynasty.*

she has been led astray by the movie and TV business. This is an industry that has often led to tragedy for the children of the famous.'

In the end, she proved a match for any of her hard-drinking, fast-living relatives from the past.

The Barrymores' roots were in England: that's where Herbert Albert Blythe punched his way into the history books by becoming the amateur middleweight boxing champion of the nation. He was the best and he loved being top of the pile.

But there was little the old country could offer him when his prowess in the ring started to fade. Casting around for a new direction, Herbert fell into acting. There was only one place where he could realize his high ambitions – America.

He set sail for New York and soon found success on Broadway with a new name, Maurice Barrymore. It seemed the faith he had in his own abilities was not misplaced.

In the final gay decades of the 19th century, he was riding high on a string of stage successes and had married America's top comedienne, Georgia Drew.

Together they had three children, two boys called Lionel and John and a girl called Ethel, but their joy was not to last. Georgia died suddenly from illness and

Maurice couldn't stand the pain. He consoled himself with a bottle. Maurice died in 1905 in a clinic, suffering from alcoholism and insanity.

Although the writing was on the wall, all three children eventually took up an acting career.

The eldest, Lionel, first studied art. It wasn't until talking movies were made that he really found top form. He won an Academy Award for best actor in the film *A Free Soul* in 1930, ironically playing a drunk when he himself was the black sheep of the family as he hardly touched the hard stuff. But it was as Dr Gillespie in the series of films about the strife and times of dashing Dr Kildare that he is best remembered.

The ravages of arthritis and the effects of a serious fall left him wheelchair-bound when he was still a young man, but it didn't end his fame or popularity. His enduring success proved a tough act to follow for younger members of the clan. He died aged 76 in 1954.

Ethel, meanwhile, had shunned the allure of Hollywood in preference for a life on the stage which brought her considerable wealth. She also showed her personal mettle when she headed the actors' strike against Broadway

Right: *Acting together for the first time in 1912, John and Ethel Barrymore both went on to find fame on the silver screen.*

management at a time when union power carried flimsy weight. It dented her popularity with the impresarios of the day, of course. But she fought back to continue her career which ended only two years before her death in June 1959, aged 80.

Her greatest accolade was an Academy Award for being the best supporting actress in the film *None but the Lonely Heart* in 1944 during one of her brief flirtations with the film industry.

But history probably remembers her best for launching the career of her firebrand brother John, Drew's infamous grandfather.

Youngest of the trio, he had resolved not to enter acting. Instead he strived to be a journalist or artist. But destiny had other ideas. When he found himself aged 20 and out of work, his sister Ethel found him a job as a bit part actor in the stage show she was in at the time.

It was enough to give the handsome charmer the acting bug. And his considerable skills earned him national stardom when a play called *Glad of It* swept to fame on Broadway.

He was the toast of the town. But John Barrymore was already drinking to success all night and all day. His huge appetite for life, like his father before him, led to booze binges which won him notoriety before he reached 30.

However, it seemed nothing could stop the steamroller that was John Barrymore's career. The age of movies was beginning and he was ready to seize the opportunities it could offer a handsome, go-ahead actor.

He made his film debut as early as 1913 in a silent film called *An American Citizen*. When talkies took cinema by storm, his silky tones were ideal and it assured his future as a matinee idol who could set pulses racing with a flashing smile and smoothly delivered words of love.

Off-screen he was wilder and more tempestuous than any of the roles he played. He married four times, fathering a daughter, Diana, by his second wife, and son, John Junior, by his third wife Dolores Costello.

As a child, John Junior saw little of his well-known dad. Soon the name John Barrymore was synonymous with drunken womanizing and he became loathed for his outrageous ways across Hollywood. And that was the only role model John Junior knew.

In 1932 John Senior was caught urinating in a ladies' toilet by the shocked wife of a producer. 'Excuse me, this is for ladies,' she uttered with a blush. 'So, Madam, is this,' said the unrepentant Barrymore buttoning his trousers.

Another incident which compounded his infamy was when he hurled a 10-year-old actress across the set because she had upstaged him during a scene. Luckily she was caught by some stage-hands without sustaining injury.

Alcohol soon took its toll. Once a brilliant interpreter of Shakespeare, the swashbuckling hero became dependent on reading cue cards because his memory was failing. In and out of sanatoriums, he was finally reduced to playing ham comedy and was the stooge on a radio show playing

Above: *John Barrymore Junior, the debonair actor who loved the high life – with catastrophic results.*

ON-SCREEN THE MATINEE IDOL WOULD SEND WOMEN INTO A SWOON; OFF-SCREEN HE WAS MORE LIKELY TO SEND THEM CRASHING ACROSS THE ROOM.

Above: *John Barrymore Junior and his first wife, Cara Williams. Their relationship was turbulent and sometimes violent.*

opposite Rudy Vallee. It was while he was rehearsing for one of these shows that he died in 1942, aged 60 and with hardly a dollar to his name.

The mercurial heart-throb left a ruinous inheritance to his children.

John Junior grew up with this tainted view of fatherhood. While he may have longed for a dad who would play baseball or read stories, he witnessed a fallabout drunk with no respect for women or the establishment.

Diana blamed her father's neglect for a failed acting career and inner turmoil which led to three wrecked marriages. She also turned to drink, attempted suicide and was found dead in her New York home in 1957, aged 38, killed by the effects of alcohol.

VOLCANIC RAGES

John Junior tried to establish himself in films but was overshadowed by the ghost of his more famous father and more popular uncle. He found himself avidly watched by newspapers, not because of his acting achievements, but for the boozing, brawling and violent rows he had with his first wife, Cara Williams, which led him into trouble with the police.

After a jail term for possessing cannabis he secluded himself in the Californian desert, returning after some years to play in unremarkable low-budget European films.

Against this stormy background, Drew entered the world carrying the burden of the Barrymore clan on her fragile, velvety shoulders.

Her mother, Hungarian actress Ildiko Jaid, was Barrymore's third wife. Even when she was pregnant, Ildiko suffered from the volcanic rages which erupted without warning in her heavy-drinking husband. It was no surprise that this union also failed when Drew was only a few months old.

When she was 3, Drew can recall her dad storming into the kitchen, pushing her mum to the floor, hurling her across the room and charging off with a bottle of drink. This was their reunion after more than two years apart.

At school, the young Drew quickly learned another of life's harsh lessons. Other children reckoned she had a boy's name. It was the kind of ammunition that kids love and they made her life a misery with constant barracking.

In the end, she left school to have an alternative education at home. While other children settled down to *Sesame Street*, Drew rebelled. She now admits she was scared at the sight of outsized puppet Big Bird.

Her bedtime stories were not nursery rhymes or Disney tales but complex tomes by Dostoyevsky and Henry Miller. Lullabies were by Janis Joplin or the Doors. Perhaps this early sampling of glitz and grit armed her for later exploits.

With her breeding, it was no surprise she was going to act and at just 11 months she made her screen debut, starring in a dog-food commercial. Concerned at the bizarre life-style led by child stars, her mother stopped auditioning her when she was 2. But by 4 Drew herself asked to be allowed to resume her career.

It was a matter of months before the chance for international fame came with auditions for the new Steven Spielberg film. Already a celebrated director, Spielberg was determined that this project would be the epic he dreamed of.

Carefully he scrutinized the 31 nervous hopefuls who lined up yearning for the part

of Gertie. One stood out as having enough sparkle and innate expertise for the demanding role. It was Drew.

For a while, Spielberg became the father-figure she yearned for.

'I wanted so badly to be accepted by him – and when I was, it meant so much to me,' said Drew later.

'I was thrilled when he invited me to his Malibu house. We'd run along the beach and build sandcastles. It was so much fun to be with him. But working with Steven was even better. Often he let me do whatever I wanted.

'He would often take me aside and ask if I could do something a different way. It made me feel so good. For once I didn't feel like some stupid kid. I felt important and useful.'

She recalls that making the film was the best time of her life. Her young head was brim-full of fantasies and make-believe, so it was a dream come true to be with the Spielberg creation E.T. every single day. It wasn't important that he was a studio-made dummy, reliant on special effects to come alive. To her eyes, he was real and she believed in him.

> **WITH A DRUNKEN FATHER, AND BULLIED AT SCHOOL, DREW'S LIFE WAS A MISERY.**

Left: *Drew enjoyed few of the pleasures open to other children of her age after she was thrust into the limelight.*

Below: *Spielberg and E.T. The blockbuster film grossed more than $700 million and was seen by at least 240 million cinema visitors after its release in 1982.*

Above: *The screen kiss that sealed Drew's fate. Thousands were captivated by her, but the pressure of superstardom nearly wrecked her life.*

'On lunch breaks I'd take my food into the room where he was kept, sit down beside him and carry on a conversation while I ate.'

She stayed at the Universal Sheraton Hotel before the release of the film with her screen brothers Henry Thomas and Robert McNaughton, by now her closest friends.

At night they would keep themselves awake by telling each other ghost stories. During the day they would chase each other around and have wild food fights. They were larking about together when the TV flashed up how record cinema queues were forming to see the new hit film, *E.T.* 'We're in that,' screamed Drew breathlessly, but she had no idea how that one film would change her life for ever.

For Drew those happy months during and shortly after filming were the last vestiges of childhood that she could cling to.

NIGHTMARE FAME

When the film opened, it was a roaring hit. She describes it as like walking into a thunderstorm. Drew became public property with an army of fans made up of children and adults alike.

Every time she ventured out she found swarms of autograph-hunters at her heels. As she walked down the street people would point and stare. Some even called her E.T.

There was no all-embracing family life to protect her. Drew Barrymore's childhood was swallowed up by stardom.

'I was expected to be a role model after *E.T.* Kids loved me and I had thousands of fan letters. But the kids didn't know what I was going through. After *E.T.* it was like an earthquake. People wanted things from me and expected me to be much older. It was very frightening,' she explained.

The wrinkly alien she had once adored

turned into a spectre which was to haunt her. She was living the glittering life of a superstar – but deep inside she knew she would have swapped the trappings of Hollywood for the comfort and security of two loving parents.

Her father ignored the international acclaim won by his young daughter. He failed to acknowledge the heights to which she had been catapulted.

Meanwhile her mother, once a hard-working actress, gave up her career to become Drew's manager. Was the girl simply an unloved meal ticket?

Of course, her mother was only doing her level best to support young Drew, but through the child's eyes, it seemed a calculated and manipulative move. By now Drew was unmistakably different from other girls of her age, set apart by her life-style and her character. It wasn't long before she embarked on the addictive behaviour which seemed to be born to the Barrymores. At first, she got hooked on behaving outrageously, almost certainly to attract the attention of her mum.

Without the discipline of school, there was little to curb her wilful ways. And with estimated annual earnings of £100,000, it seemed no one could stop Drew from going her own way.

Aged 9 she was a pert young madam acting like a 29-year-old and relishing the opportunity to sample champagne. With that first glass of bubbly started a long-term addiction to drink. It was in the same year that she learned to drive and started smoking.

At 10 she was booked to fly to Germany for a three-hour television film called *Babes in Toyland*. She teamed up with pop legend Rod Stewart who had a gig in town and was thrilled to travel on his tour bus back to a hotel.

BLIND DRUNK

While the gravelly-voiced singer retired, Drew stayed up with members of the entourage and got blind drunk. At 4 am they decided to play musical instruments including trumpets and drums as loud as they could. The impromptu session ended when the hotel manager blazed at them, threatening to throw them out if the racket continued. In league with the rest, she made sure her mother didn't find out about

the incident. But at home with mum her life was far from normal.

Together with friends in the same jet-setting world, she would dress up in seductive mini-skirts, black lace blouses, high heels and make-up. Her mum mistook

THE WRINKLY ALIEN SHE'D ONCE ADORED TURNED INTO A GRUESOME SPECTRE WHICH RUINED HER YOUNG LIFE.

the temptress garb as innocent dressing up. She would even compliment the girls on how lovely they looked. Then together they would visit a swish club. Parents instructed the youngsters to stay on a balcony overlooking the action while they danced below.

However, it gave the girls ample opportunity to sample the delights of the adult world. They would take it in turns to raid drinks left on the bar by unsuspecting clubbers. They would knock back anything that came their way.

And, of course, they took their place on the dance floor with the rest of the

Above: *Drew giving an interview. While most children of her age were doing schoolwork, she became the darling of the media.*

Right: *Drew in make-up. She looked and behaved far older than her years.*

Below: *A sophisticated Drew out on the town.*

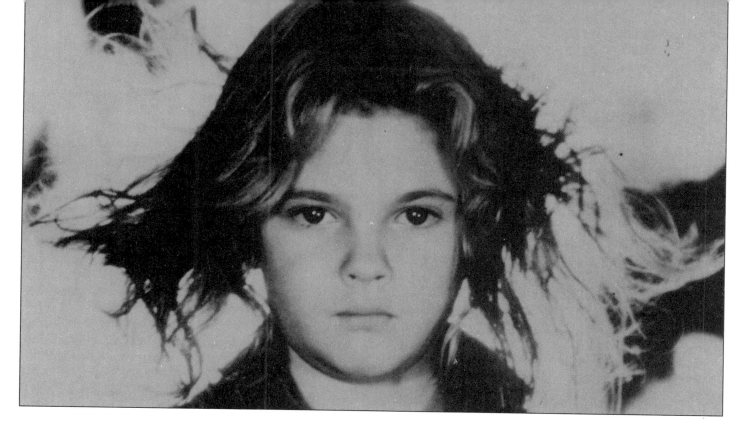

revellers, imitating the sexy swaying of the older women in the room.

It led to a banner headline: 'Drew Barrymore dancing at 2 am. Shouldn't she be in bed?'

But far from chastising the youngster, the headline made her determined no one would tell her what to do or how to do it.

It was on her way home from a club that she took her first marijuana. In the early hours she was going to spend the night at a friend's house when the young pal's mother lit up a pot-smoking pipe. Glancing around with a serene smile, the woman asked if anyone wanted to try it.

Without hesitation, Drew volunteered and soon mastered the technique of using the drug.

A few puffs left her helplessly giggling although she insisted between spasms of laughter that it was having no effect. Sure that she was in control, she wondered what taking cocaine would be like. She could not resist the prospect of experimenting.

Addiction to cocaine was no different for little rich kids like Drew than for ordinary drop-outs on the street. Quickly she was hooked and she craved her next fix of the designer drug. Without it, her palms began to sweat and she cannot remember without flinching how her head was filled with a flashing sign saying: 'Coke, get Coke'. The nightmare was well and truly under way.

A CRY FOR HELP

In her early teens Drew made a desperate bid to escape her private torment with a dramatic attempt at suicide.

It followed a row with her mum who then flew to New York. Drew found herself sobbing uncontrollably as she realized she was alone and totally lonely. Her mother's parting words were echoing in her ears: 'I have washed my hands of you, I don't give a damn what you do.' Drew was too distraught to understand the words were said on the spur of the moment and meant nothing. In an almost defiant gesture she took a knife from the kitchen and pulled it across her pale, vulnerable wrist.

She was saved by a friend who was alerted by Drew's hysterical telephone call. As Drew says later in her autobiography, *Little Girl Lost*, it was a cry for help. 'I wanted to get the most attention and sympathy. I didn't want to die.'

A family friend said at the time: 'Drew is a child who never was a child. She gets herself into adult situations. Everyone forgets she is only 14 years old.'

It was inevitable that she would end up in a clinic. Her admission into a therapy centre came after a noisy and violent row with her mother. Ignoring a midnight curfew, Drew drank, took drugs and then took exception to her mother. She rang and told her to get out of the house.

Left: *Little girl lost? In her autobiography, written when she was 14, Drew spoke frankly about her drug and drink dependency.*

THE KITCHEN KNIFE CUT ACROSS THE PALE, SOFT FLESH OF HER WRIST AND THE BLOOD SPURTED OUT.

Above: *Drew eventually found happiness after kicking drink and drugs. She once told reporters with a smile: 'I'm a girl who has lived a lotta life.'*

a regime of rules and regulations. It was easy to sneer at the soul-baring sessions to begin with and Drew only grudgingly joined in. But by the time she left a fortnight later to start a new film, she resolved to abandon the bottle.

It was easy enough at work to fight the urge for a drink – there were constant distractions, not to mention her mother's watchful gaze.

But at play the temptations were always at hand. Even friends who knew she was fighting against a drink-and-drugs habit would offer her alcohol and cocaine. The consequences were disastrous.

A fine record of 76 days without a drink was wiped out in one late-night session. With it went Drew's painfully constructed self-esteem. She vowed to escape by flying off to Hawaii.

When she returned home to pack some clothes she found a stranger in her room who snapped on some handcuffs. Her concerned mum had called agents from a drug centre who were willing to intervene to stop Drew's recklessness.

It wasn't the last time Drew would go to a centre to help control her addictive ways. And each time Drew was brought a bit closer to the realms of clean living that were her goal.

She began to learn that she had to face up to problems rather than hide behind drink and drugs. While they may have shielded her from the pain, they certainly didn't solve anything. In therapy she met other girls like herself who were running wild. It made her realize that, contrary to her beliefs, she was not isolated and alone.

The fact that Drew could write an action-filled autobiography when she was 14 is an indication of how extraordinary her early years were. She was fortunate in that her highly publicized descent from grace didn't end her career. In time producers got back in touch and she remained a hot property in Hollywood. In recent years she has proved she is no longer driven by drink. And she has reaped the rewards with major film roles including a sinister belle in *Gun Crazy* and a trickster in *Poison Ivy*.

Today she is more likely to stay at home lying on her sunflower bedspread and reading books or painting T-shirts than she is to go cavorting in clubs. The only

When she returned home just before dawn Drew was incensed to find her still there. She started throwing anything she could lay her hands on at her mum who looked on helplessly.

Suddenly, Ildiko picked up the telephone and called a friend. Drew, overcome by the drink and emotion, didn't resist their bid to take her to a clinic.

For the first time in years she was facing

addiction she has not been able to kick is a love of Camel cigarettes. She cherishes the time she spends with friends.

But it has taken years to reach this happy plateau. The hell-raising days didn't stop when the therapy was over. She was 15 when she paid £1,000 for four tattoos on her breast, backside, arm and ankle. And she continued to attend wacky parties despite her pledge of clean living.

She put her house on the market after being plagued by a night stalker who breached her home's security fences and peered in at the windows. At the time she revealed she frequently walks around California in disguise because the pressure of being recognized is so great.

BETRAYED

Her love life has been another disappointing tangle. She was paired with Balthazar Getty at 15, the son of ill-fated oil empire heir John Paul Getty III. He was there to listen and advise when she first began emerging from the haze of the addiction years. There were other more fleeting associations and finally an engagement to an engineer, but at 17 it fell apart because of the binding ties of her job.

Her life's major romance was to actor Jamie Walters. They too marked their love with a ring and dreamed of days growing old together. But their relationship floundered.

The film industry that she is mostly wedded to still pulls no punches. She played the lead role in *The Amy Fisher Story* about a Lolita who shot her lover's wife. She enacted a 10-second sex scene fully clothed.

Without her knowledge, the makers used a body double to spice up the story with lurid romps. Viewers believed the wild child was back to her old ways.

The betrayal enraged her. 'I'm not like that,' she insisted afterwards. But it seems unlikely that she will abandon her acting heritage despite the knocks it has dealt her.

'I was thrown into so much so soon. It was expected of the Barrymores.

'And I have to admit I couldn't cope with it all. Drugs and booze were both available. So I thought, why not?

'Everybody has to touch the stove to see how hot it is. I was never one of those people who could just hear about it. I always had to touch.'

SHE SOUGHT PEACE BUT IT ELUDED HER: A NIGHT PROWLER STALKED THE GROUNDS OF HER HOME AND SPIED ON HER.

Below: *Drew won critical acclaim in* **Gun Crazy,** *a love-on-the-run story of murder and mayhem.*

VIV NICHOLSON
From spend, spend, spend
to scrub, scrub, scrub

Viv Nicholson had known only poverty and drudgery when a spectacular win on the pools transformed her life. But as she tried to spend her way to happiness, she discovered that money buys tragedy as well as joy.

The winners come and go. The jackpots get bigger every year. But for millions of Britain's ever-hopeful pools punters only one name lingers as 'the' winner who cornered the market in fame.

Her name is Viv Nicholson. Her edict was 'spend, spend, spend'. And perhaps more than any other living Brit she has gone from rags to riches and back in record time.

Viv was born in a two-up-two-down terrace home – No 38, Walling Street, Wheldon Lane, Castleford – on 3 April 1936. She was working from the moment her little limbs were strong enough, picking coal off the local pit-head tip or pea-picking in the nearby fields.

Her dad George, an epileptic, worked occasionally down the pit after failing to make it as a policeman and as a soldier in the Guards. For many of those early years Viv remembers the family income (his sick pay) disappearing behind the bar of the local.

At school she was good at art, sport and Bible classes but admitted she 'got the stick a lot on my backside'. She'd often play truant, spending her dinner money at the flicks or posing in front of the boys she fancied outside their school. Weekends she'd work in her Aunt Liz's shop, help her mum look after the younger kids and then make the evening trek to the pub to pick up her dad's beer.

Even her first wages from the nearby Liquorice Allsorts factory were handed over to the old man. She'd get back half-a-

crown pocket money – if she was lucky – and had to supplement her wages working at the Queens, the town cinema, until 11 pm. It was there she met a soldier called Barry and began necking with him. He would write her explicit and raunchy love-letters and in her biography *Spend, Spend, Spend*, she vividly recalls the beating her dad handed out when he discovered them.

'He hit me on the ribs at the side which he knew would cave me in anyway. Then he picked me up and he hit me again on the other side. I kept falling. I had a bloody lump on the side of my head where I'd hit the corner of this oak chair and my eye hit the other side of it.

'... Afterwards I was bad: I was vomiting all night, my head hurt, I didn't know which part of me to hold.'

After that Viv decided that if you got beaten for NOT having sex she might as well go ahead and try it. She lost her virginity to a young miner called Matthew Johnson – he would become her first husband – in his bedroom. Quickly she got pregnant from the affair and, despite her father's grumbles, decided to marry. She was 16, he was 23.

The relationship turned into a sham almost overnight. Viv rejected Matt's advances even as she waited to have his baby, Stephen. She said later that the

Opposite: *Viv Nicholson in 1971. Her image graced Fleet Street tabloids for years.*

Below: *Viv, second husband Keith and Bruce Forsyth at the cheque-presentation ceremony.*

Above: *Viv borrowed the brolly and bowler belonging to Littlewoods' chief Cecil Moore for this famous pose.*

THEY WERE SO POOR THAT VIV'S DINNER WAS A SLICE OF BREAD, USED TO WIPE THE KIDS' PLATES CLEAN.

prospect of raising children frightened her, though she stressed she loved the child deeply, and later admitted: 'At 17, stuck in that bleeding house baby minding I was only a kind of kid myself.

'I thought what a fool I was. But I'd enjoyed what I'd done so that is what you get for what you enjoy. That's what I told myself.'

BEG, STEAL OR BORROW

Things improved slightly when she and Matt moved out of his mother's place into a council house in Duke Street, but it wasn't to last. Viv had spied the handsome young miner living next door, called Keith Nicholson, and set about seducing him. Just as quickly she became pregnant with Sue and the marriage to Matt finally broke down.

More children followed – Timmy and Howard – and Viv and Keith moved out to a bigger house shortly before the divorce

was sealed. They married, but found the going tough. Keith's trainee wage was barely enough to see them through the week.

Viv said: 'The little bit he did get wasn't blinding worth it. It didn't go far.

'But I made sure those kids really had their fill. I'd only have what was left, even if it was just a little bit of mashed potato. I'd make about four potato sandwiches out of it for me and I'd really thoroughly enjoy it.

'Then I'd get my bread and chase it round their plates for a bit of dip. I hardly once sat down to a good square meal.

'... Keith thought he was providing money for us. You see, he didn't care how I managed. He brought home £7 or £8 a week clear, and I never told him I had to beg, steal or borrow.

'He thought we were doing great guns on it because although I hardly had enough to eat we had a three-piece suite, nice red carpet, nice little table lamp, a rented TV, eventually, and a standard lamp – all got on tick, of course.'

On 23 September 1961, Keith was, as usual, keeping an ear on the Saturday afternoon football results. He knew the numbers he'd picked but was also realistic enough to know the enormous odds stacked against him getting a big win.

He was shaving ready to go out that evening and as the fifth draw came up – he needed eight for a possible jackpot – remarked to Viv: 'It's a start love, eh?'

He'd cut his chin when number 5 was announced and he cut it again when 6 came up. At 7 he was grabbing a towel to staunch the blood pouring from the neck wounds and shouting 'That's it, that's it!'

He was celebrating what he thought would be a payout of a few hundred pounds but he was way out in his calculations. Excitedly he and Viv recovered their crumpled copy of the coupon from his trousers. Then she rushed to get her dad, who returned with the local Saturday sports paper. He and Keith lay on the floor as the old man checked the numbers.

'Tha's right Keith, there's seven draws, lad.'

Then a short pause and, almost as an afterthought: 'Tha's got the eighth too, Keith.'

Viv said: 'We wanted to celebrate and we had £1 between us.

'So I borrowed a few quid from my dad, who hadn't cared much for Keith till then, extracted the family allowance from my mother and off we all went to the local.'

THE TASTE OF FAME

Viv could take none of it in, not even when they sent off the telegram claim. It wasn't until 1.45 pm the following Monday that she began to believe she could be rich beyond imagination. She was making chip butties at the time.

There was a knock on the door and a fat man with grey hair asked: 'Does Keith Nicholson live here? I'm sorry we are a bit late but we are from Littlewoods Pools.'

Keith had ticked the no-publicity box on his coupon but got talked out of it by the PR men. The Nicholsons were taken to the Metropole Hotel in Leeds, out of the way of the hunting press men, before catching a train to London on the Wednesday.

Littlewoods, who had already paid out £200,000 to a winner in 1957, knew they were in for a good press, but even the most optimistic of their marketing people could never have dreamt so much free publicity was about to come their way.

So it was that when the 7 am train from Leeds pulled up in London Viv Nicholson tasted fame for the first time. A throng of reporters and photographers besieged her on the platform. One asked the inevitable question: 'What are you going to do with the money, Viv?'

Quick as a flash back came the reply: 'I'm going to spend, spend, spend.'

And spend they did. The only thing that stopped them starting right away was the insatiable demand of Fleet Street. Viv was photographed smiling at Bruce Forsyth, who presented her with the cheque, and then close to tears when she realized it was made out for £152,319. She was snapped dancing, jumping, hugging, even high-kicking in a famous pose which used Littlewoods' chief Cecil Moore's brolly and bowler as props.

Then it was an expensive hairdo (pink champagne blonde) followed by a trip to the Palladium to see Sammy Davis Junior and a Soho nightclub. Finally she and Keith returned to their suite at the Grosvenor Hotel and bathed in champagne and brandy.

From there it was back to Castleford and a free drinks party at their local pub, the Miners' Arms. It cost £200 – eight months' wages then – and Viv later described it as a

> **THEY CELEBRATED BY BATHING IN CHAMPAGNE AND BRANDY – AND THAT WAS ONLY THE BEGINNING OF THEIR WILD SPENDING SPREE.**

Below: *There was a lot of sneering and sniping in the press after Viv bought her dream home. But she didn't care.*

Above: *The sweet-factory girl made good. Fur coats and fast cars were suddenly no more than a signed cheque away for Viv and she realised every opportunity to unload her winnings.*

Right: *The serious-looking gentlemen with Viv were her financial advisers. They had every reason to look serious. As fast as they tried to invest her 'luvverly lolly' she blew it.*

bloody battlefield. But that was only the start. Viv bought a new car – an American Chevrolet, a £500 organ and a new house, No 11 Grange Avenue. She watched the begging (and hate) letters come and go and entertained hundreds of total strangers who'd start by buying her a drink and then expect the next ten rounds to be hers. Generous to a fault, Viv never failed to disappoint them.

By now the kids were in a private boarding school and Keith and Viv were free to throw party after party, to the chagrin of their new middle-class neighbours. Many would go on for days, lubricated by a seemingly unending supply of booze.

Keith, meanwhile, could indulge his love of fast cars. He also bought racehorses and top-of-the range shotguns and would laugh at the notion of rubbing shoulders with the nobs at Ascot or blazing away at grouse on some remote northern moor.

They were halcyon days and son Tim would later recall: 'It was like living on the edge of a volcano.

'Me and the other kids never knew what she was going to do next. There would be late-night parties, with Sparrow – we all call her that – bringing people she hardly knew in for free drinks. I don't resent her getting rid of all the money although, like everyone else, I would sooner be in a nice house with a decent car outside.

'They were only living on £7 per week when they won the pools. It's no wonder it went to their heads but it's no use worrying now the money is gone. My mother is kind and generous. I've seen her spend her last pound on a round of drinks.'

In her book Viv recalled: 'I was becoming an alcoholic … it would always be somebody's birthday or something.

'We'd even throw a party for a dog's birthday because we needed people.'

Only months after the big win had sunk in the money was draining away. Viv had taken little heed of the advice offered by the financial consultants put forward by Littlewoods. Her idea of investment was putting money into fun and she was not planning to waste time.

By 1964 Viv and Keith had spent around one-third of the money. The pressure of getting rich quick was now telling on

Keith. He couldn't understand why the bank was hassling him over an overdraft when he had £100,000 invested. In anger and frustration he'd tell Viv: 'Why don't they just take it out and stop pestering me and do what the hell they have to do with it? I've my life to lead.'

He would refuse even to open bank statements and would sometimes burn tax demands. And still neither of them wanted to put the brakes on their spending.

That year they chose just about the most expensive – and lengthy – holiday they could find. Viv wanted to see Dallas on the first anniversary of President John Kennedy's death, but they also took in Los Angeles and New York, and the bills kept on coming.

By the standards of the nineties their windfall was worth more than a million, to them a bottomless pit of cash. But it couldn't last. In 1965 the pit of cash was replaced by the pit of despair.

In later interviews Viv always insisted the loss of the 'luvverly lolly' didn't worry her. She'd set out to have a good time and that's exactly what she'd done. After all nothing was for ever, was it?

DISASTER STRIKES

Then that year Keith was killed in a car crash and Viv discovered the true meaning of loss. Her world fell apart. She later spoke of him as the only one of her five husbands she'd ever truly loved.

Keith had been on his way back from Wetherby races when it happened. By astonishing coincidence – Viv later believed it was a sign from beyond the grave – her own brand-new Chevrolet broke down at almost exactly the same moment as she drove to see relations in Sheffield. In her grief she took to drinking and popping the occasional sleeping pill. On one occasion the memories overwhelmed her and she packed the kids into a car to go and visit Keith's grave at midnight, a kind of crude but heartfelt therapy to assuage the tremendous loss they all felt. Later she admitted: 'I was so bad tempered. Talk about Jekyll and Hyde.'

In those difficult months Viv found herself living off a widow's pension and social security benefit. Keith's death meant his £100,000 estate was frozen. Even the £10 they found on his body was taken away. The bank called her and told her that all she had was £10 per week to live on from a trust fund.

She recalled how one bank official told her: 'Well, what a life.

'You've had three different kinds of lives: you've had poverty, you've had the very rich and what's this got to be? It's got to be the middle class, hasn't it?'

Viv, who now owed the bank £4,000, decided to fight to get her share of the will. She survived by bouncing the occasional cheque and selling what possessions she could. It wasn't until months later that she was awarded £34,000 by a court for proving that the stake money was hers. She put £14,000 into the kids' school trust fund and blew the rest: a holiday in Malta while she searched to buy a business, another new car, and then a fashion shop in Castleford.

It was a disastrous venture and by the time the VAT and tax people had taken

> THE FRIGHTENED CHILDREN WERE BUNDLED INTO THE CAR FOR A MIDNIGHT VISIT TO KEITH'S GRAVE.

Below: *Viv could never resist posing for a camera and she made the most of her numerous wedding days. Here the lucky man is Graham Ellison. She thought he was terribly handsome … but the marriage lasted just six months.*

Above: *With fourth husband Brian Wright on their wedding day. He proved a jealous lover.*

Right: *With Gary Shaw, husband number 5. He and Keith were her true lovers.*

HAUNTED BY THE PAST,
VIV TOOK ONE PILL, AND
THEN ANOTHER, AND THEN
ANOTHER …

their share, Viv Nicholson was back where she started. Living in Castleford. And broke.

Lonely – but determined not to be – Viv set out to seek true love once more. It proved a fruitless search that saw her take on, and lose, a string of husbands. As she put it: 'Falling in love … that's what life is all about, isn't it?'

Throughout the rest of the sixties and early seventies Viv tested that theory to its limits. Sadly, true love always seemed to be one step away. Marriage number 3 was to car salesman Graham Ellison, but they stayed together for only six months. 'He was terribly handsome,' Viv would admit later. 'He used to call me Mags Diamond.'

Fourth husband was nightclub doorman Brian Wright. He proved to be a jealous lover and the relationship was marked by almost constant bickering. Wright later died, again in a car crash.

Fifth – and last – spouse was Gary Shaw. He died in her arms from a drugs overdose just seven weeks after they exchanged their vows. It left her totally distraught. Gary was later buried beside her beloved Keith.

In 1978 all the anguish of those difficult years came to a head. By now Viv was getting the first warnings from doctors to kick her 20-a-day smoking habit and give up alcohol. They argued it would be better for her health and help control her arthritis and stomach ulcers.

She did, in fact, try to go on the wagon but later declared: 'They were the most miserable three weeks of my life.

'Doctors told me I would end up in an emergency ward if I did not change my ways.

'There is no fun at all in going out for a night and sipping orange juice with a long face. I have taken my life into my own hands.'

They were brave words but Viv's past still haunted – and taunted – her. On 4 February 1978 she came within a whisker of following three of her husbands to the grave. From her Castleford home she telephoned a friend and revealed she'd taken some sleeping tablets. The friend didn't like the sound of her voice and decided to call an ambulance, just to be on the safe side.

When the crew dashed into her house at 4 am they found her lying unconscious in a bedroom. She was immediately admitted to hospital as an emergency, but later Viv insisted she hadn't deliberately taken an overdose. In one remarkably frank interview she said: 'There is a 36-hour gap in my life. I have no idea what happened.'

A SECRET FEAR

She speaks of waking up in the Pontefract Infirmary with a 'secret fear' engulfing her. It had been brought on by the glimpse of an old lady in a nearby bed. In that woman's tired, worn face Viv saw herself in years to come and began to realize her own mortality. She told of feeling a desperate urge to escape, of an obsession about getting old and of the anguish she endured watching her father take two years to finally die at the age of 60. Perhaps most telling of all she spoke of 'getting out' while she still looked good.

Viv added: 'I want to be remembered as a striking lady with sex appeal.

'When I look at actresses like Bette Davis and see how they have wilted I think it is a pity that somehow their beauty couldn't be preserved. I want the impossible. I want time to be stopped. I want to turn the clock back.'

In the interview Viv returned again and again to her 'hobby horse' – the fears felt by women as they grew older and realized that sex appeal had a shelf life. Men, she said, could still pull the birds when they got old and wrinkly. Women saw this happening and feared being left alone.

She spoke of herself as being 'halfway to Paradise' at 41 and admitted it was the 'decay of the body' that scared her.

She added: 'I know it's time I started settling down. I don't want to get to 50 and meet some guy who will just be a fireside companion.'

She spoke of how fame, and her reputation for walking on the wild side of life, had made her almost an oracle in the eyes of some young men. 'Guys come up to me with problems about their wives,' she said. 'They are mainly young men. They complain that their wives won't even discuss sex problems with them. I have to answer the best way and show that I am interested. Women who are having trouble with their husbands also expect me to know all the answers.

'In fact, I sometimes feel like the Marje Proops of Castleford.'

Released from hospital Viv returned home with a new-found optimism, yet she had hardly had time to fully recover from the overdose scare before the next crisis developed. She was stopped by police on

suspicion of drink-driving and accused of failing to provide a specimen for lab tests. In fact, a court later found her not guilty of driving while unfit through drink.

But magistrates still ordered her to pay £294 in fines and compensation and banned her from driving. Viv was outraged and promptly vowed to go to prison rather than stump up the cash for what she saw as trumped-up charges. She claimed she was 'sick and tired of being harassed by the police'.

Sure enough the fines stayed unpaid and she was given a 6-week sentence at the 'Grisly Risley' remand centre near Warrington, Cheshire. It was perhaps the lowest point of her amazing life. Stories appeared in the papers describing how she was given a job cleaning the floor of a prison corridor known among inmates as the Golden Mile.

Under the headline 'Scrub, Scrub, Scrub Viv' it was claimed she worked for just 49p per week to buy cigarettes. Yet once the sentence was over she was quickly back to her old self … and again looking for love.

JINXED

Twice she thought she'd found husband number 6. Each time her hopes were sadly dashed. First came a 25-year-old divorcé,

Above: Viv's children Steve and Sue call at 'Grisly Risley' remand centre, where Viv was taken to serve her sentence.

Above: *Viv and Bernard Curran. But wedding number 6 never happened.*

Right: *Viv with her sons Steve and Howard in March 1977.*

Son Howard Nicholson later revealed there had been a last-minute disagreement between the couple. It was two years before Viv tried again, this time to a man she met in a whirlwind romance. She accepted his proposal but then ditched him when she found out he was already married.

He pleaded that he was separated and had planned to wed her after his divorce came through. But it was no good. Viv declared he'd tried to make a fool of her and he was kicked out of her life.

It seemed, in her own words, that she was just 'a born loser' in love and marriage. In the past she had often talked of a jinx on her life, a belief heightened when the actress Susan Littler (who played her in the award-winning TV play *Spend, Spend, Spend*) succumbed to cancer aged just 33. Yet by now a subtle transformation was beginning in Viv Nicholson. For the first time in her life she had begun to take a genuine interest in religion and found she could look beyond the frustrations and pain that so dominated her days as Britain's best-known pools winner.

She was persuaded to go along to the local Kingdom Hall meeting of Jehovah's Witnesses. And she later recalled: 'Everyone was so happy I just cried.'

In August 1982 Viv appeared on the BBC 1 series *Sin on Saturday* to talk about the deadly effects of covetousness. In an interview published that day she joked that she didn't even know what covet meant until she joined the Witnesses.

Bernard Curran, 16 years her junior. He was a market trader in children's clothes and Viv would joke that she'd finally managed to marry into money.

But on the big day – fixed for 13 May 1978 – neither of them turned up. A congregation of around 600 had to kick their heels outside the Castleford register office before eventually giving up and going home.

Through them, she said, almost all traces of her old existence had disappeared.

'I was always the one to go from the sublime to the ridiculous,' she said. 'I've never been the halfway type. At a crossroads I've always wanted to go all four ways. I'd probably have finished up in a mental home if I hadn't let it all hang out. I was always rebelling against my father. But Jehovah accepts you when you're ready to give up your past and I've finally found the real me.

'It's hard work coveting things, believe me. I couldn't sleep at night for worrying about things I wanted. Jehovah's Witnesses's beliefs are contrary to everything I've ever done. But I've never been as happy in my life. You don't give up the seven deadly sins to be unhappy, do you?'

She made it clear she no longer accepted the idea of a jinx on her life, even though she'd been through a recent cancer scare (two aunts died of the disease). The cancer tests were clear and she regards the whole upsetting episode philosophically as the will of Jehovah.

As for publicity and the TV appearance – no, she didn't much like publicity, she said, but she'd made an exception for *Sin on Saturday*.

'I love Jehovah and thought I'd have a go at witnessing for Him on TV since the Witnesses never get a plug on the Sunday religious shows.'

Viv speaks with pride of the 'services' she carries out – door-to-door preaching aimed at persuading more people to join her religion. Far from the popular belief that Jehovah's Witnesses are used to slammed doors, she remembers only one rebuff that really hurt.

'It was many years ago; a lady came to the door who'd had a recent bereavement, she'd lost her father.

'I said: "Don't worry, Jehovah will return him." She said: "You can talk; how many husbands have you had back?"

'I suppose she was reacting to the bad profile the press has given me over the years. I keep a chart of the man-hours I put in. If someone new is baptized I don't take it as a personal compliment but as a sign that God is working through me.

'It's good that we work with the angels who guide us to the right doors. We are taught to be humble.'

THE SIMPLE LIFE

In one interview, in 1989, she revealed: 'Sometimes people ask: "Aren't you Viv Nicholson?" I reply: "Yes, what's left of her." But people still talk about me because I know how to live life and they've never tried it.

'They need a psychiatrist. I don't because I've worked out my problems. I studied the Bible and found it was the truth.'

Viv's life is now a world apart from that of the excitable extrovert who first shot to fame so many years ago. She now speaks with fondness of the simple pleasures in her life – completing *The Sun* crossword, reading her copy of the Witnesses' journal, *Watchtower*, or spending time with her grandchildren. She enjoys ironing and vacuuming, household chores which she finds soothe her thoughts.

And she's not too proud to work – a part-time post in a perfume shop, paying less than £100 per week, has been among the jobs she's taken.

'People ask me if I still do the pools,' she says. 'Of course I don't, it's against my religion. I miss absolutely nothing from the past. I mean, once I could drink in the pub all evening, get through money like there was no tomorrow.

'True, I had a lot of fun but it's hard work having money and I certainly did spend.

'I wouldn't want it again.'

'**THE ANGELS GUIDE US TO THE RIGHT DOORS. WE ARE TAUGHT TO BE HUMBLE.**'

Below: *In 1984, with the money long gone, Viv is just another grandmother.*

MARLENE DIETRICH
Falling in love again

She'd dreamed of being a concert violinist but fate put paid to her dreams. Instead Marlene Dietrich was destined to become one of Hollywood's most famous actresses, and notorious for her outrageous love life.

A bowed figure patiently pressed the bell of an apartment block in a Parisian avenue.

His hair was grey, his lean face lined, but there was no mistaking the identity of the caller. It was James Stewart, matinee idol and Hollywood legend. Even in his 70s, his presence was enough to cause a stir.

He waited for the door to open. He could reasonably have expected it to be flung wide for a greeting of kisses and joyous exclamations. But the welcome he had hoped for was not forthcoming. Instead the door was opened just a few inches. Peering out from the shadows was an equally famous face from Hollywood's heyday, but there were no smiles, no embraces, no warmth at all.

No, he could not come in. And no, she would not come out. After a tense exchange, James Stewart departed, bemused and anxious.

For half a century they had been friends. Now screen goddess Marlene Dietrich was refusing to meet him. As she closed the door in his face, her pain was palpable. She couldn't bear a man who had once surveyed her fabulous body with pleasure and longing to see it raddled by old age. Brittle bones beneath a withering skin were frequently fractured and left her in constant distress. The lines of agony were etched on to a face which was once as smooth as an apple. The hair was now limp and lacklustre thin. None of this was surprising.

Marlene was born at the turn of the century. Now it was the closing quarter and

she had aged in the same way as the world about her, but Marlene had no time for the toll of the rolling years.

Seven years after she kept Stewart on the doorstep he returned with fellow actor Roddy McDowall. This time they were graciously allowed an audience. Afterwards she commented bitterly: 'James has a beer belly, I can hardly walk. We are both ancient ruins.'

He wasn't the only pal she refused to acknowledge. She met film director Billy Wilder in 1928 – he was her oldest surviving associate from the film industry – but even he received a cold shoulder. 'I call her up whenever I'm in Paris. She answers in a different accent every time, either French, Polish or Czech, telling me Miss Dietrich has gone to Switzerland.

'I always call her bluff. I say: "For Christ's sake, Marlene, cut the bull. I know it's you." She then either hangs up or invents some phoney reason why she can't see me. She doesn't want to be reminded of the past.'

For 15 years the performer and party-goer who was escorted by some of the

Above: *Billy Wilder, one of Marlene's oldest friends. He said of her: 'I call her up whenever I'm in Paris. She answers in a different accent every time … telling me Miss Dietrich has gone to Switzerland. I always call her bluff.'*

Opposite: *Marlene, the screen goddess.*

century's most adored men shunned the public's gaze. Fiercely private, she allowed only a few chosen people to witness her physical degeneration. They included her secretary, a radio producer and her butcher. The lonely and frugal life she led in the years leading up to her death in 1992 were a stark contrast to her opulent existence as screen queen during some four decades.

Marlene was born as the world bade farewell to the 19th century. A consensus of opinion puts the date at 27 December 1901. She contradicted herself on numerous occasions about the date, finding pleasure in feeding the confusion.

DIVIDED LOYALTIES

Her father was a police lieutenant, Louis Erich Otto Dietrich, former Cavalry major who served with honours in the Franco-Prussian War of 1870–71. His courage in the field won him the Iron Cross. The household reflected his military background. It was well ordered and respectful, and the abiding memory Marlene had of her father was his shiny leather boots and the whip he cracked regularly to instil discipline in his daughters.

In 1883 he took a 17-year-old wife, Wilhelmina Elisabeth Josephine Felsing, the daughter of an eminent watchmaker, who bore him a daughter, Elisabeth, followed a year later by the little Marlene.

Her full name was Marie Magdalene Dietrich – the stage name she adopted telescoped her pretty Christian names – and she entered the world in Schoneberg, Germany. Later, she lived in both Berlin and the attractive district of Weimar.

At the knee of their forthright and fierce mother, Elisabeth and Marlene learned the skills of which Prussian women were most proud – cookery, needlework, flower arranging and the art of running a household. They were talents she took pride in throughout her sparkling career into her old age. Wherever she went neighbours grew used to the sight of the elegant and stylish Miss Dietrich, unrecognizable in a headscarf and pinny, on her knees scrubbing her own front doorstep.

Also in the home, she was introduced at an early age to the literary greats so beloved by the Germans: Goethe, Schiller and Heine were the favoured writers in the Dietrich household. Marlene and her sister learned their masterpieces by rote and read aloud to each other on long, quiet Sunday afternoons. It was an ideal grounding for the profession she chose much later.

She went to a well-thought-of girls' school where she was shy, religious and a dedicated pupil. While she abhorred games, her favourite subjects were French and literature. She was also an accomplished violin player. Paradoxically, she became

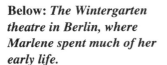

Below: The Wintergarten theatre in Berlin, where Marlene spent much of her early life.

furious when people repeatedly thought her younger than her years.

In 1911 her father died. Her mother married again, another military man who perished in the carnage of World War 1. During the war, Marlene joined other womenfolk knitting clothes for soldiers, humming patriotic songs and never complaining about the food shortages. But in her heart she was divided. The nation's enemy was France, yet French-speaking Marlene adored all that was Gallic and always had done.

It was with relief that she greeted the end of the conflict when her loyalties were no longer split. She decided to study the violin at the Konservatorium in Weimar. There, her teacher was Professor Paul Elgers. Wolfgang Rose – nephew of the composer Gustave Mahler – who was also there later recalled: 'I will never forget the sensation Marlene caused when she arrived to study the violin with Elgers. Her beauty astonished us all and the young men were lining up to take her out. But she was not at all flighty. She was very modest and shy and seemed almost unaware of her loveliness.'

An injury to her finger put an end to any dream of becoming a concert violinist. Despite opposition from her family, she plumped for a career as an actress instead.

She moved alone to Berlin where she took lessons from an eccentric English woman called Elsie Grace. In her spare time she earned commission as a gloves saleswoman and found some popularity as a dancer and singer in the town's swinging cabaret clubs. Her aim was to join the prestigious Max Reinhardt drama school but she failed her audition and had to make do with private tuition from a teacher.

OUTRAGEOUS LIFE-STYLE

Soon she was trying her luck at auditions across the city. It was during one such reading – for a part in a silent film called *The Tragedy of Love* starring idol of the era Emil Jannings – that she met her husband.

Rudi Sieber was a production assistant, aged 25 and tall with blond hair and a muscular frame. The instant she entered the building he noticed her – it was difficult not to. Marlene had honed an outrageous dress sense which had her wearing red fox furs or wolf skins instead of the plain woollen coats more usual on the streets of Berlin at the time. Not only that, she arrived at the studio holding a puppy which tugged her this way and that on its lead.

With help from Rudi she won the part of the svelte girlfriend of a prosecutor in a murder trial. Although her time on screen was limited, it was enough to sow the seeds of a legend. For her role she donned a monocle which had belonged to her father. The image was instantly seized by the underworld of gays and lesbians as a trademark.

The marriage of Sieber and Marlene was followed eight months later with the arrival of a daughter, Maria. For some eight

THE MODEST GIRL WAS QUICKLY SEDUCED BY THE DECADENT NIGHTLIFE OF BERLIN.

Below: *Marlene with her daughter, Maria, whom she loved and left.*

Above: *Marlene in top hat and tails, the garb which became her trademark.*

MARLENE FLAUNTED HER SEXUALITY AND BOTH MEN AND WOMEN LUSTED AFTER HER.

dirty insinuations and kept on his chosen way to be all he promised me and much, much more.

'We never lied to each other from the time we married. His love for me was greater than I understood then. I was not very bright when I was young … It had to do with his complete acceptance of me, all my faults included.

'He knows what is right and wrong which I don't, except in the basic rules of life. He would always steer me in the right direction: that is the essence of our relationship.

'Although we have been apart geographically we are tied eternally. I am certain no such relationship exists between any other two people.'

LESBIAN LOVE

Marlene, meanwhile, was becoming an enigma in the Germany of the 'Roaring Twenties'. As Germany shed the austerity of its Prussian past and World War 1 defeat, a liberation spread among its young, vibrant people. Marlene was part of the sexual revolution, and it appears she, ranking alongside many leading figures of the day, was flagrantly bisexual.

She was the only woman allowed to attend the annual male transvestite ball in Berlin, arriving in top hat and tails. As well as socializing with transvestite clubs, she became infamous for her performance of a duet with another woman actress clutching a bunch of violets, the floral symbol of lesbian love in the city.

Rumours about her sexuality gained momentum throughout her career. There were hordes of male admirers, of course, but her name was romantically linked with cabaret star Claire Waldoff, actresses Claudette Colbert and Lili Damita – later Mrs Errol Flynn – and society darling Mercedes de Acosta.

Biographer David Brett insists: 'Marlene denied any lesbian affairs. In fact, she was virulently anti-gay.'

Yet her own daughter Maria Riva, whose book wasn't published until after Marlene's death, details how she took women as well as men to bed.

Sailing to America at the start of the thirties, she is said to have invited a fellow woman passenger to her cabin to woo her

months Marlene gave up her ambitions to look after the baby which bewitched her. Aged 22, she found joy in feeding, dressing and walking her lovely baby.

But her contentment which grew from the homemaker skills she had learned as a girl did not provide sufficient satisfaction for a woman with a destiny.

Her place was on the big screen where her elemental appeal would explode like a storm. When she went back to the world of theatre and film, Rudi stayed at home to care for their child and he quickly realized his wife would never be tamed. Marlene struck up various liaisons, apparently discussing her infidelity openly at home.

By 1927 Rudi had fallen in love with Russian dancer Tamara Matul – she became Marlene's unofficial replacement for both little Maria and Rudi. But Rudi and Marlene never divorced. Indeed, he remained a loyal ally until his death, when she mourned as any widow would.

In her diary in later years she wrote: 'My husband is an extraordinary man and I want to pay all my homage to him. He has guided me through all my turbulent life, never thinking of himself, only for me and our daughter. He said "*merde*" to all the with champagne and violets. When Marlene produced a book on lesbian love the woman stalked out. Marlene merely shrugged and said: 'In Europe it doesn't matter if you're a man or a woman. We make love with anyone we find attractive.'

She told critic Kenneth Tynan the lesbian rumours were merely a useful diversionary tactic which added to her allure. Yet her former secretary Bernard Hall is certain where her tastes lay. 'Emotionally, she was a man. She went to bed with men to give them pleasure but her strongest feelings were for women.'

At any rate, she refused to deny the lesbian rumours. Mostly, when confronted, she would roar with laughter at the suggestion of having women lovers. The sexual grey mists she created clearly amused her.

Her first film role earned her accolades in Germany. Offers of work came pouring in, and already she was earning a reputation for being stroppy on set. On one film she refused to do profile shots because it revealed a tilt at the end of her nose. The director was furious but she remained stubborn and won the day.

But there was an appealing vulnerability in her brittle, ambitious character too. Her love of music, for example, endeared her to fellow actors. Often she would give impromptu recitals on the musical saw which she mastered in those early Berlin years. She was also known for carrying a Negro doll given to her in childhood as a good-luck charm.

Before long, the biggest break of her career offered itself in the form of the sleazy singer Lola-Lola in *The Blue Angel*. Joseph von Sternberg, an eminent Austro-American director in charge of the film, was captivated by Marlene's beauty, but he also saw a sensual talent which was tailor-made for the part. While other leading actresses were tipped for the coveted part, it was Marlene who was triumphant.

The film had Emil Jannings in the part of a stuffy professor who falls head over heels for a cabaret singer-cum-trollop. They wed but soon she is bored. Heartbroken and humiliated, the professor returns to his classroom to die.

In the film Marlene was mesmerizing in a top hat, silk stockings and black suspenders. She also first crooned the melody which became her hallmark. 'Falling in Love Again' was instantly memorable and much admired, thanks to the guttural style which was all her own. Emil Jannings was bitter at being upstaged. A scene which had the professor attacking Lola-Lola became all too real when an enraged Jannings gripped Marlene by the neck, leaving finger-marks in the soft skin for weeks afterwards. He

was dragged off by stage-hands. The tension between them reverberates through the film.

At the time of its release *Variety* said: 'It will undoubtedly do splendidly in the whole of Europe and should also appeal strongly in the States … its only fault is a certain ponderousness of tempo which tends to tire.'

Ponderous or not, it was a huge hit and had American star spotters knocking at

Above: *Marlene as Lola-Lola in* **The Blue Angel,** *a role she grew to despise.*

HITLER WANTED HER TO
BE HIS LOVER — BUT SHE
LAUGHED IN HIS FACE.

Marlene's door. She signed for Paramount Pictures and set sail for the USA, leaving Rudi and Maria in Germany.

THE HORRORS OF NAZISM

It was a well-timed exit. Her homeland was in the grip of burgeoning Nazism which spiralled during the early thirties until Hitler was finally in command. Marlene herself had no time for his brand of national socialism and was sympathetic to the Jews he persecuted.

Later she would not only turn down a personal invitation from Hitler to return to Germany – which many might have taken as an order – but also spurned the opportunity to become his lover. Her pet name for the Führer was 'that horrible little dwarf'. She commented lazily: 'He promised me a triumphal entry into Berlin. I'm afraid I laughed.'

She was furious with her fellow Germans for allowing the dictator to hold sway and bring ruination to the country and its people. At the end of the war she discovered her own sister Elisabeth was a victim of the harsh regime. The modestly living teacher had been confined as a privileged prisoner in the death camp, Belsen. Marlene ducked out of her high-flying career to nurse her sister back to health. She also supported Elisabeth financially until her death. Much later she visited the house of Anne Frank, the Dutch girl killed by occupying Nazis, and emerged wordless with her eyes red-rimmed from crying.

The horror of the Nazis was a world away, though, as she sailed from Germany in 1930. She may not have been fêted on her arrival – newspapers hardly carried a line – but she soon whipped up a storm. Marlene, who wore trousers in Berlin without raising an eyebrow, generated shock waves when she slipped into slacks in the conservative USA. In fact, she insisted on wearing them when the dismay of the studio bosses became apparent. It was a gamble which she won hands down. Before long women across the country were imitating the casual style.

Teaming up with her in the USA was Von Sternberg, who soon added to her notoriety by having her kiss a fellow actress full on the lips in her first American

Above: *Von Sternberg, the director who helped to launch her career.*

Right: *Marlene and her husband Rudi, bound for the United States on the SS Berengaria in 1937.*

film, *Morocco*. She was the manipulative cabaret singer who finally fell in love. She was reluctant to repeat the role of good-time girl but Von Sternberg was insistent. And he was right. One review read: 'A definite step forward in the art of motion pictures' while another enthused: 'Brilliant, profuse, subtle and at almost every turn inventive'. It earned Dietrich and Von Sternberg each an Academy Award nomination.

But Von Sternberg was a tyrant to Dietrich. Frequently his rantings in their native German reduced her to tears and sent her fleeing to her dressing room.

Despite their fierce battles, Von Sternberg was besotted by Marlene, to the consternation of his wife Riza. By 1931 she was suing him for divorce and Dietrich for alienating her husband's affections. And there was a libel writ after a magazine interview in Germany reported Marlene as saying Riza was an undutiful wife.

Rudi was summoned from Germany and the family – complete with Maria – put on a united front. Paramount Pictures, embarrassed at the commotion, paid Riza $100,000 to drop proceedings.

Marlene's public agony was not at an end, however. A year later a crank sent her an anonymous note threatening to kidnap her beloved daughter. Frantic, she told the police, who kept guard on her Californian home and staged a ransom drop to catch the villain. The cash, however, was never collected. Marlene put bars on the windows, employed bodyguards and armed the nanny. In the end her daughter became a prisoner in her own home, lonely, frightened and bored in turns.

The partnership with Von Sternberg was not to last. Although they made several more films together, his popularity with studio bosses waned while hers soared. He was tortured when she embarked on a series of relationships which read like a *Who's Who* in Hollywood and were to keep Tinseltown gossips working overtime for years to come.

PARAMOURS

There was Gary Cooper, her co-star in *Morocco*, who boasted a magnificent physique. Their liaison was carried out in tandem with an affair with French singer

Maurice Chevalier. Later he branded their fling as 'simply camaraderie' but his wife did not agree. She used the evidence of an association as the basis for a divorce. Much later Marlene said of Chevalier: 'I adored him. He was the finest man I ever loved.'

John Wayne was among her paramours, too. The Duke was invited into her dressing room. After locking the door behind him, Marlene purred: 'What's the time?' She went on to answer her own question by provocatively raising her skirt to reveal a garter watch around her thigh. 'It's very early, darling. We have plenty of time,' she cooed at him.

Author Erich Maria Remarque, who wrote the powerful anti-war epic *All Quiet on the Western Front*, was a suitor as well as Douglas Fairbanks Junior and Frank Sinatra. During World War 2 she bedded Generals Paton and Gavin. She freely admitted she had never felt a strong sense of possession about anyone.

Ernest Hemingway was a close confidant. Although he was apparently never a lover, his picture was kept at her bedside and they corresponded in affectionate terms.

Her greatest love of that period was brooding French actor Jean Gabin whom she met in 1939. A real-life tough guy, he wanted to abandon his Hollywood career to fight Hitler with the Free French army. He even slapped Marlene powerfully both in public and behind closed doors, sending her reeling across the room. But she adored him. At home she would cook and launder

Above: *Maurice Chevalier signing autographs. He refused to admit to an affair with Marlene.*

Above: *With Jean Gabin, the macho French actor she adored.*

Right: *By the mid-thirties Marlene was ranked the third-biggest earner in the US.*

DESPERATE FOR HIS LOVE,
MARLENE HAUNTED THE
STREET WHERE HE LIVED,
HOPING TO CATCH A
GLIMPSE OF HIM.

---

for him. Star Tyrone Power was astonished to see her bow down to remove his shoes and massage his feet before sliding on some slippers.

The pull of duty was too strong for Gabin to counter. He returned to Europe in 1943 to join the ranks against Hitler, but their affair continued in Paris after the war. It only foundered when Gabin, then 55, grew weary of her infidelities which continued in the face of her devotion to him. He finally ended the affair to marry French actress Mauban.

In 1963 she told Senator Robert Kennedy that Gabin was the most attractive man she had ever known. Why had they split? 'Because he wanted to marry me. I hate marriage. It is an immoral institution. I told him that if I stayed with him it was because I was in love with him and that was all that mattered.' Years

later, Dietrich haunted the street where he lived just to catch a glimpse of him, such was her continuing infatuation.

She felt she was mother and lover to Gabin and that was the role she favoured above all. All too frequently, she felt an urge to cherish and care for emotionally damaged men who crossed her path. It normally ended between the sheets.

Her life-style was lavish by any standard. By the mid-thirties she was earning an estimated $350,000 a year, making her the third-highest earner in the country. She would fly food from her favourite bakeries or delicatessens in Europe to her table in America. For 30 years she paid $300 a month to store a 16-cylinder Cadillac in Hollywood where she never rode in it.

But then age began to be an issue. Her lovers were all much younger, her rivals more juvenile. In her middle years she courted two men who were later to wed Elizabeth Taylor.

Michael Wilding, the foppish Englishman, was 11 years younger than Dietrich when they starred together in Hitchcock's *Stage Fright*. She was devastated when their love affair ended so he could marry Elizabeth Taylor, some 30 years her junior.

Wealthy producer Mike Todd, tragically killed in a plane crash in 1958, was the other man she was to share with Taylor, to her fury.

She then became obsessed with one lover, Yul Brynner, during a 6-year-long affair. He was married with a child and refused to leave his wife.

In her 1954 diary Marlene wrote: 'How can I stand this much longer? It will be four years in May. I must ask him to be more definite. As always I'm depressed when he leaves without anything personal being talked about.'

At last Marlene knew what it was to yearn for one love – and not to win it.

Later in the sixties, composer Burt Bacharach was the subject of her attentions. Although he was 27 years younger than she, the relationship flourished for a while with Dietrich once again in the role of *hausfrau*. Dietrich was acerbic when he abandoned her later to marry blonde actress Angie Dickinson.

'He might as well marry Julie Andrews,' she spat.

She was concerned enough about ageing to visit a Swiss clinic for rejuvenating therapy. Three times the cells of a lamb foetus were injected into her bottom, causing maximum discomfort. As she discovered, the effects, if any, were purely temporary.

THE TRAGEDY OF AGE

Afterwards she was shaken by two tragedies. She was touring in Poland in 1967 when she met 39-year-old Zbigniew Cybulski, a home-grown heart-throb with legions of fans around the country. Although bisexual, he became devoted to Marlene and she to him, the vast age difference not withstanding.

She was booked to leave on the midnight express train from Wroclaw to Warsaw. The parting was an emotional one, rendering both in tears. In an impetuous gesture, Cybulski decided to join her and aimed to leap on the moving train. It was a stunt he had carried out successfully many times on film.

But as she watched breathlessly, he slipped between the platform and the train, falling to his death. Emotionally she was scarred by the shocking experience and refused to talk about it.

Above: *With Burt Bacharach before he left her to wed actress Angie Dickinson.*

**AS THE HELICOPTER
DITCHED INTO THE SEA, THE
WHIRRING BLADES SLICED
OFF HER LOVER'S HEAD.**

The following year she visited Australia and met journalist Hugh Curnow, of the same physical stamp as Jean Gabin but aged about 30. Quickly she snapped him up to work on her biography. Although a grandmother, she still tingled at the challenge. The relationship fell apart somewhere between Australia and Paris where she whisked him away. He returned full of stories about the woman who spent evenings poring over scrapbooks reminding herself of a glorious past.

When she went back to Australia to take part in the Adelaide Festival of Arts, he was covering an oil discovery off the coast of Victoria. A helicopter being used to photograph the rig suddenly ditched and the whirring blades decapitated Hugh in an instant. The grim news was broken to Marlene just before she went on stage. Unflinchingly she gave her performance, but the incident wounded her irreparably.

For many, reaching 70 would have been a time to retire gracefully from the public eye to enjoy some well-earned rest. Marlene continued on the showtime beat, mainly because she needed the money.

But her health was not good. The aches

Right: *Leaving London Airport after falling on stage in 1974. Her body became increasingly frail.*

Opposite: *On stage in London, 1973, on one leg of a gruelling world tour.*

and pains of old age and hardening arteries in her legs made her scratchy. Never was it more striking than when she toured Japan and a violinist played a wrong note. Viciously, she turned on the orchestra and sizzled: 'Don't think I have forgotten Pearl Harbor.'

On stage she wore a rubber body suit to enhance her fading figure. A strenuous world tour sapped her energies. There followed a series of disastrous falls including one in which she broke her hip and another when she fractured a thigh bone.

Depressed by the deaths of Von Sternberg, her husband Rudi and Gabin, she faded from public view at last. Then the inducement of earning $250,000 for two days' work on the film *Just a Gigolo* enticed her back to the screen. The movie was savaged by critics. It was taken as a sign, if any were needed, and Dietrich hid herself away in penury.

Behind the doors of her Paris flat, she laced her morning cup of tea with whisky to help dull the pain of her tender limbs. She would avidly read newspapers from across Europe or devour Dick Francis novels and spend hours on the telephone to friends all over the world.

Marlene continued a disorderly approach to eating and drinking. As she had done throughout her working life, she would often forgo food during the day to feast around midnight, troubled as she was with insomnia.

Bizarrely, she used a police whistle to summon her staff at any hour. Often the crack of a gunshot would ring out. Reclining on her pillows, she used a starting pistol to scare pigeons from her window boxes.

A photographer who lurked outside her apartment in the hope of snatching a picture was treated to a whack around the head with her handbag. Another who hired a crane snapped the outraged recluse hidden behind a writing pad.

Dietrich was a proud if distant grandmother who refused to brook any talk of *The Blue Angel*, the film which carved out her career and which she grew to loathe.

She collapsed and died while looking at family snaps, alone save for a paid helper. It's probably just as she would have chosen.

CHRISTIAN BRANDO
Rich kid loser turned killer

Scarred by the traumas of a desperately unhappy childhood, addicted to drugs and obsessed with guns, Christian Brando was a killer-in-waiting. The writing was on the wall for the son of the famous filmstar.

He fancied himself as an aspiring titan of Hollywood, just like his father.

The same smouldering good looks, the hypnotic eyes, the effortless charm so few women could resist. Yet when Christian Brando finally fulfilled his craving to become a household name it was the crime reporters – not the Tinseltown critics – who penned the front-page stories.

In a scene which could have been culled straight from father Marlon's most acclaimed picture, *The Godfather*, Christian stood accused of murder. He'd pumped a single bullet into the head of 26-year-old Dag Drollett, who was the lover of his pregnant half-sister Cheyenne, 20.

The fact that the killing happened at Marlon's sprawling 12-room mansion at Mulholland Drive, deep in California's South Monica Hills, added spice to the scandal. And from the moment the local night duty cop answered an emergency call to hear 'This is Marlon Brando. There's been a shooting at my house,' even the most jaded of Hollywood gossips sprang to attention.

Not since 1958 when Lana Turner's daughter stabbed to death Johnny Stompanato, her mother's lover, had the movie world become so engrossed in a crime story. And as the trial unfolded they would not be disappointed. Every nuance, every tragic twist of the Brando dynasty was finally laid bare.

How Christian was among nine children produced for Marlon by a string of wives. How he became trapped in a vicious custody battle, dropped out of high school and became sucked into a spiral of drug abuse and booze that perfectly fitted the classic 'poor little rich kid' syndrome.

And how, at 32, he pulled the trigger of an SIG-Sauer .45 pistol and threw away his future in a pique of rage.

EXOTIC PASSION

From the start, Christian's life seemed destined to be a roller-coaster ride.

What started as a passionate love affair between Marlon and the boy's mother, Anna Kashfi, ended in hostility and bitterness as they squabbled their way through the child custody courts. The couple had met in Hollywood in 1955, three years before Christian was born.

Brando was quickly transfixed by the beautiful, olive-skinned woman whose taste for sari dresses so ignited his passion

Above: *Marlon in a scene from perhaps his most famous movie,* **The Godfather.**

HE PUMPED A SINGLE BULLET INTO THE LOVER OF HIS PREGNANT HALF-SISTER.

Opposite: *Christian, aged 13, arrives at London's Heathrow Airport. Brando Senior had just brought his son back from the hippy commune in Mexico following Anna's kidnap attempt.*

Above: *The scene of the murder. In this house on Mulholland Drive, Hollywood, Christian gunned down Dag Drollett.*

IT WAS TO BE A FAIRY-TALE ROMANCE — WITH THE BITTEREST OF ENDINGS.

---

for the exotic. He promised her all the help he could in pursuing a film career and the pair began dating almost immediately. But within months they were faced with personal crisis. Anna contracted tuberculosis and was confined to a hospital bed. Once past the worst ravages of the disease doctors ordered that she must take time to convalesce and agreed to release her into Brando's care.

By now deeply in love, Brando bought her an engagement ring. She responded by telling him he was soon to become a father. A secret marriage ceremony in October 1957 appeared to have set the seal on the fairy-tale romance. In her own words Anna once recalled those halcyon first weeks as she waited for Christian to arrive.

'After we married I was like the queen of a strange castle at his house in Mulholland Drive.

'My days were spent in idle splendour. I had maids to wake me up and cook me lunch.

'I would spend the morning painting before driving in a Mercedes to my favourite restaurant for lunch with friends. In the afternoon I would laze around until it came time for the maids to dress me before I went out to some dazzling party.'

Anna described how she would be dressed by names such as Chanel, Yves St Laurent and Christian Dior, and how her pearls, hand-made shoes and designer accessories only ever needed to be signed

for – nothing so crude as a cheque or cash for Marlon's girl.

But if the seal on the romance ever truly existed, it was smashed to fragments within weeks. A newspaper published an exclusive story revealing the new Mrs Brando's claim of coming from Indian stock was pure fiction. In fact she was Welsh. Anna's father, factory worker William O'Callaghan, said his daughter had no Indian blood and was merely brought up there while he worked on the Indian railways.

BRUTAL REJECTION

Brando's blind love turned to blind rage. His personal aides were ordered to wring the truth out of Anna by testing her life story at every opportunity. At first she was aloof and dismissive, but as the questions kept firing in she became hysterical, then rambled incoherently and finally wrapped herself even deeper in a cloak of inventions and half-truths.

Brando responded in typical style – by rejecting her company at home for his old bachelor life-style and the hordes of Hollywood beauties falling over themselves to attract his attentions. Anna hit back by publicly accusing him of flirtatious behaviour.

But despite it all, Brando stayed with her until Christian was born. Soon afterwards she packed her bags and left, taking the baby with her, and then collapsed, suffering from a nervous breakdown.

Before baby Christian was a year old, Anna had dragged Brando into court claiming he had physically abused her. He meanwhile accused her of trying to break into his home. It was the start of a marathon legal tussle in which Christian would be torn between his warring parents like a rag doll. By the time the boy was 6, however, Brando had established a clear advantage.

Anna admitted she had a problem with alcohol and drug abuse and her appearance before the court made it clear she desperately needed treatment. As she gave evidence she went on a violent rampage and was even arrested for attacking three people. The judge granted Brando temporary custody and further ruled that Anna could not even see her son unless there was a lawyer present.

With an apparent victory behind him, Marlon began weaving a new, tangled web to his personal life. He married – and divorced – Mexican actress Movita Castenada, with whom he had another son, Miko, and a daughter, Rebecca.

Then, while playing his role in *Mutiny on the Bounty*, he met a Tahitian woman who totally captivated him. Actress Tarita Teriipia – to whom he is still married – gave him two more children. The youngest, a girl, they named Cheyenne.

By 1971 Christian Brando was seeing his mother again, but her joint custody agreement was blown apart in spectacular style when she paid $10,000 for her boy to be kidnapped and brought to a hippy commune she had joined in Mexico.

A team of crack private detectives eventually returned a bemused Christian to his father. For a couple of years the young Brando was destined to enjoy a stable – and utterly idyllic – life on his father's Tahitian island. When Marlon was called away, either to film or pursue his interest in helping the American Indian human rights movement, hired nannies would take care of his needs.

As his teenage years moved on he was sent to a private Californian school where the darker side of his mixed-up personality soon began to show through. Far from trying to pitch in as just another ordinary kid, Christian would boast about his mega-rich life-style and loved to be known as 'the son of Marlon Brando'.

It was the one slice of self-respect he'd retained in a childhood that had lurched from trauma to crisis. At school he was, predictably, a failure. He hadn't the willpower to knuckle down to exams and had no desire to achieve independence through a career of his own.

He would even question his undoubted ability to attract girls, convincing himself they only wanted to make love to him because he had such a famous father.

In 1981, aged 22, he married a make-up artist called Mary McKenna, but hopes of a stable relationship and family life proved fanciful.

Christian became fascinated by guns – the bigger and more powerful, the better. He grew more and more dependent on booze and cocaine, drifting slowly down

Below: *Marlon and Tarita Teriipia. She totally captivated him.*

*Above: **Christian and his half-brother Miko, who later worked for Michael Jackson.***

CONVINCED THAT NO ONE COULD EVER LOVE HIM, HE RESORTED TO BOOZE AND COCAINE — AND VIOLENCE.

Right: *Christian with a girlfriend, Laura Fuoni.*

into the gutter with Hollywood's motley bunch of no-hopers and hangers-on.

A TIME BOMB

One gang he joined, the Downboys, were stunned at his passion for weaponry and desire to play 'death games'. One member of the gang later told reporters: 'We knew he'd kill one day.

'If only we'd turned him in to the police Dag might still be alive.

'Christian could have killed any of us at any time. When he's spaced out on drugs and booze he's a wild man, a time bomb waiting to go off.

'I saw him trying to kill four people and he didn't even know he was doing it.'

Others told how Christian would launch himself into fights using steel-capped boots and even a claw hammer. All the time the shady, third-rate agents were closing in – promising bit-parts in B-movies. Theirs was a secret agenda. The real aim was to cash in by securing some snippets on his personal life and flogging them to some trashy magazine.

When Christian finally got his 'big break' it verged on farce. He was to play a hitman in an Italian-made gangster movie called *The Issue at Stake*. But the funds ran out and the project collapsed in turmoil and recriminations.

While in Italy, though, Christian did get a genuine chance to break free of the leeches and pushers that now monopolized his private life. He was an instant hit as a male model and drew high praise from leading agents around the world. One, New York-based Andreas Julietti, said of him: 'Christian had a rugged, boyish-yet-male Don Johnson style – a great formula.

'If someone came to me with his portfolio of pictures I would snap him up.

'He displays great character in modelling … and he has the physique.'

Modelling could have been Christian's ticket to the fame after which he still hankered obsessively. Sadly, addled by drink, and unable to control his coke habit, he turned his back on the opportunity and lurched back to life as a professional waster.

By 1983 he was languishing on Marlon's Tahitian island paradise, Tetioroa, entertaining friends who had both the money, and the will, to help finance his high-spending habits. And it was in the summer of that year that he delivered a treacherous blow to one of his closest friends.

Bill Cable, a bit-part actor had brought his wife Shirley to stay on the island. Christian decided it would be fun to seduce her. He would contrive to have the three of them running naked along the long, sandy beaches or to share drinks with Shirley at sunset.

In an interview she later admitted: 'Christian explained that he had only invited us so that he could get closer to me.

'There was an animal magnetism about him, a smouldering sense of danger. He had charm, but it was a rough kind of charm.

'Although I felt myself being drawn to him I didn't want to sneak off and have sex with Christian. I knew that ultimately it would destroy everything that Bill and I had together.'

NAKED SEDUCTION

Shirley related how she challenged Christian one evening as they strolled together, naked, along a beach. She wanted to know why he was trying to double-cross his best friend by romancing her.

With a grin Christian told her: 'To hell with Bill, I go for broke.'

CHRISTIAN LIKED TO PLAY IT ROUGH WITH HIS WOMEN – HE LIKED TO PROVE 'WHO'S BOSS'.

Below: *Bar and beach, Tetioroa. Christian used the island as his personal paradise.*

Above: *Dag, his mother and Cheyenne. Cheyenne never took Christian's threat to kill her lover seriously.*

Then they made love at the water's edge.

Shirley always insisted she knew she was playing with fire. Her new-found lover had told her how he liked to play rough with his women and how sometimes he liked to prove to them 'who's boss'. Christian told her that on one occasion he was punching a girlfriend hard in the face while he held her by her twisted hair in the other hand.

Suddenly his father entered the room, alerted by her screams, and placed a huge hand on his shoulder to jerk him violently away.

Marlon told him: 'You punk! Touch this girl again and I'll flay your skin off your back.'

Shirley, however, insists: 'I'm a lady and he always treated me like one except towards the end.

'He did a lot of bad things but he never physically harmed me.'

As the days turned into weeks on Tetioroa the tension between Bill Cable and Christian built up into a full personal crisis. Shirley decided to leave, in the hope they could sort out the love tangle between them.

But when six weeks later the two men in her life followed her back to Los Angeles their friendship seemed in tatters.

The affair continued to simmer behind Bill's back, at cheap motels or Christian's Hollywood Hills home, bought for him by his father.

Shirley would later describe him as 'an incredible lover, very sensitive to a woman's needs'.

Christian, she claimed, would melt into her arms after sex and regress to his childhood, calling her 'Mommy' and curling up into the foetal position.

'I think that's where a psychiatrist would say all his problems stem from,' she said.

'A deeply disturbed and unhappy childhood has left him scarred mentally beyond belief.'

'Christian,' she said, 'lost his virginity at the age of 13 to a 25-year-old stripper who hoped to use him as a way to get close to Marlon.'

Shirley went on: 'One day after we made love I asked him why he had never straightened himself out. He said: "Listen babe, the old man has blown a packet on shrinks for me and it ain't done any good for me.

"The problems I got no one can solve. There ain't anyone else like me."'

In the end it was drink that drove Christian and Shirley apart. He was cracking a six-pack of malt liquor for breakfast every day – no matter what state he'd arrived home in the night before.

He'd tell friends how his father desperately tried to dry him out, first by sending him to detoxification clinics, then by isolating him for six months on Tetioroa.

Both attempts failed. Christian would even boast how he learned to make his own hooch on the island using fermented coconut and banana juice. He proudly claimed the concoction would 'send an elephant loco'.

THE SMELL OF DEATH

Throughout the booze-and drug-induced haze of the late eighties Christian would increasingly look to his extended family as a rock in troubled waters.

He didn't know Cheyenne well but saw her as something of a fellow spirit – rebellious, independent and strong willed. In fact their lives shared an obvious parallel and each perhaps guessed a little of the other's torment. Christian would even admit to detectives that he was 'over protective' of his half-sister.

Cheyenne had grown to cherish her father's superstar reputation and spoke of him in glowing terms. But, like Christian, when it came to school she rejected his plea to study and became a teenage drop-out. If booze was Christian's weakness, drugs – especially marijuana, tranquillizers and LSD – were hers.

In 1989 she was severely injured when a car, driven by her lover of three years, Dag Drollett, crashed. It left her with deep psychological and emotional scars and as her father would later observe laconically: 'She's been doing a lot of strange things since then.'

When, in the autumn of that year, she became pregnant with Dag's child, Brando insisted that the couple fly to stay with him in Los Angeles. Tarita would come too, to care for the young mother-to-be, and Brando could be sure his grandchild would be given the best medical care money could buy. In truth, he had no confidence in Tahitian doctors. But Dag's parents were concerned. His father Jacques, a high-ranking retired government official, warned in striking terms that the union was doomed.

And in words that sounded chillingly like a premonition he told Dag: 'Stop this life with Cheyenne.

'She's not balanced. You're going to meet a tragedy with that girl. Your life

together smells of tragedy, it smells of death.'

Afterwards he would recall his strange feeling on the night of the killing – still unaware that a tragedy had taken place.

Jacques said: 'I cannot easily describe it. I just didn't feel well inside.

'I said to Françoise [his wife], "I have to go home."'

That fateful night, 16 May 1990, Jacques had been in the Tahitian capital Papeete to attend a reception in honour of the French President François Mitterand.

His overpowering sense of dread is still recalled by Polynesians as further proof of the magic of the South Seas. No one can

Above: *Jacques Drollett. He had some kind of premonition the night his son was shot.*

ever be sure if that feeling descended upon him at the very moment of Dag's death. But it is possible.

For as the limousines full of dignitaries drew up outside Papeete's Gauguin Museum in the mellow evening sundown, it was late in the evening over in Los Angeles.

The next day, Jacques discovered the awful truth in the worst possible way. An LA TV journalist rang him to say: 'Your son has been shot through the head. He's dead.'

'At first I thought it was a joke,' Jacques recalled. 'I thought that someone was having a sick joke on me. When I learned this was the truth I didn't know what to do.' Back in Los Angeles that 16 May night Cheyenne had decided to accept Christian's invitation to dinner to get a change of scene. She hoped it would give them a chance to know each other better, away from the influence of their family.

Dag meanwhile stayed at home to eat with Marlon and Tarita. At Musso & Frank's restaurant on Hollywood Boulevard brother and sister talked – and drank – and gradually opened up their innermost thoughts.

Christian asked her about her relationship with Dag. She told him it was good, but didn't all couples fight occasionally? Christian seemed to get angry even though she promised that the fights were only verbal. Suddenly he was talking about killing Dag.

THE LUST TO KILL

After dinner they drove to the apartment of Christian's then girlfriend, actress Laurene Langdon. Cheyenne recalled how he stormed into the bedroom and came out carrying a knife and a large gun. He again talked about killing Dag but, she later insisted to police, she did not take his threats seriously. On the way to Brando's home he vowed for a third time that he was bent on killing her lover. Cheyenne told how he followed her into the house and confronted Dag in the TV room. She heard a short conversation followed by a single shot. Christian then walked out holding the gun and said simply: 'I killed him.'

Later, brother and sister's accounts of Dag's final moments would be hopelessly at odds. Christian told police later: 'It was an accident.

'The gun was under the couch. I got it because he hit my sister. My sister is pregnant. Two guys with a gun wrestling. It goes off and he's dead.

'When we came back here it got crazy. He went nuts … he grabbed the gun and we fought over it. The gun had a bullet in the chamber and it went off.

'Man, death is too good for the guy. If I am going to knock someone off it wouldn't be in the house. It was an accident. I told him to let it go. He had my hands then "Boom!" Jesus, man, it wasn't murder.'

Cheyenne's statement was quite different. With a frankness that delivered potentially explosive evidence to prosecutors she told one cop the killing was 'not an accident like everyone was trying to make it out to be'.

And she went on: 'It's a murder, in case you didn't know it.' Almost immediately she was put on a plane back to Tahiti with her mother – the travel arrangements were made by her father. Her claim was never tested in court and she refused to return. Later she would give birth to a baby boy, Tuki, born with his mother's drug dependency and looked after in his first weeks of life by Tarita.

Cheyenne, still vowing she would never forgive Christian, later took an overdose. She lapsed into a coma but recovered under the love and care of her mother.

So what of Brando himself? He had become the main witness to a drama more incredible than anything he'd played on screen. Within minutes of the shot ringing out he had dashed on to the scene of the killing. Frantically, pointlessly, he had tried to revive Dag. Then, at 10.58 pm, he made the call to his local police station.

An ambulance, a fire crew and two police cars were despatched to Mulholland Drive. Fire captain Tom Jefferson was first through the double gates to find Brando confronting him. 'He's in the TV den. I've tried mouth to mouth but I can't get a response.'

Jefferson and his men ran into a large white room dominated by a huge TV screen built into one of the walls. There, slumped on a luxury padded sofa, was Dag dressed in blue surfer shorts. A blanket had

Above: *Tuki. He was born with his mother's dependency.*

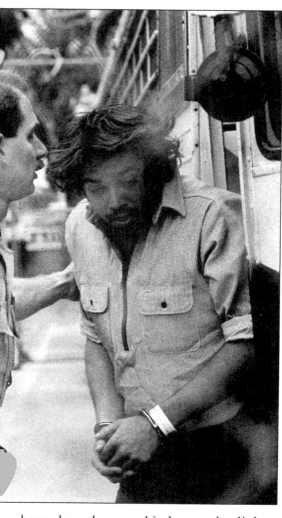

mean to shoot him,' he said. Seconds later his hands were handcuffed behind his back and he was hearing the words of a murder charge.

THE MESSENGER OF MISERY

As Dag's corpse was removed in a body bag the ambulancemen were halted by Brando and asked to open it. Then he gently bent forward to kiss the father of his unborn grandchild.

Later he would tell reporters: 'That night the messenger of misery came to my house.'

Suddenly Brando, the silver-haired screen genius who never really rated acting as a proper job, found his life turned upside-down.

> **THE TV** REMOTE CONTROL WAS STILL CLUTCHED IN HIS HAND AND HIS EYES LOOKED AS IF THEY WERE WATCHING THE FLICKERING SCREEN, BUT THERE WAS A GAPING BULLET-HOLE IN HIS HEAD.

Left: *Christian on his way to court.*

Below: *Dag's funeral turned into a media circus.*

been draped across his legs and a lighter and tobacco pouch were clenched in his left hand while a TV remote-control console was clutched in his right.

On the wall the TV remained on, channels flipping up constantly as though Dag was still trying to choose what he wanted to watch.

His eyes were still open and he seemed to be staring at the screen, but a bullet-hole gaped wide in his left cheek. Outside policeman Steve Cunningham leapt from his patrol car to be grabbed by a fireman.

'There's a guy in the house shot dead,' the man screamed. 'Brando's son is the suspect. He's still in there somewhere.'

Warily Cunningham pulled out his pistol and approached the open front door. The first person he met was Marlon.

'Where's your son?' he asked.

'I don't have any idea,' replied Brando. 'I can't believe Christian shot him.'

Cunningham found Christian in his half-sister's room sitting on the floor with his arm around her. She was crying. 'I didn't

Above: *Marlon in court. He said later, 'My son isn't a mad dog killer.'*

First he pledged his beautiful £3 million home to secure Christian's bail. Then he broke almost 40 years of media silence to call a press conference in his son's defence. In an often rambling monologue he said: 'It's tough for any of you to go through the experience of being famous.

'It robs you of your personality. Most people believe what is written about them. Let them call me names, it doesn't hurt me. But my children aren't used to that.

'My son isn't a mad dog killer and I hate to see him portrayed that way.'

Dressed immaculately in crisp white shirt, navy blue blazer and slacks, the two-times Oscar winner went on: 'Christian has been depressed and I don't think he should be punished simply because he has got a father who has been well known.

'It's become a zoo, or some kind of animal show, where my son is portrayed by the carrion press as the mad dog killer, but that picture has been run to death.

'There is another view. There is another Christian.'

Marlon said he'd had to fight to bring up his children 'with a sense of the real world'.

'They all work for a living,' he said. 'Christian is a welder. Miko works for Michael Jackson. My daughter Rebecca worked as a waitress.

'My other daughter,' here he paused, clearly forgetting her name, 'my other daughter Petra worked for a law office and wants to be a lawyer, and Teho is working.

'I've got nine children. You have to forgive me.

'They have all put in time. They're not all standing around waiting for my millions.

'I've had them open the door on their birthdays looking for the Porsche. And it's not even there. I couldn't even spell Porsche.'

Then, recalling the custody struggle he fought for years over Christian with Anna Kashfi – coincidentally at the same Santa Monica court where his boy was to be tried – he said: 'I fought like hell.

'I was in court about 15 times on visitation rights and custody and by the time he was 14 the judge let him make up his own mind who he wanted to live with. He didn't choose his mother.'

Asked directly if his son was innocent Brando replied: 'I believe Christian. He has never lied to me.

'You might think that every father will believe his son. But when I sat him down he said: "I've always told you the truth."'

Christian's trial, when it finished, produced a predictable result. He escaped the first-degree murder rap but pleaded guilty to voluntary manslaughter and was sentenced to ten years in the St Luis Obispo penitentiary, California.

Apparently he shows little remorse. When his appeal for a reduced sentence came up in 1991 a fellow prisoner told the judge Christian spoke often about the killing. He told other convicts: 'I'd do it again. Dag beat and abused my sister.'

Not surprisingly, sentence was upheld. But what of his mother Anna, the woman he'd railed so hard against during the case and whom he'd refused to even acknowledge? Like Christian, her story also became one of rags and riches.

The $800,000 settlement she got from Brando back in 1960 quickly dwindled into nothing. She claims the lawyers bled her dry. In recent years she has taken to living in a ramshackle trailer home, drawing a $60 per week social security cheque. And when she visited St Luis prison Christian turned her away. The irony is that as a kindergarten teacher she is adored by dozens of children. All she has to remind her of her son is a glazed pottery cast of his hand and an embroidered picture made for her by Christian before Brando won custody. A message on it reads: 'The best things can never be kept, they must be given away – a smile, a kiss and love.'

> **CHRISTIAN SHOWED LITTLE REMORSE FOR THE BRUTAL KILLING, BOASTING IN PRISON: 'I'D DO IT AGAIN.'**

Below: *Christian on trial. The verdict of the court was manslaughter.*

IVANA TRUMP
A fairy-tale romance?

Brought up under the miseries of Communism, the beautiful Ivana fought for her happiness and found love in the arms of a dashing American tycoon. But all her millions could not protect her from the ultimate betrayal.

At the foot of a steep snowy slope, a 4-year-old Czech girl lay in a crumpled heap, skis awry, not knowing whether to laugh or sob.

The winding route at the centre of panoramic white mountains had looked so simple. It was an ambitious path on a sharp curve that might have daunted skiers twice her age, but this gutsy girl with sparkling eyes and skin like a cherub never thought of turning back.

At first her descent was precise and controlled, but suddenly she found herself out of control and racing at dizzy speed towards the foot of the slope. Her skis were like arrows shooting her into the unknown. Beyond the slope edge was a cliff where she would plunge into goodness knows what.

Unable to halt herself with a snowplough stop on skis, the youngster remembered her father's words of advice during earlier skiing tuition. She summoned her courage, let herself go limp and flopped on to the ice-hard ground.

She bruised her head and her bottom. More than that, her pride was dented. She longed to cry but feared it would mean the end of skiing on the adult runs where she craved to be. After just a few moments lying on the snow, the young body swathed in woollens began to flex. Realizing no bones were broken, she got back onto her feet and on to her skis ready to march back up the mountain and give it another go.

Ivana Zelnicekova could not have known it but those early tumbles in the picturesque mountain ranges of her native Czechoslovakia were symptoms of what destiny had in store for her later on. It was the first time Ivana found she had to pick herself up, dust herself off and start all over again – but not the last.

For Ivana has lived a fairy-tale life which has taken her from the heart of grim Communism into the headquarters of glossy capitalism on the arm of a dashing tycoon. To most people, the lives led by characters in American soaps like *Dynasty* and *Dallas* were a fantasy. For Ivana, a sumptuous US life-style of private jets, limousines and lavish parties was an everyday reality.

But just as it seemed she had her heart's desire, her charmed existence was smashed apart when her husband deserted her for another, younger lover. The public mud-slinging that followed would have been enough to make lesser women crumble but Ivana was from a determined mould. She

Above: *At Ascot in 1991 Ivana's flamboyant clothes raised eyebrows.*

IVANA'S HAPPY FAMILY LIFE HAD BEEN PUBLICLY SMASHED TO SMITHEREENS AND IT SEEMED IMPOSSIBLE THAT SHE'D EVER BE ABLE TO PICK UP THE PIECES.

Opposite: *Ivana learned to ski in order to escape from Communist repression.*

Above: *Prague, capital of Ivana's native Czechoslovakia – a beautiful city dulled by Iron Curtain politics.*

THE DRAWN FACES OF HER FELLOW WORKERS ENSLAVED IN DRUDGERY FILLED HER WITH HORROR AND MADE HER DETERMINED TO ESCAPE.

Right: *A hearts-and-flowers romance led quickly to marriage after Ivana met Donald Trump.*

vowed to build her own empire on which her faithless husband could gaze with envy.

And that's just what she has done.

ESCAPE FROM MISERY

Looking at the little girl whose knocks on the ski slopes only made her more dedicated, it would be difficult to chart a more extraordinary life.

Ivana, now 45, was the daughter of an electrical engineer who grew up against the grey backdrop of Communism in post-war Czechoslovakia.

Under the knuckle of the Nazis during World War 2 the Czechoslovakian people had found little comfort. And there was no joy in store either when the war ended and another totalitarian regime held sway.

Those who ventured opinions about politics and the economy were swiftly dispatched by the Communist rulers. Ordinary folk were forced to look over their shoulders before speaking on even the most innocent of subjects. Religion was frowned on behind the Iron Curtain. Families which had sought solace in the embrace of the Catholic Church found themselves bearing the full weight of official opposition.

The street corners were haunted by the grey-coated policemen, their faces like sullen masks. They were the tools of the regime employed to keep good order at any price. Even now Ivana confesses to suffering an involuntary shiver when she sees a uniformed policeman.

The bleak way of life caged so many spirits but Ivana was convinced she would escape its clutches. Her early years were tinged with the kind of glamour hardly known in that grim era. She found herself by chance picked as a child actress by a popular director to appear in several films.

It was a thrilling time, but the young Ivana decided the excitement of make-up, lights and cameras paled against the adrenalin which came from torpedoing down a mountainside on a pair of skis.

Anxious to give their only daughter the best, her parents focused her on a sporting career from an early age. They reckoned it was the best chance she had of milking the Communist system which cosseted its sports stars, and might even give her a chance to escape.

Ivana was a natural athlete: her slender, strong limbs soon thrust her leagues ahead of other child skiers. Her devotion to the sport and an innate competitive edge marked her out as a winner.

As if she needed any convincing, she spent two weeks inside a shoe factory when she was 12 years old which left her petrified and full of resolve to flee the constraints of Communism. The drawn faces of fellow workers enslaved in drudgery filled her with horror.

'I promised myself that I was never ever going to do that kind of work again,' she recalled.

So she concentrated on her skiing, spending every weekend she could on the country's most challenging runs. By 1972 she was accomplished enough to be considered for the Czech Olympic skiing team.

Not surprisingly, her education was orientated around sport. She studied for a degree in physical education at the prestigious Charles University in Prague. Her glorious good looks were not wasted either. She worked as a model, well paid by Communist standards even if the frippery of the job was abhorred by the bull-headed rulers.

It was through her love of skiing that she seized her first chance to flee the repression

of Czechoslovakia. She met Austrian ski instructor Alfred Winklmayr through mutual friends. For the price of a pair of skis, he agreed to wed her – so providing a ticket out of her homeland. The service took place in Prague in November 1971. That night the couple returned to separate beds and he went back to Austria soon afterwards without consummating the marriage. It was ended in a Los Angeles divorce court the following year.

Now Alfred Winklmayr has remarried and lives modestly as an estate agent in a suburb of Sydney, Australia, where he emigrated after that first marriage of convenience. He remains intensely loyal to the woman whose career he helped to launch in the freedom of the West.

Tracked down by reporters in 1990 when the cracks in the Trump marriage began to show he said: 'She's certainly come a long way since I knew her but we are still friends. I've been trying to follow events but it's not easy to keep up with everything.

'Ivana's been receiving a lot of criticism lately but I can tell you she's not the kind of person to take it without a fight.'

A DREAM ROMANCE

Ivana used her newly found freedom from the Communist tentacles to live and work in Montreal where she was a successful skier and model. It was during the Olympics, held there in 1976, that she first laid eyes on Donald Trump, 48, the man who arguably made her, then tried to break her.

It was the stuff of which slushy romance novels are made. Their eyes met across a crowded room. A fizz of electricity left them both shaken. The busy reception they were at might as well have been empty of people – they only had eyes for each other.

After nine months' long-distance courting they were married in April 1977. Later Ivana revealed what thrilled her about Trump.

'What really attracts me is that fabulous energy. Donald is a great leader in the way he motivates people.

'Energy. He had a great head on his shoulders and that he was handsome didn't hurt either. Values, hard work. His sense of reality. Not smoking, taking drugs, drinking. No cheating, lying or stealing.'

He was embarking on a career in wheeling and dealing. He admitted he was hooked on what he called 'the power of the deal'. With clear-headed Ivana as wife and business ally, there would be no stopping them.

Such was his talent for making money, he went on to become America's 19th richest man. The empire of the man who became something of a billionaire boardroom showman was astonishing. The jewel in his crown was Trump Tower, a shiny skyscraper 58 storeys high in the heart of fashionable New York. It comprised apartments, offices and a luxury shopping mall. Also in New York were the prime-site developments of Trump Plaza and Trump Palace.

Add to that the Plaza Hotel, the Grand Hyatt Hotel and the city's ice rink and you

Top: *Donald in Trump Tower.*

Above: *The Trump shuttle airline service, just one arm of Donald's amazing money-spinning empire.*

Above: *Ivana and her three children: Donny, Ivanka and Eric.*

Above right: *Chef Anton Mosimann on his home ground with Ivana.*

Below: *Ivana's own hotel, which she steered to success.*

learn a fraction of what Trump owned in New York alone.

There were three casinos in Atlantic City, an estate in Florida, the Trump shuttle airline service, a splendid yacht and a weekend retreat in Greenwich. The list of his acquisitions seemed endless and all were hallmarked with the Trump name – as was a Monopoly-style board game, a television show called Trump Card, a Brazilian horse race, the Trump Cup, and the cycle race known as Tour de Trump.

'I believe I've added show business to the real-estate business,' he told *Playboy* magazine. 'That's been a positive for my properties and in my life.'

Ivana found herself at the hub of a world most can only wonder at. She slipped into the role of society hostess with relative ease. Apart from their three children, Donny, now 16, Ivanka, 13, and 7-year-old Eric, there were swanky charity bashes to support and lunch parties where she could gossip and giggle. But while it might have kept many women happy, Ivana was keen to make her mark.

Donald recognized the business asset he had in his gorgeous wife. 'She's incredibly good at anything she's ever done, a natural manager – she may be the most organized person I know,' he commented while they were still in harmony.

So Ivana was put in charge of Trump Castle, one of the trio of casinos in Atlantic City. As chief executive, she proved her worth as a money-spinner by rewarding him with a turnover of £20 million a year.

A year later he bought the fabulous Plaza Hotel and presented it on a platter to Ivana. She had big plans for the hotel, featured in the hit films *Funny Girl* and *Crocodile Dundee*.

'I want to make it one of the world's memorable experiences. I want it to represent the glamour of the New York of 1907 when it first opened.'

In came a team of designers who lavished marble on the bathroom suites and antiques in the hallways. Donald told the world she was running the 1,000-room landmark for 50 pence a year – and all the dresses she could buy.

In fact, her extravagant fashion spending had prompted some cutting criticism among society watchers. She is said to have paid $37,000 for a beaded Christian Lacroix jacket alone. The garish colours she favoured raised eyebrows too.

Then she did for American fashion what Princess Diana had done for Britain's top designers. Her European sprees came to an end and she bought quality imitations drawn and made in the USA at a fraction of the cost they commanded as originals in a French or Italian fashion house. The common-sense move won her friends at home, especially as she went on to lure top names in the rag trade to her revamped hotel, giving a stage to home-grown talent.

HER EXTRAVAGANCE ONCE
PROVOKED JEALOUS
CRITICISM — SHE PAID
$37,000 FOR A SINGLE
JACKET.

Left: *Setting the style for a generation of women, Ivana went to fashion shows with personalities such as Bianca Jagger.*

She revealed how her clothes would last for several seasons.

'A Christian Lacroix dress costs $24,000. I could buy a Porsche for that. At some point you have to draw the line.

'Usually I wear something two or three times and then I put it to sleep for a year with tissues and covers and bring it out a few seasons later.

'Or else I give it to my mother and she gives it to my friends in Czechoslovakia.'

In addition to a will to win, she admits her Czechoslovakian roots have helped her succeed.

'Most of the people there work and you either have the drive or you don't,' she admitted.

As a working mother, her day would start at 7 am with a work-out with her personal trainer before arriving at her office before 10 am. For efficiency, her appointments for the day were neatly typed on a sheet which she slipped into her bag.

At lunchtime she often missed the chatty lunches so loved by American society women in favour of a wholefood snack at her desk. 'I have a disciplined diet and I don't eat junk food,' she explained.

By 5.30 pm she would be on her way back to see her children, oversee their homework and preside at a family dinner. Both she and Donald were keen to instil decent values in their children. Pocket money was restricted and a huge emphasis was put on education. Sometimes in the evening she went clubbing with her husband. Often she would read in solitude or busy herself arranging fresh flowers which she adored around the apartment. Twice weekly she went to the hairdresser and, unlike many others in her income bracket, she applied her own make-up.

If 'The Donald', as she affectionately called him in her attractive East European accent, had a business trip abroad, she always found the time to go with him, providing invaluable assistance as hostess with business brains.

Home was a 50-room suite high in the imposing Trump Tower. There were handmade crystal chandeliers, a king-sized bed with gold canopy, a marble-paved dining room, 24 ct gold-leaf stencils, a solid bronze front door and even a 12 ft waterfall.

Below: *The 50-room suite in Trump Tower, opulent and splendid, which the Trumps called home.*

IVANA THOUGHT SHE HAD
EVERYTHING — UNTIL THE
RUMOURS MADE HER
SUSPECT SHE NO LONGER
HAD HER HUSBAND'S LOVE.

Come the weekend it was time to adjourn to an out-of-town retreat where she kept her figure in trim by playing tennis or swimming.

A CRUEL AWAKENING

Ivana clearly adored her husband and she was devoted to and fiercely protective of their handsome children. Under scrutiny from the public they seemed a model all-American family who might one day end up in the White House. At the end of the have-it-all eighties, Ivana did indeed seem to want for nothing.

Then rumours that Donald was being seen around town with another stunning blonde came to her ears. Catherine Oxenberg, actress and daughter of Princess Elizabeth of Yugoslavia, and former Olympic skater Peggy Fleming were mentioned in the press. But reporters were wide of the mark.

The object of his attentions was Marla Maples, a former Miss Georgia, fan of motorcycling and trampolining and former

girlfriend of football star Sean Landetta. She was quite unknown in the New York circles frequented by Ivana.

Matters came to a head shortly after Christmas 1989 when the two women in Donald Trump's life met at the swish winter resort of Aspen, Colorado.

Audaciously, Trump and Maples arrived at the jet-set playground in the same plane and left the airport together in an incongruous black limousine. Marla jumped out of the car to stay in a holiday home with a girlfriend while Trump met his wife.

Ivana gradually began to suspect that something was amiss. She overheard a telephone conversation between her husband and a friend relating to the illicit affair. She believed her rival to be called Moolah and didn't have a clue what she looked like. Finally she came face to face with Marla at a mountain-side café called Bonnie's Beach Club.

Marla asked her acidly: 'I'm Marla and I love your husband. Do you?'

Ivana told her to 'get lost', a statement she was later to regret for being unladylike.

Other diners saw the Trumps skiing away with Ivana wagging her finger and chastising the wayward Donald. He wearily replied: 'You're over-reacting.'

Despite his wandering eye, Ivana loved her husband and urged him to save their marriage by calling off the relationship with Marla.

Meanwhile, the American press got into a frenzy. In the USA the couple had been regarded as royalty. News of cracks in the institution of the Trump marriage was met with a huge volume of newspaper coverage which relegated other world events, like the release of South African Nelson Mandela, to corner slots.

At Ivana's 41st birthday lunch in a top New York restaurant – attended by 30 close friends, mother Matka and her mother-in-law Mary – crowds greeted her shouting: 'Take the money.'

As the wronged wife, she was earning more sympathy and respect across America than ever she could have expected as a brittle society beauty. Women who had previously looked on Ivana with envy and even loathing began to identify with her and the impossible position she found herself in.

Below: Donald Trump with his pregnant mistress Marla Maples. She came face to face with Ivana at a Colorado ski-cafe and told her: 'I love your husband. Do you?'

Friends encircled her during her pain and urged her to dry her tears, set her jaw and brazen out the agony of the very public split. Among her famous supporters were tennis player Martina Navratilova, designer Calvin Klein, TV personality Oprah Winfrey and actress Robin Givens.

Meanwhile, Donald found backing from boxer Mike Tyson, Cher, Liza Minnelli and Frank Sinatra.

For almost three months the couple tried to work out their differences – but to no avail. Trump had not fallen out of love with Ivana but had toppled head over heels for 27-year-old Marla. It was a hopeless triangle.

A sour clash began with Ivana demanding millions in cash, as well as the Plaza Hotel, of which she was president, and a Boeing 747 jet.

His response was to throw her out of the hotel office she ran.

By the end of March both sides signed a separation agreement along the lines of their 1977 nuptial agreement. Trump agreed to pay $350,000 in cash to Ivana, as well as an annual sum of $350,000 until she remarries, and $300,000 in child support.

A BITTER ENDING

Divorce came later that year in Manhattan Superior Court. In a swift hearing Judge Phyllis Gangel-Jacob declared: 'I grant you a divorce from Donald John Trump on the grounds of cruel and inhuman treatment and particularly Donald Trump's flaunting of his relationship with Marla Maples.'

Afterwards Ivana said: 'It's very sad for me, for the children, for our families and for everyone concerned.'

After 13 years, it was the start of the single life again for Trump, but it coincided with a disastrous slump in his business activities. It seemed his Midas touch was deserting him. Rumours that he would have to borrow heavily simply to survive in business were rife. He had a battle on his hands.

Ivana too was struggling with a crisis: she felt shattered by the split of the marriage she had held so dear. It came in the same year as her beloved father's death.

'It hurts, of course,' she explained. 'But my mother helps me tremendously. Maybe because of my upbringing in a Communist country where you really did have to keep your thoughts to yourself, I don't open up very much. It still takes time until I open up, even with my friends.'

But a Manhattan journalist threw her a lifeline. Shirley Lord invited her to do a cover for *Vogue* magazine. At first it seemed a brutal suggestion.

'You must be joking. I'm going through the worst time of my life and I look terrible,' replied Ivana.

Dully she accepted the challenge, certain it would be a disaster, but she was reckoning without the talents of a make-up artist and hairdresser who together turned out a new woman. It was a woman Ivana liked the look of – softer colours on her face, quieter lipsticks – and she adopted the image to face the nineties.

She also lost an incredible 2 stones in weight. In 1992 she displayed the remarkable poise and flair she had re-created after the body blow of divorce when she took to a catwalk at a Paris fashion show, to gasps of appreciation from

Above: *After his divorce from Ivana many thought Donald would revel in a bachelor boy lifestyle. But his return to the single life after 13 years coincided with a devastating collapse in his business fortunes and Donald became a more subdued figure in society circles.*

WHEN DONALD TRUMP DESERTED HIS WIFE – THE MIDAS TOUCH DESERTED HIM.

Above: *Ivana causes a sensation on the catwalk in Paris.*

Above right: *Beautiful hair: 'the best revenge'.*

a delighted crowd. The picture was so breathtaking it appeared in *Penthouse.*

'I couldn't have gone out in front of 2,000 people if I didn't feel good about myself, about my body – and if I didn't have my sense of humour,' she said afterwards.

She still had Donald to contend with, however. He had won a victory which he had longed for – a gagging order on Ivana to stop her revealing details of their life together, uncomfortable in the knowledge that revenge was on her mind.

She had already taken a public swipe at him by recording an advertisement for Clairol shampoo in which she swung her glossy mane and stated: 'Beautiful hair is the best revenge.'

Ivana published a novel called *For Love Alone*, written with former TV scriptwriter Camille Marchetta. It's about a Czech girl, Katrinka, who skis brilliantly, escapes her homeland and marries a tycoon. After an unhappy split following his affairs, they divorce and she marries an even richer man.

While admitting she wrote about things she knew, Ivana stoutly denied the novel mirrored her life with Trump. She would not give her ex the satisfaction of featuring in her drama, she announced.

He disagreed and sued her for $25 million. Months of bitter wrangling followed with accusation upon counter-accusation eagerly seized on and spat out again by the newspapers.

Trump accused her of violating their nuptial agreement by living with her boyfriend Ricardo Mazzuchili, a 50-year-old Italian engineer, and demanded that the divorce cash he paid her should be returned.

For her part, Ivana demanded the $4 million housing allowance which formed part of the now disputed agreement and claimed he had failed to pay her alimony.

It wasn't until 1993 that the couple managed to negotiate a secret deal which made peace between the parties.

Ivana had the satisfaction of watching her husband's fortune dwindle. After they separated she told interviewer Barbara Walters she thought she had Trump's last $9 million.

Refusing to be beaten, Donald made two business comebacks in typically flamboyant style, assuring his rivals he was still a force to be reckoned with.

Ivana was quick to drop her second name. It was a statement which said she no longer needed the man who was once her husband.

She launched a successful cosmetics, jewellery and clothing business, appearing on American TV to sell her wares. They are inexpensive copies of her favourite designs and have been a hit with the American public. During a weekend she sells about $3 million worth of merchandise. She is well rewarded for public speaking engagements and in huge demand. Also, she has more books in the pipeline including further love stories and a how-to book on going-it-alone following divorce.

'I am not poor and I don't mind work,' she declares. 'The divorce was very difficult but I am an optimistic person. You have to pick up the pieces and make the best of it. The money I received from Donald was put in trust for the children. I make my own money. Always have.'

In December 1993, Donald Trump and Marla Maples wed in a lavish ceremony. It took place at Trump's Plaza hotel and Marla wore a tiara worth more than £1 million to go with her designer wedding gown. Although top New York socialites were on the guest list, their daughter Tiffany, aged two months, did not appear. Neither did Trumps three children from his marriage to Ivana who preferred to continue a skiing holiday in Aspen, Colorado.

Above: *Ivana found happiness again with new love Ricardo Mazzuchili.*

JIMI HENDRIX
A tragedy in waiting

Once the brilliant and shocking Jimi Hendrix had excited a whole generation of kids with his unique brand of music and sexuality, but the burden of fame tore him apart as the fans who'd once screamed their admiration turned their backs on him.

To the flower children of the sixties Jimi Hendrix was the pop star turned prophet, a musical genius who could, literally, make his guitar talk.

Even more than Bob Dylan or the Beatles, Hendrix had a magical stage presence that entranced all those lucky enough to witness it. More than that, he was the figurehead who fuelled a million sex, drugs and rock 'n' roll fantasies for his adoring teenage fans.

There were the legendary three-in-a-bed sex sessions. All-night parties overflowing with heroin, cocaine or LSD. Delightful society-shockers like his faked orgasms on stage with an electric guitar. And, of course, his sheer ear-splitting, gut-wrenching exclusive brand of blues rock.

Like many a pop hero who came before – and after – him, Hendrix was both a magnificent showman and a master of his art. Yet he never came close to mastering his destiny.

His three years of fame would end in a lonely, pathetic death – the apparent victim of a large dose of sleeping pills which led him to inhale his own vomit. Some insist he committed suicide; others say he took an accidental overdose. Even more outlandish is the claim that he was somehow murdered.

Yet, however he passed away in his adopted London that September day in 1970, one thing is sure: Hendrix deserved a better end.

He had been born 28 years earlier in Seattle, Washington, a city he mostly loathed. His dad was a gardener and although money was tight James Marshall Hendrix grew up as part of the classic American middle-class culture attending predominantly white schools.

HIGH SCHOOL DROP-OUT

He and kid brother Leon had a sober, god-fearing father who perhaps

Opposite: *The wild man of rock. He virtually made his guitar talk.*

Below: *Pop star and prophet, Hendrix fuelled a million teenage fantasies.*

JIMI CLAIMED HE WAS
THROWN OUT OF HIGH
SCHOOL FOR DARING TO
HOLD A WHITE GIRL'S
HAND IN CLASS.

over-compensated for the wild ways of their mum, Lucille, a woman of Cherokee Indian ancestry. Jimi would later tell how she would drink and engage his dad (also James) in blazing rows. Often as not he would be packed off to his grandma's place in Canada until things calmed down.

Lucille died when Jimi was 10, a personal trauma he never shook off.

Above: *Hendrix was a natural performer. He'd also picked up a few tricks from stars such as Little Richard, the Isley Brothers and Wilson Pickett.*

Despite her boozy, devil-may-care approach to raising kids he always referred to her fondly as his 'groovy mother'.

Not long after her death the young Hendrix began to show his first interest in rock 'n' roll. He'd already played around on harmonicas and violins from the age

of 4. Now he would pick up an old kitchen broom and pose with it slung low across his thighs as a make-believe electric guitar. His father bought him his first, cheap, acoustic instrument when he was 11 and on his next birthday he was upgraded to an electric.

In those early days of endless practice sessions in his room, Jimi naturally found himself drawn to the great blues singers of the fifties and early sixties. B.B. King, Elmore James, Muddy Waters and, later, Bob Dylan all shaped his style. To James Senior (who had only ever managed to play the spoons) it was all an amazing revelation.

Jimi was kicked out of high school in 1957 – he later claimed it was 'for holding a white girl's hand in class' – and began picking up any casual work he could find. In summer he could work cutting grass for his father; in winter he took anything that would pay.

All the time he was getting better and better on the guitar, experimenting with wah-wah and feedback, the sounds that would later become his trademark.

His first gig was at a National Guard armoury where he and a few friends trotted out the Tamla Motown and rhythm and blues numbers their audience demanded. Later Jimi would observe: 'I dug listening to Top 40 R&B ... but that doesn't mean I like to play it every night.'

In 1963 he joined the US Army's 101st Airborne Division on the grounds that he might as well sign up sooner as later. Although he hated the Army he reckoned his National Service would be that much worse if it arrived just as he stood close to making a breakthrough in the music business.

Jimi made 25 jumps in what was regarded as one of the Army's toughest training grounds. Asked what made him do it he would delight in replying: 'The Sergeant ... and the fact you got more money.'

The 26th jump, however, went slightly wrong and Jimi took a bad landing, breaking his ankle. He was discharged after a 14-month stint and found himself quickly on the road as a professional backing musician. He worked with the likes of Little Richard, the Isley Brothers and Wilson Pickett, and also on some of the trendy star 'package tours' of the time.

These left him rubbing shoulders with B.B. King, Sam Cooke, Solomon Burke, Chuck Jackson, Ike and Tina Turner and the twisting sensations Joey Dee and the Starlighters.

THE BIG BREAK

It wasn't until 1965 in Greenwich Village that he finally formed his own band – Jimmy James and the Blue Flames – a name that later caused him to crack up in self-mocking laughter.

The following year Jimi got the big break he'd dreamed of.

Chas Chandler, bass player with the Animals, had decided to move into management and record production. He'd heard from Rolling Stone Keith Richard's girlfriend, Linda Keith, of a brilliant young guitarist who was setting the cafe bars of Greenwich alight with a fresh, raw talent. They watched him perform in the Cafe Wha, and Chandler was hooked.

He urged Hendrix to come back with him to England, then almost the centre of the pop world. Jimi liked the idea but was cautious. Were the backing musicians any good? What about the equipment? He didn't want to compromise his act by blowing second-rate amplifiers every night.

Chandler soothed his doubts but it was only when Jimi asked him about Eric Clapton that the deal was sealed. Jimi said: 'If you take me to England will you take me to meet Eric?'

Chandler told him: 'When Eric hears you play he'll be falling over to meet you.'

That night Chandler watched Jimi perform 'Hey Joe' several times. It was a song he'd recently discovered and had been itching to record. Hearing it pounded out in the Cafe Wha seemed to be an omen and he became convinced he was watching a future megastar.

In one later interview he admitted: 'Jimi wasn't known at all at this time but I hadn't any doubt in my mind. I thought he was fantastic.

'I thought there must be a catch somewhere. Why hadn't anyone else discovered him?'

In September 1966 Hendrix arrived in England and found himself tasting stardom for the first time in his life. He was booked into the swish Hyde Park Towers Hotel by Chandler and taken on a rapid tour of London's trendiest clubs, where almost the only clientele were musicians, agents and managers. Chandler knew he needed to find his protégé a backing band quickly, but the people had to be right. As it turned out everything fell into place.

That same month a bespectacled kid called Noel Redding arrived in London from his native Kent with 10shillings in his pocket. He'd read in the *Melody Maker* newspaper that the Animals wanted a new lead guitarist and he turned up at Chandler's Gerrard Street offices to offer his services. Chandler told him the job had gone, but how did he fancy trying to switch to bass and play with the still unknown Hendrix?

Jimi and Redding strummed together for a few hours and Jimi decided he'd got the right man. Redding ruefully admitted to Chandler: 'I'll switch to bass. I don't see anyone else playing lead guitar with this bloke.'

A few days later Hendrix had his drummer. Mitch Mitchell had just quit a band run by Georgie Fame and was looking for work.

The Jimi Hendrix Experience was born.

Below: *The Jimi Hendrix Experience was a band thrown together by chance. Noel Redding had arrived in London to audition as a lead guitarist but after playing with Hendrix he switched to base. 'I don't see anyone else playing lead guitar with this bloke', he told his manager.*

Above: *Hendrix, Mitchell and Redding show they can pose with the best of them.*

THEY WERE AT THE POINT OF GIVING UP – THE JIMI HENDRIX EXPERIENCE WAS A FAILURE.

Right: *Eric Clapton. He once said of Hendrix: 'Christ, nobody told me he was that good.'*

Their first single, 'Hey Joe', was rejected by a Decca Record company executive who tardily informed Chandler he didn't think Hendrix had 'got anything'. It was to be one of the greatest blunders in the history of rock.

Chandler took no notice and got the 45 distributed anyway through a newly launched company. He sold five guitars to pay for a promotions party at London's Bag O'Nails club.

Jimi got the offer of more support work but it was hardly big money – £25 a night. Chandler later confessed he was down to his last 30 shillings and when Jimi had his guitar stolen Chandler had to sell his last bass to replace it. For a while it looked like the Jimi Hendrix Experience was going to be a bad one for all concerned.

Then 'Hey Joe' stormed into the charts and their problems were solved. From £25 a gig the Experience was earning £1,000 a night by the spring of 1967. Redding and Mitchell got 25 per cent of the takings, with Hendrix himself getting 50 per cent.

THE WILD MAN OF ROCK

Jagger, Lennon and McCartney were among the first in the queue to watch them. Quickly Chandler capitalized on the publicity, designing an outrageous stage package for Jimi which was unveiled during a tour with the Walker Brothers. Apart from a sleazy sex romp with his guitar, Jimi began setting fire to it with the aid of lighter fluid – an act that filled theatre managers across the land with a sense of dread.

A concert in Monterey followed with the Experience acting as support for the Mamas and Papas and Otis Redding. The 7,000 fans had never heard of the black guy in the outrageous psychedelic gear, but after he played a stunning version of 'Like a Rolling Stone' they went berserk. It was almost half an hour before the fans had quietened down enough for the Mamas and Papas to take the stage.

From September 1967 to the summer of 1968 Jimi Hendrix was simply the biggest pop star in the world. His talents had at last been recognized in the USA following acclaimed gigs in San Francisco and New York. In London the album 'Are You Experienced' raced up the charts. Fashion magazines clamoured to get him on their covers, reporters jostled for interviews, photographers trailed the band everywhere and millions tuned in to *Top of the Pops* to see him strut his stuff.

Flower-power teenagers saved their pocket money to get kitted out in the Hendrix look. Typically this would include military-style embroidered jackets, bright silk cravats, frilly shirts, patterned bandannas, velvet purple waistcoats, ethnic bead pendants, long-fringed white leather jackets, bell-bottomed trousers with button leg detail and a large, floppy black fedora hat.

In Britain Eric Clapton – himself dubbed 'God' by rock fans – was at one time being lined up to perform a duet with Jimi.

He went to one gig and, with his usual modesty, politely declined, saying: 'Christ, nobody told me he was that good.'

Another big-name strummer of the time, Johnny Winter, summed up Hendrix's talents as well as anyone.

'He could create feelings nobody else could,' said Winter. 'His guitar was like an

extension of his soul. It wasn't even a guitar, or notes, or music. It was him. He was just projecting Jimi Hendrix.'

And Mitch Mitchell revealed: 'He had huge hands, his thumbs were nearly as long as his fingers. Like many blues players he could use this to his advantage – hooking it over the neck of his guitar as an extra finger.

'Jimi could, and did, play anything – left-handed, right-handed, upside-down, behind his back, over his head. He could even play with his teeth.'

Often those closest to Jimi's guitar genius were the roadies who watched him warming up for a gig. At that time amplifiers and speakers were crude by today's standard and the problems of feedback – the noise made when the electrical field generated by a guitar interferes with a sound system – were the bane of many a band's life on the road.

Jimi simply used it as just another way to make music. Combined with a fuzz box and wah-wah pedal the effect was genuinely unique.

His road manager Eric Barrett would tell how Jimi would wire up massive banks of speakers and souped-up amplifiers through a special box of gadgets, itself linked in to the fuzz and wah-wah systems. Sometimes Barrett would try to test a guitar on it – but all he got for his trouble was a wall of feedback noise.

Barrett said: 'Jimi could control it all with his fingers and I still don't understand to this day how he did it. It was all part of his genius.

'We carried two dozen fuzz boxes and two dozen wah-wah pedals. We had so many spare parts – 13 guitars and pieces of guitar that he had smashed. He enjoyed smashing guitars – it got his frustrations out and the kids went berserk.

'Out of all the bits I'd build another guitar and he'd go and smash it again.'

Despite the on-stage violence – a hallmark of live Hendrix – roadies and stage managers around him at the time spoke consistently of the gentle man behind the wild image that had been so carefully crafted on his behalf.

Jimi hated any of his entourage feeling left out, often insisting on introducing a newcomer personally to the rest of his team. This attitude also translated into his

attitude to fame. He was keen for Mitch Mitchell and Noel Redding to get their fair share of the glory.

Off-stage Hendrix's musical choice was inevitably Chicago, or Led Zeppelin – he was an admirer of Jimmy Page – Cream or Bob Dylan. He worshipped Dylan and even grew more confidant in his own vocals after realizing that Dylan's nasal whining was one of his greatest attributes. Jimi's all-time favourite song was rumoured to be 'All Along the Watchtower' but, according to Eric Barrett, he could never remember all the words and would often end up singing the first verse four times over.

His music ranged from the sad and tender, such as 'The Wind Cries Mary', to the bluesy 'Red House' or the driving rhythms of 'Can You See Me'. In almost everything he wrote, the first few bars made it unmistakably Hendrix.

FREAKING OUT

The band's outrageous reputation brought the predictable backlash from Conservative MPs and some over-zealous churchmen who considered him the devil incarnate. In June 1967 it was claimed no fewer than 30 Stockholm

Above: *The Experience fly in to Heathrow Airport in 1967. Jimi was then simply the biggest pop star in the world.*

THE VIOLENCE AND SEXUALITY OF HIS STAGE ACT DROVE THE KIDS BERSERK.

hotels had banned Hendrix from staying with them.

It was all superb publicity and, naturally, record sales rocketed. Hendrix even managed to shrug off the disastrous decision to tour America with the Monkees, a band billed as the New Beatles at the time. Their fans were mainly love-struck teeny-boppers; Hendrix's the rebel-student type. Unsurprisingly the teenies turned out in force to see their idol Davey Jones and the Experience died a death at the first few concerts. A way out had to be found and Chandler let it be known that a right-wing group called the Daughters of the American Revolution had demanded Hendrix be banned for his indecent act. The Experience were able to quit the tour with heads reasonably high while the Daughters carried on their campaign blissfully unaware of the unwitting part they had played.

Friends of Hendrix later claimed this tour was the first sign of what became known as 'Jimi's downer', a progressively blackening mood that led him to start flirting with LSD and drug cocktails.

Shortly after the New Year of 1968 the Experience arrived in Sweden on a three-day tour. The band booked into the Opelan Hotel in Gothenburg and it seemed all three were happy if tired from a round of almost constant live shows and recording stints.

Then on 4 January the world awoke to find Hendrix was in police custody. He was accused of damaging his room by smashing windows, mirrors and chairs. Night staff had reported screams coming from the room. Police said they arrested Hendrix after three members of the tour entourage sat on him to calm him down.

Jimi was taken to hospital to have stitches in the self-inflicted wounds on his hands, presumably caused where he'd struck the window. He had clearly been out of his mind on a drugs- and booze-induced rampage and claimed later he could remember nothing of what went on. But the incident clearly frightened and disturbed him, so much so that it formed the basis of his song 'My Friend' from the 'Cry of Love' album. Jimi had temporarily lost control of his mind and he didn't like the feeling.

He was fined the sum of his earnings in Sweden and left the country immediately to prepare for a new tour of the USA. That tour provided the first clear signs that Jimi was getting tired of his wild-man-of-rock image. There was none of the crazed guitar riffs or half-screamed-half-sung vocals. At one concert he played only four numbers in his second set, apparently infuriated that an amplifier had blown.

In the months ahead Chas Chandler realized Jimi was starting to drink far more than his usual three whiskies a day. It was also becoming obvious that he'd started taking the 'flower-power drug' acid, or LSD, at almost every opportunity. Chandler urged restraint, realizing Hendrix was tempted to 'drop' a tab of acid whenever it was available. Later the manager recalled: 'There were so many people hanging around him. He couldn't be himself.

'We had an argument about it and he said "OK, no more." Then someone would turn up at the studios with a bag of goodies and pour some more down his throat.'

Jeanette Jacobs, one of Jimi's closest and oldest friends, observed: 'He would say to me: "What do you want?"'

'I would say: "What do you mean?" And he'd say: "In the next room you can get anything for free."'

'I asked who they were and he said they were fans trying to get him stoned. Not to hurt him but to turn him on. There was anything you could think of – uppers, downers, white lightning, purple hearts, take your pick.

'You wouldn't believe it. They really thought he could take it all at once. It's a drag to think that the people who loved him could have killed him. Not intentionally, of course.

'He was an idol, maybe a genius, and they thought he could take everything. He enjoyed experimenting but I never saw him take anything except acid.'

It was too much for Chas Chandler. Sick of the studio hangers-on, whom he saw as parasites on Jimi's talent, he decided at the end of 1968 to quit as Jimi's manager. As he put it so succinctly later: 'All I was doing was sitting there collecting a percentage. ... He wouldn't listen to anyone. And I had no way of saying anything. He was tearing himself apart for no apparent reason. I wasn't wanted any more so I split and flew back to England.'

BUSTED

In November 1968 it was announced that the Jimi Hendrix Experience had split up. In an interview Jimi suggested Mitch and Noel wanted to do their own things, producing or managing other performers. Noel, it was said, was reluctant to spend hour upon hour in the studio when the band could be out playing live. Hendrix insisted he was not abandoning Britain and paid tribute to his UK fans for not forgetting him. At that time his single 'All Along the Watchtower' – the classic Dylan song – was bursting into the top 20. But it was far removed from Hendrix's new work and had not even been his choice of release. He seemed like a man full of ideas but desperately unsure how to translate them on stage or vinyl.

Money was by now almost meaningless to Hendrix. He'd give vast sums to his family and in Los Angeles once gave $3,000 – then almost a year's wages for ordinary folk – to two girls for a shopping expedition.

Another story had him buying a brand-new Stingray car, taking it on the road for a day and smashing it up. Without a second thought he headed straight back to the showroom to buy another, only for the same thing to happen again four days later.

Ironically the first time he was prosecuted for possession of drugs he was totally innocent. Customs officers at Toronto airport discovered heroin in his luggage. He was arrested and warned by lawyers that he could go down for ten years.

Fortunately police uncovered the truth. Hendrix had complained of a headache and one of his girl groupies had thrown a package in his bag, promising 'Here, this'll help your head'.

Jimi was acquitted and the fear of an innocent man facing punishment convinced him to be more discreet – at least temporarily – about his use of hard drugs.

By now America had really woken up to the boy from Seattle, heralded in the media as the Black Elvis. Leaders of the Black Power movement thought he would be the

Top: *Playing in Sweden, where he had a huge following.*

Opposite top: *Jimi and his road manager, Eric Barrett.*

Opposite below: *Another airport, another pose. Jimi arrives in London en route to the Isle of Wight Rock Festival.*

Bottom: *The Experience are interviewed by Godfrey Winn. Jonathan King lurks in the background.*

Above: *Performing in 1969. By now the strain was starting to show.*

HENDRIX WAS TAKING **LSD** AT EVERY OPPORTUNITY – THE FANS THAT ADORED HIM WERE KILLING HIM WITH DRUGS.

Right: *The Isle of Wight Festival. Hendrix had lost much of his genius but got through the concert.*

perfect figurehead and began courting him as an active supporter. Jimi turned out at a few functions but it was clear he couldn't be dealing with the politics of colour. Some say he found it inconceivable that any human being could really be racially prejudiced, and so felt the struggle was somewhat pointless.

But he did send a $5,000 cheque to the Martin Luther King Memorial Fund, a rare contribution to a current-affairs issue. Later he was quoted as saying: 'I just want to do what I'm doing without getting involved in racial or political matters. I'm lucky that I can do that … lots of people can't.'

By the end of 1969 Hendrix was based permanently in New York, venturing out only to play a couple of concerts at the Royal Albert Hall in London and the legendary Woodstock free festival. However, early in 1970 he re-emerged with a new backing group – the Band of Gipsies – featuring Bill Cox on bass guitar and Buddy Miles on drums.

They knocked out one live album in New York but to most fans it was a poor substitute for the previous Experience. At a later concert in the city Jimi stormed off in a huff after a few numbers, claiming the band wasn't working together well.

Afterwards he admitted he

was never happy with the Gipsies' album and suggested it had been a rushed affair brought out under pressure from record company executives who wanted the tracks he 'owed' them.

In August 1970 Jimi flew back to Britain for what was to be his last live appearance, at the Isle of Wight Rock Festival, perhaps still the most prestigious ever held in Europe.

Jimi was tired – he'd flown to London straight from a party to launch his Electric Lady recording studios in New York – and then found himself scheduled to go on stage at 3 am.

He, Bill Cox and Mitch Mitchell were left hanging around in straw-strewn tents for hours, then endured a further delay while equipment was tested and re-tested. Finally he appeared before a tense, expectant crowd under a starry sky with the words: 'Yes, it has been a long time, hasn't it?'

The first few numbers didn't work out well and Jimi was forced to take the mike again and murmur: 'Let's start all over again. Hello, England.'

At the end he got the thunder of applause befitting his pedigree but he knew, and every fan staring up from the

damp fields knew, that this was not the Hendrix of old. A month later he was dead.

Hendrix had been staying in London at the Notting Hill basement flat owned by his then girlfriend, German Monika Dannemann. She was a stunning blonde skating instructor whom Jimi had met a year earlier in Düsseldorf. Rumour had it that they planned to marry.

SUICIDE?

On 16 September Hendrix showed up without warning at Ronnie Scott's Jazz Club in Frith Street, Soho. He knew his old pal Eric Burdon was playing there with a new group, War, and Burdon had earlier hinted he wanted Jimi to play with them.

Burdon later recalled: 'We knew things weren't all that good with him but we did our best to let him know that we were there to help him.'

Jimi started poorly but his performance improved throughout the set. There was little to suggest he was overtly depressed or unstable.

The following day Monika called Burdon to tell him Hendrix was ill. He immediately reassured her and promised Jimi would be OK. Later he was to change his mind and urge her to call an ambulance.

That evening Monika and Jimi arrived home around 8.30 pm and shared a hot meal and bottle of wine. He washed his hair in the bath and then sat up with her talking and listening to music until the early hours. Then, at 1.45 am, Jimi suddenly announced he had to go to meet some people – he refused to call them friends – at a nearby house. He said he did not want Monika with him but agreed that she could drop him off there in the car.

After leaving him at the address Monika returned at 3 am to take him home to bed. She later told of making him a fish sandwich and then sitting and talking to him right through to 7 am. She finally took a sleeping tablet but woke again at 10.20 am to find Hendrix dozing. She left to buy some cigarettes but by the time she returned he had been sick. For the first time it occurred to her that he had swallowed sleeping tablets.

Monika checked his pulse and called an ambulance, which took about 20 minutes to arrive. There is little doubt that Hendrix

was still alive as he was ferried towards St Mary Abbotts Hospital, Kensington.

Monika would later maintain: 'He did not die from the sleeping tablets because he had not taken enough to be an overdose.

'The reason he died was because he couldn't get air. He suffocated on his own vomit.'

Above: *Monika Dannemann, Jimi's German girlfriend, arriving at the Westminster coroner's court for the inquest.*

> **DESPITE THE KIND APPLAUSE, JIMI READ THE SIGNS – HE WAS FINISHED.**

The following day the headlines screamed the inevitable to a shocked world: 'Jimi's last, lost days', 'Jimi Hendrix dies in drugs mystery' and, inaccurately, 'Jimi Hendrix dies – drug overdose'. One Sunday paper even called him the 'prophet-in-chief of the drugs generation'.

Three days later Eric Burdon appeared to support the suicide claim. He told the BBC that Jimi had left a suicide note and that as one of the star's closest friends he intended to carry on the Hendrix legacy.

The theory was immediately pooh-poohed by Jimi's manager Mike Jeffrey who said: 'I've been going through a whole stack of papers, poems and songs ....many could be interpreted as a suicide note. I just don't believe it was suicide.'

The Kensington coroner, Dr Thurston, agreed. He said there was no evidence to suggest a deliberate attempt was made by Hendrix to take his own life. His report concluded: 'The question why he took so many sleeping tablets cannot safely be answered.'

One theory is that he wanted to make a cry for help, to tell those around him that he was unhappy and didn't know how to break free from his cycle of despair. Others say he simply couldn't find sleep with one tablet and took a further eight in his impatience.

The effect on British musicians who knew him, and indeed the entire nation, was of deep shock combined with a sense of disbelief. Wasn't he so young, so famous? Hadn't he so much more to give?

THE END OF THE PARTY

Eric Clapton, it is claimed, cried for three days when he heard the news. And Chas Chandler, being met that day by his father at Newcastle station, remembers: 'I couldn't believe it. I was numb for days. But somehow I wasn't surprised.

'I don't believe for one minute that he killed himself. That was out of the question. But something had to happen and there was no way of stopping it.

'You just get a feeling sometimes. It was like the last couple of years had prepared us for it. It was like the message I had been waiting for.'

Noel Redding in his memoirs *Are You Experienced* suggests Hendrix was capable of killing himself. He claims Jimi slashed his wrists at the end of one particularly taxing US tour in 1968. Intriguingly, Redding also says he does not rule out foul play in the star's final hours.

'There is no question that Jimi was in a mess and involved with some pretty creepy people,' he said. 'Jimi's death was the most lucrative act of his sad career.'

That comment is at the root of Redding's anger and frustration at the way he and Mitch Mitchell were later treated. Hendrix's estate was estimated at more than $100 million by the early nineties, mostly the royalties from four studio albums and 15 compilations of concert recordings. But much of the money has been enmeshed in a series of highly complex legal arguments.

At one point even Jimi's father – the man surely first in line for a share of his son's wealth – was given a yearly allowance barely amounting to the price of a new car.

Redding says the mass confusion that

Above: Shown here on his wedding day, Eric Burden claimed Jimi had left a suicide note. The coroner came to his own conclusion.

Detectives established that nine pills were missing from a bottle in Monika's flat. But why should Jimi have risked downing them when he was so aware of the dangers?

erupted around Jimi's fortune followed the death of his manager, Mike Jeffrey, in a plane crash in 1971. From then on, he and Mitchell have had to live in relative penury – despite their massive contribution to the success of the Experience.

In 1990 Mitchell was finally forced into parting with his most prized possession, the white Fender Stratocaster guitar that Hendrix gave him after playing that final Isle of Wight performance. It fetched a record £198,000 at the London auction house Sotheby's and Mitchell kissed it goodbye with the words: 'I would like to think it would get passed on to people who have access to play it.'

In death, as in life, Jimi milked every moment. Even the funeral in his Seattle home town turned into a massive knees-up with musicians such as John Hammond and Buddy Miles jumping on stage in a rented hall to pay tribute. As Mitchell later put it: 'We had a good party. It was the way he would have wanted. We gave him a good send-off.'

To a generation of sixties fans, Jimi Hendrix had been a hero among heroes. A musician who could at once show Jeff Beck's amazing speed, Eric Clapton's imagination and Pete Townshend's raw energy. His sad pathetic death was the final chapter in one of pop music's most moving stories.

Yet there may still be an epilogue. On Saturday 11 December 1993 the London based *Daily Mail* reported on its front page that Scotland Yard officers had sensationally re-opened their investigations into Jimi's death. They had received new evidence from another of his girlfriends, Kathy Etchingham, who had commissioned her own private detective. British Attorney General Sir Nicholas Lyell was said to be considering quashing the coroner's original open verdict and holding a new inquest.

For the fans it brought back memories of Hendrix's words in his favourite song 'All Along the Watchtower'.

Prophetically he sings: 'There's too much confusion.

'I can't get no release.'

Below: *Jimi Hendrix. 'The music will be played loud and it will be our music.'*

JUDY GARLAND
Born to sing

The future seemed rosy – fame and fortune were hers at an early age. Yet despite a wonderful voice, a powerful personality and hordes of adoring fans, Judy Garland was doomed to be trapped on the wrong side of the rainbow.

Audiences went wild for her, children were entranced by her and men fell at her feet. But although everybody loved her, she failed to love herself – or at least not enough to stop the slide into a drink-and-drugs oblivion.

Singer-actress Judy Garland was simply one of the most versatile and popular stars of the century and she loved her fans in return, from the bottom of her soul. She never failed to be genuinely moved by the public's displays of affection.

Despite her glorious voice, her impressive theatrical skills, an appealing face and hordes of devoted followers, she could not find the happiness she craved. The girl who won a million hearts as Dorothy in *The Wizard of Oz* found her own yellow-brick road was a path to self-destruction and distress.

At first it seemed nothing could halt the glittering career of the open-faced Judy who fizzed and effused over the screen. But then her own great talent enslaved her. She found herself on a treadmill, unable to stop the cycle of demands on her time, energy and money, addicted as she was to performing. She was dragged to the depths, eventually losing that amazing voice and dying in June 1969 aged 47. It was the end of a career marked not only by ovations and adulation, but also by a 30-year dependency on drugs and a string of nervous breakdowns.

How could a woman who commanded so much love and respect be the author of comments such as: 'If I am such a legend, why am I so lonely?' She also admitted: 'I seldom know who really likes me.'

In fact Judy was never given a chance to outgrow the childhood fears and insecurities that haunt us all. While everyone wanted to know about her singing and dancing act, no one was interested in the vulnerable, tortured person underneath.

A STAR IS BORN

That uneasy illusion of Judy being a commodity rather than a person with needs and desires was rooted in her childhood. Judy was the third daughter of Frank and Ethel Gumm, baptized Frances but known among the family as Baby.

The place was Grand Rapids, Minnesota, where her dad Frank ran a theatre and film house. Before her had come two sisters, Mary Jane and Virginia.

Already, Frank, Ethel, Mary Jane and Virginia were established entertainers at the theatre. Frank had inherited warm, lilting tones from his Irish ancestors which he duly passed on to his daughters. Ethel, meanwhile, was a piano player for both the film shows and the act. The Four Gumms, as they were known, were well received in Grand Rapids.

Opposite: 'Miss Show Business' at London's Dominion Theatre in 1957. Her powerful performances moved fans to tears.

Above: *Dorothy in* **The Wizard of Oz** *tends to the Cowardly Lion, played by Bert Lahr. Judy was a 17-year-old yet convincingly portrayed a child of 9.*

HER FATHER'S
HOMOSEXUALITY WRECKED
THE YOUNG GIRL'S LIFE
WHEN SHE LOST THE HOME
SHE'D LOVED.

From the moment she was born, little Frances was surrounded by the sights and sounds of showbusiness. She was the apple of her proud father's eye – he loved nothing better than to lull her off to sleep with the ballads of the day. From the first, the theatre was her playground and she was keen to join the family in their stage routine from the moment she could toddle.

Her first public performance was when she was 18 months old: her sisters let her sing 'Jingle Bells' in a neighbourhood talent show they were producing. She repeated the number soon afterwards when she sneaked up on stage at the theatre during a Christmas Eve show in 1924 for an unscheduled debut. Her bold voice and cute image earned her waves of applause from the audience. Her parents realized she was now in on the act so the Gumm sisters became a trio.

Soon their horizons spread beyond the theatre. Their mother was driven by a dream of her girls making it big, but there was no doubt the three loved to be on stage and performed with a delightful, confident charm which won them critical praise.

Little did they know there was more than just a vision of fame that kept Ethel pursuing new frontiers. She had a secret torment that she would never share with the girls. Ethel had been devastated to realize that her loving husband was in fact a homosexual whose covert activities threatened to have them run out of town.

Ethel had known about her husband's inclinations since before their youngest child was born. So upset and disgusted was she by what she discovered, she even sought to have an abortion but was talked out of it by a doctor friend.

It wasn't long before snippets of his gay exploits were the talk of the town. Until now, Ethel and Frank had been pillars of the community. A full-blown scandal would have made their previously comfortable, uncomplicated lives intolerable. In 1926 they decided to leave Grand Rapids and headed for Los Angeles.

It was the first proper tour the girls had undertaken. Frances relished this gypsy world of putting on a show in town after city until they reached their destination. They were thrilled by Los Angeles, its size and buzzing atmosphere. They returned to Grand Rapids only to sell up and move for good.

Above: A superstar, yet Judy once said: 'If I am such a legend, why am I so lonely?'

Above right: In happier days, Judy celebrates her 18th birthday with her mother and movie mogul L.B. Mayer.

Frequently, Judy the star regretted the move which took her out of the close-knit community which she had loved. As shadows grew over her life, she wondered more than once if she might have been fulfilled had her family only stayed in the cosy town where she was born. She never fully understood that her father was a homosexual and that his leanings might have wrecked any semblance of happiness in small-town America.

Finally, Frank found a theatre to run in Lancaster, a town melded into the Southern Californian desert where cowboy legend John Wayne had gone to school. The Valley Theatre, as he called it, was the new venue for the Gumm sisters, and the townsfolk their new audience.

Later, residents remarked on the charisma and energy of the smallest sister which shone out to almost eclipse the talents of the other two. Her vibrant personality – which suffered not a fleck of affectation – soon made her popular with both young and old. Everyone could hear her practising in her loud, almost abrasive voice as they passed the house.

They would hear Frank perhaps joining in the singing with Ethel on the piano and

could smell the mouthwatering aroma of Grandma cooking up doughnuts in the kitchen. Amid this vision of homeliness, it was Grandma, all floury hands and sweet smile, who first christened bubbly Baby Gumm as 'Miss Leatherlungs'.

THE SEARCH FOR STARDOM

The energetic Ethel soon became discontented, however. She yearned for her girls to get the glory they seemed to richly deserve. She would take Frances into Los Angeles, some three hours distant, in search of the big break.

The effort wasn't in vain. When she was 6 years old, Frances, together with her sisters, was on KFI radio in Los Angeles. They were a hit and it paved the way for more performances. The trips to the city became more frequent, the partings from Frank longer and longer.

Eventually, the women of the family found a base in the city to give showbusiness their best shot, leaving an unhappy Frank running the picture house in Lancaster.

Their lives were perpetually unsettled after that. The girls hopped between Los Angeles and Lancaster, depending on the shows and slots in which they appeared. They were beginning to make sacrifices, reluctantly, for their budding careers. School dances were missed, friendships curtailed, family Christmases abandoned, romances put on the rocks by the continuing demands of the shows.

Neighbours began to remark unkindly that Ethel Gumm was neglecting her husband. Others felt she was forcing her

children to perform and tour. One described her as 'a pushy movie-mother who thought she was better than the local yokels'.

Usually the girls would appear as second, third or fourth billing at vaudeville theatres around the area. Their popularity was only increasing at a moderate rate. Could it be because theatres were constantly misspelling their name so they appeared as the Glumm sisters? In a bid to improve their fortunes, they changed the surname to Garland. They were, said one theatre critic, as pretty as a garland of flowers and the image stuck.

After a performance in 1934, the *Los Angeles Times* read: 'The Garland Sisters scored a hit, with the youngest member of the trio practically stopping the show with

Top: *The brat pack.* **From left to right:** *Freddie Bartholomew, Peggy Ryan, Mickey Rooney, Deanna Durbin, Judy Garland and Jackie Cooper.*

Above: *With Mickey Rooney, another child star, who watched Judy crumble under the acute pressures of superstardom.*

*Above: **With her first husband, orchestra leader David Rose. She was heartbroken when they split up a year after marrying.***

GRIEF-STRICKEN AFTER HER FATHER'S PREMATURE DEATH JUDY WAS FILLED WITH HORROR AND LOATHING BY HER MOTHER'S AFFAIR.

---

her singing.' Other newspapers carried on in the same vein during that year and the next. Each was to rave about the three sisters but most particularly the outstanding youngest girl.

The signs were pointing to a solo career. Frances's sisters were, in any case, courting and hoping to be married. It was only a matter of time before she came to the attention of an agent. Eventually she was summoned for an audition at MGM in September 1935, to belt out a melody in front of movie mogul L.B. Mayer himself. Well known for his keen eye for talent, Mayer instantly presented her with a 7-year contract which she signed with the new Christian name she had chosen for herself, Judy.

Her parents were delighted. Ethel said: 'Hollywood can't hurt my daughter! As long as Judy is the girl I know she is, movies or movie life can't hurt her. She is happiest when she is busy and you know the old saying "the devil finds uses for idle hands". Judy wants to go on making pictures, minding her own business, developing her mind, building a sane and normal future for herself.'

THE SHADOW OF DEATH

Her solo career started with an appearance on a radio show with star of the day Wallace Beery, but her bubble burst that November when her father Frank died suddenly after a short illness, aged 49. He was never to see the huge achievements of the daughter he helped to mould and make great.

It was devastating for Judy, who later called his death 'the most terrible thing that ever happened to me in my life'.

For her it was the start of an idolization which would last a lifetime. Recalling her father, Judy later said: 'I loved my father. He was a wonderful man with a fierce temper … and an untrained but beautiful tenor voice. He had a funny sense of humour and he laughed all the time – good and loud like I do. I adored him … And he wanted to be close to me too but we never had much time together.'

Little did she know that he had been forced to leave the theatre in Lancaster due to mismanagement which left him thousands of dollars in debt, nor that whispers of his indiscretions with schoolboys were echoing around the arid town. There was even talk of an arrest in Los Angeles. Her continuing promise at the start of the thirties was merely a good excuse for Frank to cut loose once more.

His death also helped to drive a wedge between herself and her mother. While blissfully unaware of her father's flings, she had found her mother during an assignation with another Lancaster man, to her horror and shame.

The seed of suspicion that Ethel was a dominant, pushy type who cared only to bask in her daughter's reflected glory began to grow. Judy once said of her mother: 'She was a lonely and determined woman and I guess I'm the same way.'

But she went on to blame her mother at least in part for much of her misery. They exchanged some contrary insults in an embittered battle of wills. Judy said Ethel was 'the real wicked witch of the West who was no good for anything but to create chaos and fear'. In turn, Ethel remained convinced she had done her level best for Judy and was simply assisting the girl's expressed ambition to become an actress.

By the time Judy was 30, mother and daughter were estranged. Ethel, the mother who had once called her youngest daughter loving, generous and unselfish, branded her as self-centred. 'That's my fault, I made it too easy for her,' she complained. 'She worked but that's all she ever wanted, to be an actress. She never said "I wanted to be kind" or "loved", only "I want to be famous."'

Ethel went to court to gain financial support from her by-now famous daughter. With a second, failed marriage behind her, she worked as a clerk at Douglas Aircraft in Santa Monica. Finally she had a heart attack in January 1953 and was found slumped between two cars, collapsing as she hurried to work.

Shocked, Judy went to the funeral with her sisters. Observers declared both mother and daughter always loved each other in their hearts.

However, only the germ of this personal disaster was forming when Judy was in those first heady days with the world's best-known film studio.

THE TRICKS OF THE TRADE

Her first movie was made in 1936; it was called *Every Sunday Afternoon* and starred Deanna Durbin. Judy then learned the tricks of the trade in a further six films alongside established stars including Betty Grable, Robert Taylor, Buddy Ebsen and Mary Astor.

In the same stable of child stars were Freddie Bartholomew and Mickey Rooney. The diminutive Rooney, who first met Judy at a Los Angeles stage school, struck up a lasting comradeship with her which he recalled in his autobiography, *Life is Too Short.*

'It was the perfect new name for the 15-year-old singer Frances Gumm. Judy was just right: cute, peppy and full of bounce. When I knew her at Ma Lawlor's Profession School she had more bounce than everyone else put together. Gumm was the wrong image: sticky, soft, chewy, tutti frutti, Garland was full of joy.

'And I will never forget her performance at the Pantages Theatre in Hollywood. She planted both feet wide apart as if she were challenging the audience then sang: "Zing went the Strings of my Heart" with the kind of verve that made all our heartstrings go bing, ding, ping, ring, ting and zing.'

He witnessed how Judy, the young individualist, was under pressure to conform to the likes of the leggy beauties who traditionally made it big in Hollywood.

'Judy … was no glamour girl. In the first place she had a bad bite and her teeth were out of alignment. This, of course, was something MGM's dentists could fix.

'But there were some things about her that the studio couldn't fix. She was a little too short, a half inch under 5 feet tall. Her legs were long but they seemed to be hitched to her shoulders which were too broad for her body. She looked, well, different.'

When she saw herself in her second film with plaits and gingham dress, she described it as the most awful moment of her life. 'I'm like a fat little pig in pigtails,' she moaned.

Rooney pinpointed her fabulous physical attributes. 'In fact, Judy was an all-American beauty in more ways than one. She had marvellous, warm eyes that invited you to share her secret mirth and a cute little nose that wrinkled when she laughed.

'She had an expressive generous mouth that hardly ever uttered a line that wasn't funny, or, in her later years, outrageous or filled with feeling. If I had not been so tainted with the same phoney Hollywood notions about who was beautiful and who was not, I would have fallen in love with her myself.'

But Judy was learning young about the

Above: *Judy with Vincente Minnelli, the film director, who was 20 years her senior. He was the father of her first daughter, Liza, who also found fame in show business.*

AT 17, HOW COULD SHE HAVE KNOWN THAT THOSE HARMLESS TABLETS PRESCRIBED BY THE DOCTOR WOULD MAKE HER A JUNKIE FOR LIFE?

penalties of being different. The loyalty and allegiance she found in Rooney was a big comfort, but it wasn't enough. Even Mayer himself compounded her troubles. He would call her 'the fat kid' or even 'my little hunchback'.

Her big break came four years after joining the studio. She was picked to play Dorothy in *The Wizard of Oz* when rival studio Twentieth Century Fox refused to release Shirley Temple for the role.

Her confidence oozed all over the screen. That, alongside her moving rendition of the song: 'Somewhere Over the Rainbow', made Judy hot property.

FEAR OF FAILURE

But although at 17 she was little more than a child, the catapult to fame brought with it adult pressures. For about the first time in her life the effervescent kid whom neighbours found so natural and endearing became highly strung.

Perhaps it was the weight of performing in films, being the focus of the camera, lights, director and everyone else, that put her on edge.

Or maybe it was the constant invidious comparison to other svelte sex symbols of the day. Confused, the young Judy construed it was ideal to be thin, tall and sultry, none of which were her natural strengths.

To keep her nerves under control, she started popping pills prescribed at the studio. How could she have known then that those apparently harmless tablets would make her a junkie for life? By the time she was 20, she had suffered her first nervous breakdown. She had another the following year.

A lifetime of frustrating insomnia started. And the harder she worked, the less sleep she managed to achieve at night.

She considered herself plump and tried desperately to diet. She yearned for physical and dramatic perfection. It was a gilt-edged recipe for depression.

Much later she recalled how early fame had affected her: 'I had so many anxieties, so many fears. I'd had them as a child and they just grew worse as I got older and more self-centred. The fear of failure, the fear of ridicule. I hated the way I looked. I cried for no reason, laughed hysterically, made stupid decisions, couldn't tell a kind word from an insult.'

To escape the loneliness and insecurity, she married orchestra leader David Rose.

Right: *On stage, where she overcame her nerves to belt out songs which thrilled her audiences.*

Below: *With Lorna, aged 4, and Joseph, 2, in 1957.*

He was 12 years older and seemed to represent all that Judy was lacking in her world – stability, warmth and guidance.

But fate wasn't kind to the young romantics. Rose was drafted into the army within weeks. A year later he asked for a divorce on the grounds the pair had grown apart. Judy was wounded, despite his assurances she was in no way to blame for the collapse of the marriage. She continued working at a frenetic pace, finding time to entertain the troops when she wasn't making movies.

Within five years she was married again, this time to director Vincente Minnelli. Although 20 years older than her, he gave Judy time to mature and thrive. Her happiness was complete when she gave birth to a baby girl, Liza, in 1946.

BREAKDOWN

Still, Judy found the strain of working for the studio giants intolerable. Using pills as her prop, she was suffering poor health, but studio schedules and her own compulsion to perform wouldn't allow her to put her feet up. With the bouts of illness flared up tantrums and tears. Judy gained a reputation for being difficult on set.

It was during convalescence after a nervous breakdown in 1949 at the Peter Bent Brigham Hospital in Boston that her love of and dedication to children became obvious to herself and those around her. Judy spent hours at the bedside of a 6-year-old girl who refused to talk after being abused by her family. Quietly, comfortingly, Judy chatted about her life, her shows and the people she had met. The girl never said a word.

But when the day came for Judy to say goodbye, the youngster couldn't bear it. "Don't go. Don't go away," she pleaded as Judy prepared to leave, the first words she had uttered in months. Could Judy have found her niche if only she had stayed at home to be a full-time mother? It was another question that tormented her over the years.

Judy's contract expired in 1950 after 15 years and 30 pictures – and MGM decided she was too much trouble to take on again. At the same time, Minnelli decided to bring the curtain down on their marriage.

Judy was gutted by the double disaster.

It led to a frantic attempt to slash her neck and wrists, more a case of self-mutilation than suicide but enough to convince the Hollywood gossips she was finished.

And so it happened that when Judy was aged just 29, she was making her first 'comeback'.

It was to happen in London at the renowned Palladium in April 1951 in front of a buzzing crowd peppered with stars. Characteristically, Judy cowered in the wings – the prospect of performing in front of the excited throng terrified her. It was down to her friend Kay Thompson to get her onto the stage with a push from behind. But once on stage she sparkled.

To use a tired but apt statement, she took the place by storm. *The Daily Telegraph* said: 'It was not only with her voice but with her whole personality that she filled the theatre. Miss Garland's charm is a complete absence of affectation. She presented herself with no particular preparation and no preamble and just did what she must have been born to do ... sing.'

It was followed by a country-wide tour where she received the same rapturous reception and then some dates back in the USA which also played to critical acclaim. The roller-coaster tour only stopped when Judy, exhausted and suffering critical pains in her chest, collapsed on stage during a matinee performance. Her body was pleading for a rest. Judy refused to listen and went back to work after only four days.

COWERING IN THE WINGS, THE STAR WAS PETRIFIED WITH STAGE-FRIGHT.

Above: *With Liza, Lorna, Joey and her third husband, pilot Sid Luft. Their stormy marriage lasted for 11 years.*

Above: *Judy gave a stunning performance in the film* **A Star is Born,** *which also featured James Mason.*

Below: *As one of the host of big-name stars, Judy packed a punch as the persecuted Jewish woman in* **Judgement at Nuremberg.**

Her new-found burst of energy was due in part to a fresh love in her life. In 1951 she became engaged to ex-test pilot Sid Luft and wed him the following year. They had two children, Lorna and Joseph, known as Joey.

Her stage revival an unqualified success, she found the courage to go back into the studios and record a movie, *A Star is Born.* James Mason was her co-star, although both Humphrey Bogart and Cary Grant had been sought for the role.

Word had it Judy was up to her old tricks of temperamental walk-outs and fainting fits which cost the production time and money. Afterwards Judy explained: 'I'd be the last to deny the picture took an awful long time and went way over budget. But there was a reason for all that.

'I'm a perfectionist; George Cukor [director] is a perfectionist and so is Sid. We had to have it right and to make it right took time. It was a good picture; as good as we'd hoped it would be.'

It won her one of two Academy Award nominations although the golden prize of an Oscar was to elude her.

Throughout the fifties Judy performed at dates in the USA, Britain and the rest of the world, but she was still dogged by ill health. First laryngitis threatened her shows after it consumed her voice. Then there was the constant struggle against weight gain, frequently caused by fluid retention. Finally, in 1959, her very life was in the balance when she contracted hepatitis. Many would have given up the bright lights and the glory for a life at home, but

Judy was a born trouper – she loved to do her stuff in front of audiences and cameras.

More than that, she was persistently plagued by cash worries. No matter how much she earned, there were always more bills and increased demands. The lovable tramp who performed 'Couple of Swells' so memorably seemed to have a permanent hole in her own pocket.

It is thought she earned $10 million during her career. Unfortunately her mother seems to have managed the starlet's income badly. Agents and managers carved off a slice of her earnings, as well as the expenses for her entire entourage. Then there were hefty back-tax demands – Judy had no idea why – and she was always broke.

Valiantly she went back to work, making a special effort to sing in support of John F. Kennedy, a valued friend.

In 1961, she filmed *Judgment at Nuremberg* and brilliantly portrayed the German woman persecuted by Nazis on a trumped-up charge.

A review in *Weekend* magazine described how fellow star Maximilian Schell was captivated by her performance.

'Max Schell's usually solemn face was alight with admiration. "She is fantastic," he said. "She is just a whole human being. Every dimension is there. And such warmth! It is as if she is enveloping you, as if she is trying to embrace the whole world."

'He was right. The magic, the old alchemy was very much present. This was no burned-out star staying airborne on a broomstick of temperament, laryngitis and law suits.'

The marriage to Sid Luft was a stormy one. They split and were reconciled three times before a final parting. It was after one of these break-ups that Judy fled to London with Lorna and Joey, terrified Sid was going to have the courts pronounce her 'an unfit mother'.

Although the threat came to nothing, it was another turn of the screw, putting her under extraordinary pressure. The marriage staggered on until May 1963 when it was finally finished. That was just before she embarked on her own television series, something she swore she would never do. The production of the shows was fraught with difficulty and received only mixed reviews. All Judy's old infamy came back to haunt her.

CATASTROPHE

Judy was exhausted, from both work and continued ill health, including a painful kidney infection and a suspected heart attack. She was warned to temper her use of pills. Nevertheless, as her nightly quest for sleep ended in failure, she found herself reaching for a remedy in the long hours before dawn.

Her existence was getting more and more nightmarish too. She would ring up friends at all hours, starting impossible conversations about paranoid visions. Friends grew weary of soothing her panic attacks and few could blame them.

In May 1964 she undertook a series of tours in Australia. It started blindingly well in Sydney but the Melbourne date was a well-chronicled catastrophe. She was an hour late, tripped as she walked on stage and sang with a voice that could have scoured pans. She sang only a handful of songs before fleeing the stage in tears.

Quickly she moved on to Hong Kong to escape the publicity. Within days she was in a coma, struck down by broncho-pneumonia and pleurisy. Again she nearly died but fought back. Later she married Mark Herron, the man who discovered her unconscious and drove through a tropical typhoon to take her to hospital.

However, the marriage in November 1965 lasted only five months. Judy was hurt again, unable to understand how the relationship had collapsed, following as it did a year-long engagement.

There were more concerts at which she was croaky, tired and unable to finish. Lonely outside the theatre, she tried to write poetry to escape her problems but was stung by the bevy of criticism.

Judy had one final grab at happiness in the last months of her life. She met and married Mickey Deans, a discothèque manager who fell under her spell. He was touched by her vulnerability, enjoyed her tactile ways and realized she was not

WHEN SHE TRIED TO SING JUDY DISCOVERED TO HER HORROR THAT THE OLD MAGIC HAD DESERTED HER.

Left: *A feeble wave as Judy fled Australia after a disastrous show.*

Above: *Marriage to Mark Herron. The actor looks delighted to have wed Judy but the relationship floundered within six months.*

unpredictable, just scared. It wasn't her temperament to blame for perpetual upsets but mostly her health. And he was outraged at the way showbusiness hangers-on would leech from her, helping to cause her cash problems.

Appalled when he discovered the extent of her dependency on pills, Mickey limited her to 40 a day. But he was helpless in the end – which came while they were visiting her favourite city, London, in June 1969. They had spent a lazy day, playing the piano and watching TV. They curled up in bed together and Mickey, suffering the

Above: *Judy and Liza, two show business legends, embrace in mutual admiration following a show in 1965.*

Right: *The final marriage, to Mickey Deans, came in March 1969. Just three months later he discovered her body after she died from a barbiturate overdose.*

ravages of a sore throat, knew nothing more until he woke up in an empty bed to the shrill ring of a telephone and tried to find her.

There was no response from behind the locked bathroom door. Judy had collapsed and died from the effects of too many barbiturates.

Her body was flown back to New York for a funeral. Before she was buried more than 20,000 people filed past her as she lay in a white steel casket at Campbell's Funeral Home in Madison Square Garden. Hundreds more turned out for the 20-minute service at which James Mason read the eulogy.

He read: '... I travelled in her orbit only for a while but it was an exciting while and one during which it seemed that the joys in her life outbalanced the miseries.

'The little girl whom I knew, had a curl right in the middle of her forehead; when she was good she was not only very very good, she was also the most sympathetic, the funniest, the sharpest and the most stimulating woman I ever knew. She was a lady who gave so much and richly, both to the vast audiences she entertained and the friends around her who she loved, that there is no currency in which to repay her ...'

Mickey Rooney said: 'Judy's not in pain any more but I am still sad about her leaving. There will never be another talent like Judy, never anyone who can sing with such heart. Other people sing the words. She never lost the thought behind the words, never lost the poetry.'

Liza recalls her legacy from her mother. 'My mother gave me strength and magic and humour. Her humour was so immense, people don't realize that. And she gave me my drive.'

Perhaps it was that drive which drove her to death.

SPECTACULAR
FAILURES

GENERAL CUSTER
The last blunder

The ancient tribes, pushed to their limits by the land-hungry settlers, refused to surrender their holy lands. The arrogant General Custer was determined to make the Black Hills of Dakota run red with Indian blood.

George Armstrong Custer was a model soldier, the kind of man through whom wars are won and of whom legends are made. The legend of General Custer, however, is not one by which he would wish to be remembered.

Born on 5 December 1839 at New Rumley, Ohio, he graduated from the famed US Military Academy at West Point and was plummeted straight into the tragic American Civil War. He distinguished himself in this conflict by his pursuit of the Confederate Commander-in-Chief, General Robert E. Lee. By the age of only 23, he had rocketed to the rank of brigadier-general.

It was then that the vanity that eventually led him to an ignominious death first reared its arrogant head. He became a glory-seeker, desperate for mentions in dispatches. He grew his blond locks to shoulder length, and commissioned dozens of sketches and portraits of himself, with which he adorned his quarters.

His flamboyance and insufferable ego made him hated by his fellow officers, who were able to get their own back when, after the Civil War ended in 1865, he was relegated to the rank of captain. His driving ambition made him try all the harder, however, and he curried favour with senior officers until, within a year, he had regained the rank of lieutenant-colonel.

A LAUGHING STOCK

Custer was still a laughing stock among his peers. Perhaps it was one of them who reported him to his superiors for an offence that would have cost any other man his career. The long-haired egotist had found himself a wife, Libbie, and decided to spend a vacation with her – without troubling himself to seek permission from his senior officers. His absence from camp was discovered and Custer was hauled before a court martial. The sentence: suspension for a year without pay.

The delight back at camp must have been immense. It was the last anyone thought they would see or hear of the arrogant buffoon. In typical Custer style, he used his period of penury to write – about himself, of course! He portrayed himself in

Opposite: *George Custer; the truth about his bungling was kept hidden for years.*

Below: *Indian chief Sitting Bull, who had 50 pieces of flesh carved from his body to prove his courage in the preparations for Custer's last stand.*

GENERAL SHERIDAN'S DIPLOMACY WAS SIMPLE: THE ONLY GOOD INDIAN WAS A DEAD ONE.

the role of hero in a series of adventures that bore more relationship to fiction than fact. Unfortunately, it is these writings that perpetuated his image and restored his reputation. The truth, however, was that while writing his early memoirs, he was running up bills which, as he later moved from fort to fort, he never quite managed to pay off.

Custer's luck remained with him. In 1868 he was reinstated. Unbelievably, he was given the exalted rank of general and placed in charge of the illustrious 7th Cavalry. He was also given a special mission, one that required the virtues of a diplomat as much as those of a soldier.

General Philip Sheridan, nicknamed the 'Angry Bear' of the frontier forts, is best known for his pronouncement that 'the only good Indian is a dead one'. He is certainly not remembered for his diplomacy or compassion. Perhaps that is why he appointed the newly promoted General George Armstrong Custer, who also had none of these virtues, to solve one of America's thorniest problems. At the tender age of 28, Custer was ordered to bring to heel the ancient tribes of the Plains Indians.

THE WHITE MAN'S GREED

For decades, the Indians (mainly Cheyenne and Sioux) had been slowly pushed westwards by land-hungry settlers. Land treaties allowed the native Americans freedom of movement but in the 1860s the greed of the white man produced an increasing number of clashes between the new and old residents of the plains. Wandering bands of Indian buffalo-hunters were becoming an annoyance to the authorities – because they wanted the land on which the buffalo roamed. For these wholly commercial reasons, it was decided to push the Indians into reservations. Many refused, preferring a precarious existence on the plains to mere survival on reservation handouts. The government wanted 'these renegades, these outcasts, these anti-socials' to be made to see the error of their ancient ways.

Why Custer should have been chosen as the man to get this message across can only be a matter of conjecture. His career as a soldier had been extremely patchy, and he was desperate to rehabilitate himself with the senior staff. He needed success and yearned for glory. It must have been made clear to him by General Sheridan that a handful of despised Indians must not be allowed to stand in his way.

In fact, Custer's mission was: 'To proceed to Washita River, the winter seat of the hostile tribes, and then to destroy their villages and ponies, kill or hang all warriors and bring back all women and children'.

The general was delighted to accept the task. In the autumn of 1868, he rode out towards the west, revelling in the nicknames the Indians had given him – 'Hard Backsides' because of the long chases he made without leaving the saddle, and the 'Long-Haired One' (or *Pahuska*) because of his flowing, straw-coloured locks.

His first foe was to be a peaceable old chief called Black Kettle, leader of the Southern Cheyenne, who had settled with his tribe of 200 families on the bank of the Washita River – the same river mentioned in Custer's secret orders.

Winter was about to set in and Black Kettle had asked to be allowed to move his tribe to the protection of the nearest white military outpost, Fort Cobb, about 100 miles distant. General William Hazen, the fort's commander, had refused, ordering Black Kettle and his deputation to return to the Washita. The general had, however, given them a firm assurance of safety. He had promised them that they would be allowed to remain by the river until after the snows had melted.

Did General Hazen know he was lying? Or did General Custer decide to overrule him? All that is certain is that before dawn on a foggy December morning, Custer's men surrounded the Cheyenne camp. Puzzled, Black Kettle saddled up and rode out through the mist to find the leader of the whites and talk with him.

SLAUGHTER OF INNOCENTS

As the Cheyenne chief left his camp, the cavalry charged. According to Indian legend, he was shot dead as he raised his hand to greet the approaching soldiers.

A massacre followed. Custer's secret orders were to kill the warriors, but it is estimated that only ten of the victims were warriors. The other 100 were men, young and old, women and children executed indiscriminately. Another 50 women and children were taken prisoner as a warning against retaliation. As a final blow, hundreds of ponies were slaughtered so that the survivors would have no means of flight.

This act of ignominy was but the first of a series of merciless campaigns throughout the winter against all other Indians in the area. Custer encouraged the reputation of himself as a pitiless warrior against whom no Indian dare stand. For a while, he succeeded. Then he met his match – in the Sioux chief Sitting Bull.

The word 'Sioux' is an alternative to Dakota, and in 1868 the Black Hills of Dakota had been given for all time to the Indians who lived there. This treaty suited the white man because the hills were thought valueless. But in 1874 Custer led an expedition into the region and reported: 'The hills are full of gold from the grass roots down.' The local military authorities tried to renegotiate a treaty but the Indians would not budge. Their hills, the 'Paha Sapa', were holy places, the centre of their spirit world, and they would not give them up.

A commission was sent from Washington to meet not only the Sioux but also the Arapahos and Cheyenne, all of whom had claims to the Black Hills. The tribes were unwilling to sell their land or to exchange it for other territory. Sitting Bull warned: 'We want to sell none of our land – not even a pinch of dust. The Black Hills belong to us. We want no white men here. If the white man tries to take the hills, we will fight.'

The reaction of the white man was predictable. The treaty was torn up and Custer pushed a trail through to open up the wealth of the Black Hills. In the Sioux language it was known as the 'Thieves Road'. The War Department leapt into action, issuing a hypocritical ultimatum that any Indians not on their official reservations by the end of January 1876 would be considered hostile and that 'military force will be sent to compel them'.

At this, Sitting Bull proved himself a better diplomat than the commissioners or the War Department. He protested in the

most measured terms that he had received news of the ultimatum only three weeks before the deadline. It would be impossible for his tribe to move camp in midwinter. The government was confounded. Genocide could not be sanctioned, and there was no good excuse to implement such a policy.

Instead of acting openly, the War Department resorted to subterfuge and deceit. On 7 February they ordered General Sheridan to attack the Indians. He entrusted the task to his fiercest commander, General George Armstrong Custer.

This was to be Custer's greatest hour. He left the safety of Fort Abraham Lincoln, in North Dakota, and journeyed westward. Every night of his journey, he sent a dispatch to New York newspapers, relating tales of his own courage and imagination. He also kept a 'private' diary – which he meant to be published later for his own self-glorification. In it he wrote: 'In years long-numbered with the past, my every thought was ambitious. Not to be wealthy,

Above: *One of Custer's scouts, Curley, a member of the Crow tribe. He was one of the few to survive the massacre at Little Big Horn though his life was not spared out of any racial loyalty. Sitting Bull's warriors were too busy slaughtering white men.*

THE GREEDY WHITE MEN THOUGHT THE HILLS WERE FULL OF GOLD AND WERE HAPPY TO MASSACRE INDIAN WOMEN AND CHILDREN TO GET THEIR HANDS ON IT.

Above: The *Battle of Little Bighorn*, 1876.

AT THE HEIGHT OF THE FEASTING AND CHANTING, SITTING BULL HAD **50** PIECES OF FLESH TORN FROM HIS BODY TO PROVE HIS COURAGE.

not to be learned, but to be great. I desired to link my name with acts and men, and in such a manner as to be a mark of honour, not only to the present, but to future generations.'

The campaign against the tribes settled around the Montana–Wyoming border began slowly. Cavalry would attack an isolated Indian encampment and burn its tepees. Often they would shoot the horses. Feeling increasingly isolated, the scattered Indians began to band together for safety in the Powder River and Tongue River basins. Eventually, a 'mega-tribe' came into being, comprising at least 10,000 Indians, of whom some 3,000 or 4,000 were warriors. They lived in a veritable forest of tepees and makeshift tents stretching three miles along the west bank of the Little Bighorn River. The Indians termed the camp the 'Valley of the Greasy Grass'. The whites knew the area as simply 'Little Bighorn'.

A GREAT POWER

Here were gathered the Hunkpapas, as well as Blackfoot Sioux, Arapahos, Sans Arcs, Brules, Minneconjous and Cheyenne. But the camp's leader was the Hunkpapa chief Sitting Bull, of whom a cavalry scout named Lewis Dewitt left us this description:

'Sitting Bull had a great power over the Sioux. He knew how to lead them. He told the Sioux many times that he was not made to be a reservation Indian. The Great Spirit had made him free to go wherever he wished, to hunt buffalo and to be a leader of his tribe.'

By June 1876, they all knew that a great battle was imminent. The Sioux feasted on buffalo meat, danced and chanted around their fires. Sitting Bull had 50 pieces of flesh cut from his body to prove his courage. Then he went into a trance. When he was revived, he told the tribe that he had seen a wonderful vision. He had seen white soldiers 'falling like grasshoppers' into his camp while a voice said: 'I give you these because they have no ears.'

On the night of 24 June 1876, while the Sioux held a holy sun dance to strengthen their resolve for battle and to ensure that the spirits of their dead would fly heavenward, General Custer arrived at the valley of the Little Bighorn. In his desperation for battle, he had outstripped his other units (he had made 60 miles in just two days) and turned up across the river from Sitting Bull's camp with 12 troops of US Cavalry – just 611 men.

Other detachments were on the way. Major-General John Gibbon had marched east from Fort Ellis, and General Alfred Terry had marched west from Fort Abraham Lincoln to meet up with him on the Yellowstone River. The two were now moving up the Little Bighorn with their combined force of 1,500 men.

Another 1,000 soldiers, led by General George Crook, straggled far to the south on the journey from Fort Fetterman. They were slightly less anxious for battle, already having encountered a war party of Oglalas, led by their fearsome chief Crazy Horse. The Oglalas had made a daring sortie to ambush Crook's men in the valley of the River Rosebud. Indeed, they almost succeeded in wiping out the force, such was the hopeless leadership of the general. He was saved, however, by the bravery of a party of Indian allies he had brought along as mercenaries: 250 Sioux-hating Crows and Shoshonis.

Custer was unaware that Crook was delayed and that his force was in total disarray. He knew that his other fellow generals were on their way, however, and was anxious that they should not share the glory of victory.

Now knowing the size of the Indian camp, Custer should have been concerned at his tactical disadvantage. He also should have reviewed his decision to turn down General Terry's offer of extra men and Gatling guns, which he believed would have held up his progress. And he certainly should have heeded his own Indian scouts, who begged him to hold back for two days until Terry and Gibbon caught up with them.

But General Custer was too arrogant to heed any such advice. He was too vainglorious to delay attacking Sitting Bull for one day longer …

At dawn on 25 June, Custer launched his attack. He advanced with three of his 12 troops, while another three moved forward under Captain Frederick Benteen and a further three under Major Marcus Reno. The remaining troops were left with the supply train.

Major Reno's modest force of 140 men crossed the Little Bighorn River and successfully attacked from the rear, taking by surprise the Hunkpapas, Blackfoot Sioux and Crazy Horse's Oglalas in their villages at the southern end of the camp. Women and children were cruelly shot down as they ventured from their tepees.

At the moment of Reno's attack, Custer and his much larger force of 225 men were scheduled to be attacking the Indians from the other side. But Custer was still four miles away – stumbling along the river bank looking for a suitable crossing. Likewise, the third column, under Captain Benteen, was still some miles from its target.

A GOOD DAY TO DIE

Reno could not sustain the attack alone. Sitting Bull's chief lieutenant, Gall, who had just seen his wife and children cut down by the troops, rallied his warriors for a counter-attack. Out-flanked,

TERRIFIED WOMEN AND CHILDREN WERE COLD-BLOODEDLY SHOT TO PIECES AS THEY SOUGHT SANCTUARY.

Below: *Custer's last stand, from an engraving. Even though the defeat was brought about by his hasty pursuit of glory, he was still seen as a hero.*

CUSTER KILLED.

DISASTROUS DEFEAT OF THE AMERICAN TROOPS BY THE INDIANS.

SLAUGHTER OF OUR BEST AND BRAVEST.

GRANT'S INDIAN POLICY COME TO FRUIT.

A WHOLE FAMILY OF HEROES SWEPT AWAY.

THREE HUNDRED AND FIFTEEN AMERICAN SOLDIERS KILLED AND THIRTY-ONE WOUNDED.

SALT LAKE, U. T., July 5.—The correspondent of the Helena (Mon.) *Herald* writes from Still water, Mon., under date of July 2, as follows:

Muggins Taylor, a scout for General Gibbon, arrived here last night direct from Little Horn River and reports that General Custer found the Indian camp of 2,000 lodges on the Little Horn and immediately attacked it.

He charged the thickest portion of the camp with five companies. Nothing is k— n of the operations of this detachment, except their course as traced by the dead. Major Reno commanded the other seven companies and attacked the lower portion of the camp.

Above: New York World *told how the Indians had massacred 'hero' soldiers. The report appeared on 6 July 1876.*

outnumbered, and exhausted from their forced march, Reno's men retreated.

The vengeful Crazy Horse told his men: '*Hoka-hey!* It's a good day to fight. It's a good day to die. Strong hearts, brave hearts to the front, weak hearts and cowards to the rear.'

Now Sitting Bull, directing the battle from the high ground of his tepee, could vent his wrath against the hated *Pahuska* …

He ordered his chief lieutenant, the ferocious Gall, to ford the river to the rear of Custer's force and to take it from behind. The general was taken completely by surprise. In panic, he ordered his men to retreat to a nearby hill and take up defensive positions.

Struggling up this rise, with Gall's men screaming for blood at their heels, General George Custer must at last have lost his arrogant smirk. For there, atop the hill and staring down at him was Crazy Horse – with 1,000 mounted warriors. Custer was at a loss for words. He could not voice his next command. His troops were terrified. There was nowhere to run. Their leader, the 'Long-Haired One', was not invincible. He was suddenly proved to be one of history's biggest bunglers.

The force of 225 that Custer had led to war with the promise of victory and glory now stared death in the face. Crazy Horse's men delayed their revenge for a few moments as they stared down in disdain at the cowering cavalry. Then they charged.

The soldiers dismounted. Without a shred of cover, they grouped themselves in a broad circle and set about defending themselves with the resigned bravery of lost men. Whooping and shouting and screaming, the shrieking Sioux shot away at the cavalrymen. They fell by the score until a remaining few at the edge of the battle held up their hands in surrender. They were immediately hacked to death.

But where, Crazy Horse demanded, was *Pahuska*? Suddenly, Custer stood alone – in Sitting Bull's words, 'like a sheaf of corn with all the ears fallen around him'. He had been unrecognized at first because he had had his long hair cut short for the battle. But now they knew him, the Indians descended on him like flies to carrion.

Sitting Bull, Crazy Horse and their men celebrated their victory and mourned their dead. They had defended their people and their land with determination and valour. But in Washington Custer's Last Stand was labelled a savage massacre.

The body of the incompetent, arrogant, vanquished General Custer was recovered and given a hero's burial at West Point. Meanwhile, a series of punitive missions was launched against the victorious Indians, who quickly scattered.

Sitting Bull fled with 3,000 warriors to Canada, the 'Land of the Great Godmother', Queen Victoria. In 1881 he returned to the US and surrendered, spending two years in prison before being allowed to rejoin his tribe at Standing Rock reservation, North Dakota. Nine years later he was accused of once again inciting unrest among his people. Resisting arrest, he was shot in the back.

Crazy Horse also surrendered and moved to a reservation. But in 1877 he was taken to Fort Robinson where, while trying to escape, he was bayoneted to death. His last words were: 'Let me go, my friends. You have got me hurt enough.'

Custer, on the other hand, remained a hero. His phony legend of heroism took a century to dispel. The blindly blundering story of the man who by treachery and butchery helped wipe out entire nations has only recently been told.

Above: *Following the battle, Americans come to pay their respects at the graves of the men who died.*

Left: *Fearsome Oglala leader Crazy Horse. After Indian women and children were brutally murdered by the cavalry, he showed no mercy at Little Bighorn.*

CHRISTOPHER COLUMBUS Who really discovered America?

Columbus was determined to sail to the ends of the Earth in search of the riches of the Orient. Instead he stumbled across America, firmly believing that the West was really the East ...

Ask any schoolchild: 'Who discovered America?' and the answer is likely to come straight back: 'Christopher Columbus'. But should the great navigator really get the credit for being the first man to open up the New World to the Old? Or did the Chinese, Phoenician, Irish, Viking or Ancient Greek sailors get there first? And, to rewrite history even further, did Columbus really mean to discover America? Was not his voyage one of the most enduring errors in history?

Christopher Columbus was without doubt the most pioneering voyager of his age, a brave and ambitious sailor who discovered America in 1492 when he traversed the unknown Atlantic from Spain to the West Indies. Generations of schoolchildren have grown up believing the great navigator opened up this Brave New World.

What they have not been taught is the astonishing catalogue of errors that led to his remarkable ocean voyages ...

Christopher Columbus was born Cristoforo Columbo, son of a clothmaker in Genoa, Italy, in about 1451. Little is known of his early life, but he went to sea as a youth and joined the Portuguese fleet after being shipwrecked off Lisbon in 1476.

A DREAM OF RICHES

A proud, stubborn, ambitious mariner, he was convinced the world was round – an unpopular theory in his day, but one that was gaining support among the scientific

brains of Europe. He believed that the coast of spice-rich Asia and the gold-rich lands of the Orient lay west of Europe, and he dreamed of opening up a new sea route from Spain to the isles of the East Indies.

Ironically, many of the theories which were to lead Columbus to the New World were based on fallacy and wholly misinterpreted conclusions. He had read and reread in the *Apocrypha* that 'Upon the third day Thou didst command that the waters should be gathered in the seventh part of the Earth; six parts hath Thou dried up ...' And he had concluded that only one-seventh of the globe was therefore covered by sea. Columbus decided that, to make up the other six-sevenths, there must be a vast land mass to the west. The Atlantic Ocean could not be that big, after all!

For years, while sailing the shipping lanes around Portugal and Spain and down the coast of Africa to the Canary Islands, he had been planning an Atlantic crossing. The Italian captain first explained his dream in 1484 to King John II of Portugal. He sought the monarch's patronage for a voyage westward to discover a new route to the spice islands of Asia, which he described as being within easy sailing

Above: *Genoa at the end of the 15th century. Columbus was born here, but he accepted patronage from the Spanish royals to make his questing voyage.*

Opposite: *Explorer and adventurer Christopher Columbus believed a short sortie west from Portugal would lead him to the riches of the Orient.*

Right: *Columbus sets sail from Palos. He bids a fond farewell to his sponsors King Ferdinand and Queen Isabella of Spain.*

Below: *The three-masted* **Santa Maria,** *which bore Columbus and his crew across the Atlantic. It was later wrecked.*

distance. The disbelieving king turned him down.

Eight years later, he put his project to Spain's King Ferdinand and Queen Isabella – and it was accepted.

He assembled a humble fleet of three tiny, wooden-hulled ships in the bustling port of Palos, on Spain's southern coast. On Friday 3 August 1492 a gentle breeze carried Columbus and his 86 fellow seamen out of the harbour.

Led by his flagship, the 70-foot *Santa Maria*, and followed by her attendant vessels the *Pinta* and *Nina*, the small fleet headed for San Sebastian in the Canaries. Then on 6 September, eager not to miss the prevailing easterly winds, the ships turned westward into the open Atlantic.

MUTINY

The great navigator was at last on his way, heading for the greatest discovery – but also one of the biggest blunders – of any explorer.

The crew were more than a little fearful of what lay ahead. They were voyaging beyond the horizon of the known world. The mighty Atlantic Ocean seemed endless. And so it almost proved. The square-rigged ships at first made good progress in the following wind, but by mid-September, with land still not in sight, his men became worried. They feared they might never see Spain again.

The uneducated crew saw no glory in the mission, and they could not give a fig for its commercial aims – to bypass the Moslem-controlled trading routes to the Indies. All they were worried about was their safety and their comfort; few had bunks to sleep on and the inadequate food was already running low. There was even talk of mutiny.

For one man, however, the thought of sailing into the unknown held no terror. Christopher Columbus had no thought of turning back. Instead, perhaps to allay his crew's fears, perhaps doubting his own estimate of the distance to the Indies, he began to keep a false log. From 19 September, in a meticulous manner, he started underestimating the miles his ships were sailing each day.

The *Santa Maria*, the *Pinta* and the *Nina* were sometimes battered by high seas, at other times becalmed for days. They rode out the perils of the Sargasso Sea, and sailed ever west. Columbus was desperate for his expedition to succeed, but he was also mindful of the rewards that would be heaped on him by a grateful king and queen upon his return.

Hopes that the fleet was nearing land were often raised and dashed. More and more seagulls began to show ... then land birds. Sadly, the jubilant crewmen were probably deluding themselves that this meant a continent was just over the horizon. Most of the birds they saw were migratory.

On 11 October, however, the men of the *Santa Maria* spotted a green branch floating in the water. And at 2 o'clock the following morning, Rodrigo de Triana, a seaman on board the *Pinta*, raised the cry: 'Land!'

On 12 October, 37 days after leaving the Canaries, the fleet hove to off an island which Columbus named San Salvador (now believed to be Watlings Island in the Bahamas). Elated, he wrote in his log:

'There we soon saw naked natives ... A landscape was revealed to our eyes with lush green trees, many streams and fruits of various types.' The next day he wrote: 'I saw that some of the men had pierced their noses and had put a piece of gold through it ... By signs, I could understand that we had to go to the south to meet a king who had great vessels of gold.'

MONUMENTAL ERROR

On October 17 he noted: 'On all these days I have been in India it has rained more or less ...'

Columbus was referring to the new lands as 'India'. He still thought he had made his landfall on the eastern coast of Asia. And in the light of this monumental

error, he began his exploration of the New World – firmly believing that the West was the East.

Christopher Columbus sailed among the Caribbean islands until he reached the north coast of Cuba, thence on to Hispaniola (now Haiti and the Dominican Republic). Still believing that the Asian mainland was somewhere over the horizon, he wrote in his log on 28 October: 'I dare to suppose that the mighty ships of the Grand Khan come here and that from here to the mainland is a journey of only ten days.'

The fleet never attempted to reach the unseen 'Asian' mainland. Instead, after eight months at sea, they returned in

THE ROUGH CREW WHISPERED WORDS OF MUTINY – THEY FEARED THEY'D NEVER SEE THEIR HOMELAND AGAIN.

Above: *Columbus stopped long enough to raise the Spanish flag on Hispaniola before rushing back to Spain with news of his discovery.*

triumph to Spain, where Columbus was made 'Admiral of the ocean sea and governor of the islands newly discovered in the Indies'.

It was only later, after Spanish and Portuguese voyagers had explored and mapped the Americas, that Christopher Columbus received the posthumous accolade of discovering a new continent. But did this obsessive Italian émigré, hired by a foreign paymaster, really discover the New World?

UNCANNY RESEMBLANCE

Researchers suggest that it is possible that many other races, equipped with vessels far more primitive than his, could have reached it before him. People have been settled in America for 12,000 years – a fact ascertained using carbon dating, a process that accurately pinpoints the date of an artefact or other object to within 100 years.

The first settlers in America were probably descendants of Mongoloid tribesmen who reached the continent by crossing the land bridge across the Bering Strait from Siberia to Alaska. This much we know of the indigenous people, the first Americans. But who were the first people from other continents to reach America?

Some theoreticians claim that the Chinese, who were masters of technical and cultural affairs long before the Europeans, were the first outsiders to land in America. They point to the discovery of sculptures amongst the remains of ancient Central American nations and their uncanny resemblance to idols used in the Buddhist religion as proof that the Chinese arrived there in about 2000 BC. Another people who may have set foot in America before the time of Christ are the Phoenicians. Herodotus, the Ancient Greek historian, mentions the Phoenicians and wrote in 600 BC that sailors of Tyre and Sidon were hired by Pharaoh Necho of Egypt to sail around Africa. They accomplished this astonishing feat, and went on to sail the Atlantic in triremes – galleys with triple decks of oarsmen. It is thought that they reached the Azores, the site of the discovery in the 18th century of a hoard of gold Carthaginian coins.

However, the greatest backing for the claims arises from the discovery of an inscribed stone in a Brazilian coffee plantation in 1872. The translation reads: 'We are sons of Canaan from Sidon, the city of the king. Commerce has cast us on this distant shore, a land of mountains ... We voyaged with ten ships. We were at sea together for two years ... So we have come here, 12 men and three women on a new shore which I, the admiral, control. But auspiciously may the exalted gods and goddesses favour us.'

Is that proof that Phoenicians discovered the Americas long before the birth of Christ, and of course many centuries before Christopher Columbus? The argument rages to this day – against claims from many other lands and peoples.

CRYSTAL TOWERS

A 6th-century Latin manuscript which has survived contains evidence that the Irish may have been the first Europeans to cross the Atlantic. The *Navigatio Sancti Brendani* tells how St Brendan set sail in AD 540 with a crew of 14 monks. His mission was to 'find the land promised to the saints'. The *Navigatio* says that Brendan was an experienced sailor from Kerry in the west of Ireland and that his primitive boat was a 35-foot ketch, covered with the hides of oxen and greased with butter to keep it waterproof.

The document tells its story in colourful language that some sceptics believe makes it merely a fairy-tale. But, studied closely, it makes sense to many. The vessel took a northerly course, eventually coming across 'a floating tower of crystal' – probably an iceberg, thousands of which litter the northern approaches to America. They went through an area of dense mist – possibly the famous fog-shrouded Newfoundland Banks, where the warm Gulf Stream mixes with the violent Arctic currents. The manuscript does get fanciful, for Brendan claims they were guided by whales and angels disguised as birds before they reached land. The men landed on a tropical island surrounded by clear waters and inhabited by pygmies. This, say those who believe this theory, could have been one of the islands in the Bahamas group. Later he went on to find another land, which may have been Florida.

There is little hard evidence to confirm

HAD THE IRISH SAINT REALLY SAILED TO AMERICA FROM THE EMERALD ISLE IN A PRIMITIVE KETCH COVERED WITH THE HIDES OF OXEN AND GREASED WITH BUTTER TO KEEP IT WATERPROOF?

the claims of this ancient text, and it could be regarded as just fancy, were it not for the fact that the great Norse sailors testify in their sagas that the Irish were indeed the first to reach America. The Viking voyages, made in their famous longboats with imposing prows and shallow sides, are now established as historical fact. The Vikings made their journeys in short legs from Scandinavia, via Iceland and Greenland, establishing settlements en route. They were well supplied, developing a method of preserving their meats by trailing them in the salted water, and drinking water from cowhide pouches.

In the saga recounting the deeds of the great navigator Leif Ericsson, it is recorded that he reached the New World in AD 1000. He called it Vinland, describing it as a land of beauty and contrasting climates. The sagas, not written by him but based on his records, are believed to refer to the area now known as New England.

The discovery some years ago of eight houses, cooking pots, kitchen implements, boats and boatsheds at a site on the northern tip of Newfoundland offers, says Norwegian historian Dr Helge Ingstad, 'the first incontrovertible evidence that Europeans set foot in America centuries before Columbus's voyage of 1492'.

Another find, relating to the Norse adventurers is also the subject of controversy. In 1898 a farmer clearing land at Kensington, Minnesota, came across a stone covered in the characters of a strange language. The Kensington Rune, as it later became known, was said to tell the story of a 30-strong party of Norwegians and Goths who went west from Vinland in 1362, ending with a massacre in which ten of the party were killed. Again, experts are divided as to whether it is the genuine article or a clever fake. But those who believe in its authenticity say that its language is too complex for it to be a crude forgery.

Other finds may offer positive proof of the Vikings' first foothold on the continent. One such is the Newport Tower, in the centre of Newport, Rhode Island. The circular structure is supported on eight columns and could be old enough to have

Above: *Columbus returned to Spain, where he told Queen Isabella he had found a new route to Asia. He was rewarded with the governorship of the newly discovered province.*

AT A DESOLATE HILL THEY DISCOVERED AN EERIE SACRIFICIAL TABLE USED DURING MACABRE CEREMONIES.

Right: The family man. Columbus was father to two sons, Diego and Ferdinand.

Below: A map of the four great voyages charted by Christopher Columbus, from a book published in 1889.

been constructed by the Vikings. But some say that the building is merely the remains of a church built by much later, Christian settlers.

SACRIFICIAL TABLE

Among this mass of Irish, Viking and Phoenician contenders for the discovery of America is one more – another Celtic expedition. A desolate place called Mystery Hill in North Salem, north of Boston, consists of a collection of ruins of a kind usually associated with the great megalithic sites of Europe. There are the remains of 22 huts, passageways and cooking pits, and an eerie sacrificial table with a speaking tube through which voices can be projected – presumably for use during macabre ceremonies.

The huge blocks of granite comprising the passageways are held in place by their own weight, and many thousands of artefacts from different periods have been

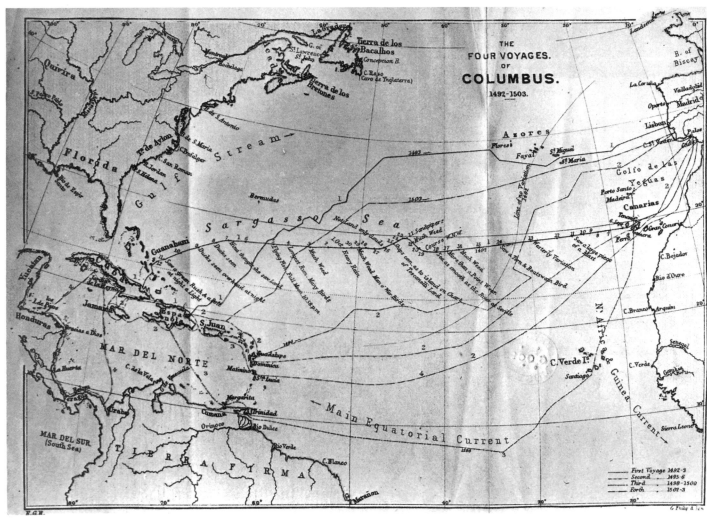

THE FOUR VOYAGES. OF **COLUMBUS.** 1492-1503.

found there. Stones bearing chiselled inscriptions in the ancient Celtic form of rune writing called Ogham have been found too. Is this evidence of yet another race laying claim to America? Or is it perhaps not the work of the Celts, but of Ancient Greeks – perhaps even the great hero of Homer's legendary tale, Odysseus, arriving there on his voyage to the far frontiers of the world? The theories are endless.

What is now certain, however, is that it was not Christopher Columbus who first set foot in the Americas. For centuries, the crediting of the Italian navigator as the founder of the New World has been an astonishing mistake.

Even Columbus himself slowly began to realize that his earliest theories about the land to which he had sailed might be challenged by the evidence of history. In the ten years following his first crossing of the Atlantic, he made three further epic voyages, and only towards the end of his explorations did he begin to doubt whether he had in fact found the eastern coast of Asia.

On his third voyage in 1498 he began to wonder whether he had found a new continent. He had taken a more southerly course across the Atlantic and had made landfall on the island of Trinidad. While exploring in the nearby Gulf of Paria, he came to the place where the mighty Orinoco River of South America flows into the sea. In his log of 14 August 1498, he wrote: 'I believe that this is a very large continent which until now has remained unknown.'

AN IGNOMINIOUS END

In 1502 Columbus set out on his fourth voyage. For nine months, in gruelling weather, he explored the coasts of Honduras, Costa Rica and Panama. Then, in May 1503, he struck north in a desperate bid to reach the new Spanish settlement of Santo Domingo, on the island of Hispaniola. He failed. With his storm-battered ships – worm-eaten, leaking and altogether unseaworthy – he spent 12 months as a castaway on Jamaica before being rescued with his crew and taken back to Spain.

It was an ignominious end to the last

great voyage of the great navigator. He returned home still believing that the islands he had discovered on his first two voyages were off the eastern coast of Asia. He still believed that a passage through to Asia must exist between these islands and the great new land to the south.

Twice he had stumbled across the New World without really knowing it. He died on 20 May 1506, never to know that the land he had discovered was in fact the vast continent of America.

The result of his error was that the land that Christopher Columbus had risked his life four times to reach was named after one of his rivals. Fellow Italian adventurer Amerigo Vespucci explored much of Brazil's coastline – and it was the accounts of his discoveries that eventually won him the honour of having the great new continent named after him.

It is Christopher Columbus, though, who will probably continue to be credited as the man who discovered the New World. He may have made a giant error, but his discovery is part of the history of mankind and paved the way to the modern world. The tragedy for Columbus himself is that he died without ever knowing how stupendous his achievement was.

Above: *Columbus still gets all the credit for discovering the New World, even though there's evidence that ancient peoples made the journey there centuries before he set sail.*

TRAGICALLY HE DIED WITHOUT EVER KNOWING HE'D DISCOVERED ONE OF THE EARTH'S GREAT CONTINENTS.

DAILY SKETCH, MONDAY, OCTOBER 6, 1930

SURVIVORS' VIVID STORIES OF AIRSHIP DISASTER

DAILY SKETCH

INCORPORATING THE DAILY GRAPHIC

ONE PENNY.

MONDAY, OCTOBER 6, 1930.

No. 6,699. [Registered as a newspaper.]

THE LAST OF THE GIANT R101: WONDERFUL AIR PICTURE

R101 MEMORIAL NUMBER

...aster in which R101 crashed in flames near Beauvais, Northern France, within eight hours of ...killed, there being only eight survivors. Her commander, Flight-Lient. H. C. ...another of the victims, initiated the construction of R101 and ...than air vessels.

THE R101
A flight to hell

Lord Thomson of Cardington thought that the world's mightiest airship would carry him to personal glory – blind ambition prevented him from seeing that the R101 would be his ticket to a blazing hell.

The R101 airship was a disaster long in the making. It was designed and built to satisfy the power and prestige of politicians. And it was flown in the face of all advice and protests in order to satisfy the whim of one man. The R101, this mightiest of British inflatables in the age of airships, was used to boost the already over-inflated ego of Lord Thomson of Cardington, the secretary of state for air. His arrogance cost the lives of all but six of its 54 passengers and crew in an inferno on a French hillside in 1930.

The most unnecessary disaster in the history of flying began seven years earlier, however, when in 1923 the Conservative government was persuaded by the Vickers aircraft and engineering firm that giant airships could be used for passenger services linking all major parts of the Empire. The government would commission them and Vickers, the most experienced builders of airships in Britain, would, of course, be paid to build them.

Vickers, greedy for the contract, were horrified when the Conservatives fell before a decision could be made, and in 1924 the first Labour parliament came to power on promises of nationalization and state control. Socialism was the order of the day and success for the fiercely capitalist firm of Vickers was not to its liking.

ASTONISHING DECISION

The new prime minister Ramsay MacDonald and his advisors then made the most astonishing decision. They decided to commission not one, but two airships to exactly the same specification: the R100, a capitalist airship, and the R101, a socialist airship. The R100 was to be built by Vickers and the R101 by the Air Ministry. By some extraordinary set of rules, the government would then decide which of the two would win its accolades and its orders.

No one was more astonished by this than Nevil Shute Norway – now better known as novelist Nevil Shute. At the time, he was Vickers' chief calculator, and he wrote: 'The controversy between capitalism and the state enterprise had been argued, tested and fought in many ways but the airship venture in Britain was the most curious of them all.'

Above: *Lord Thomson, the man who made the success of the R101 a life's ambition.*

Opposite: *Cover of the* **Daily Sketch***, which graphically illustrated the scale of the disaster.*

Below: *The R101 was visually stunning but it was plagued by design faults. It should never have left the ground.*

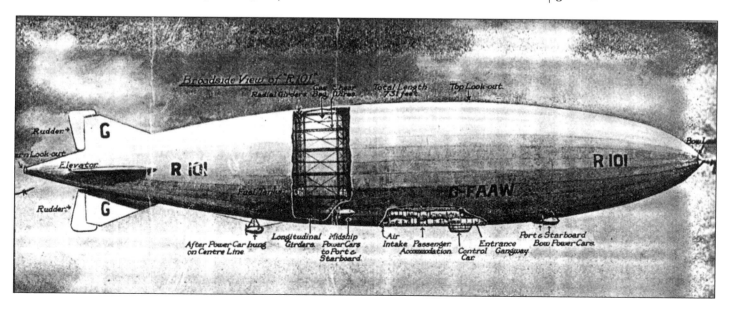

THE DESIGN WAS BEAUTIFUL – AND LETHAL.

Below: *The Royal Airship Works, Cardington, where the ill-fated R101 was constructed.*

Lord Thomson, Labour's air minister, was responsible for the R101. So fanatical about the project was he that he adopted the name of the nationalized aircraft factory as part of his title. It was therefore as Lord Thomson of Cardington that he oversaw the building of the airship at Cardington, near Bedford. The first problem facing the design team was the ministry's decision that petrol engines would be unsafe for their airship. The Cardington team argued fiercely against deisel engines but were overruled. As a consequence, 8-cylinder diesel units were ordered – engines originally designed for railway locomotives. They weighed twice as much as the R100's petrol-power units, were far less efficient and vibrated alarmingly.

Such was the weight of the engines and other equipment built into the R101 that when the airship was first inflated and tested it was discovered that its lifting power was about half what it should have been. The team immediately began taking out of the craft all the gadgetry which they had confidently built into it. The effect was disastrous …

The gas valves were so sensitive that they leaked perpetually. The propellers broke when put into reverse, and a heavy backward-facing engine had to be fitted in order that the airship could manoeuvre when docking. The hydrogen bags which would keep it aloft rolled around inside the craft. The airship was unbalanced. It bucked up and down dangerously as soon as it was tethered at its mooring mast. The craft's outer casing split time and time again and ended up being covered with patches, and the fins, though beautifully streamlined, tended to stall.

Of course, many such problems were also encountered by the Vickers R100 team, led by designer Barnes Wallis, who was to become famous in World War 2 for his dam-busting bouncing bomb. But they were overcome – despite some less than salubrious conditions.

The R100 was being built in a leaky World War 1 airship hangar at Howden, Yorkshire. Writing much later about how untrained local labour was being used for much of the manual work, Nevil Shute complained: 'The local women were filthy in appearance and habits, and incredibly foul-mouthed. Promiscuous intercourse was going on merrily in every dark corner.'

Shute never gave an opinion as to whether this was the reason that the R101 was finished first! But, by hook or by crook, it was and a VIP crowd was invited to Cardington to watch it being floated out of its hangar.

DISASTER AVERTED

A few weeks later, on 28 June 1930, the largest airship in the world – 200 yards long and filled with 5 million cubic feet of hydrogen – was flown to Hendon to take part in an air display … and immediately

THE CROWD APPLAUDED THE AIRSHIP'S ACROBATICS, BLISSFULLY UNAWARE THAT DISASTER HAD NARROWLY BEEN AVERTED.

Left: *R100 flying over Farnborough. It took longer to build than its government-sponsored rival, but it flew beautifully.*

appeared to embark on a sequence of aerial stunts. It twisted and turned, then suddenly dipped its nose and dived spectacularly before pulling up sharply. The 100,000-strong crowd applauded, but they were even more impressed when moments later the aircraft, already too low for comfort, repeated the manoeuvre and pulled out of its dive just 500 feet above the ground.

The entire show had, of course, been entirely unplanned. The crowds were unaware that the craft's sweating coxswain had been struggling at the controls to avert disaster. Neither were they told that when the R101 was examined afterwards more than 60 holes were found in the hydrogen bags. The highly inflammable gas was pouring out everywhere.

The public was blissfully innocent of these problems. The Air Ministry technicians were frantic in their attempts to solve them. They had already cut their airship in two, inserted an extra gas tank in the middle, put the craft together again and once more hauled it to its mooring tower. Surely the extra lift would solve their problems. But within minutes, the whole skin of the airship began rippling in the wind, and a 90-foot gash opened up along its side. The next step was to begin disposing of every piece of non-essential equipment. Out went the expensive power steering and many of its more luxurious touches.

The R101's outer cover was a constant source of embarrassment. It rotted so quickly that a story went around that the culprits were construction workers who, too lazy to return to ground level, had habitually urinated from the topmost part of the airship. The chemical reaction of urine with the solution of dope on the outer skin was said to have been detrimental. It is known that as the airship emerged from its hangar one day in June 1930, a rip 50 yards long appeared in its side. It was repaired

but exactly the same thing occurred the following day.

At this time one courageous Air Ministry inspector reported: 'Until this matter is seriously taken in hand and remedied I cannot recommend the extension of the present permit-to-fly or the issue of any further permit or certificate.' His report was never published and was quietly pigeon-holed by the ministry mandarins.

Production of the rival R100 was meanwhile continuing apace. The Vickers airship lacked the beautiful lines of its sister craft but had one significant advantage: it could actually fly!

The Vickers team announced that their airship would embark on its flight to Canada in the summer of 1930. The Cardington team suggested a postponement both of the Canada trip and of their trip to India. Vickers, gleeful at their rivals' problems, refused to call off the R100's journey. On 29 July 1930, seven years after

Below: *R101 at its mooring tower. Wind constantly ripped its outer skin and hydrogen poured out of dozens of holes in the gas bags.*

Above: *Sir Sefton Brancker doubted that the R101 could survive a major voyage. He discovered, to his cost, that he was right.*

Below: *The luxurious lounge where passengers relaxed, in ignorance of the problems besetting the ship in flight.*

Vickers first proposed the giant airship project, the R100 set off for Canada. It completed the round-trip successfully and without fuss.

By now, Lord Thomson was beginning to fluster and bluster. He saw his pet project as a battle between capitalism and socialism, a battle that the socialists were losing. It did not help his case that the private-enterprise sister ship had so far cost the taxpayer somewhat less than his R101. The noble lord's airship must not be shown to be second-best. It had to fly – and soon.

Re-covered, lightened and lengthened, the R101 made its trial flight on 1 October 1930. The craft's oil-cooler having broken down, there was no opportunity for any speed trials. Poor-weather tests had not even been embarked on. The airship had not flown at full power. Neither had the R101 been issued with an airworthiness certificate … so the Air Ministry wrote one out for themselves.

HELPLESS!

The very day before the flight, a final conference about the trip was held at the Air Ministry. Lord Thomson piously warned: 'You must not allow my natural impatience or anxiety to influence you in any way.' No one believed his caution was sincere. After all, he had already announced: 'The R101 is as safe as a house – at least to the millionth chance.' And he had issued an official directive to everyone concerned in the project: 'I must insist on the programme for the Indian flight being adhered to, as I have made my plans accordingly.'

Nevil Shute wrote later: 'To us, watching helplessly on the sidelines, the decision to fly the R101 to India that autumn of 1930 appeared to be sheer midsummer madness.' He said of Thomson: 'He was the man primarily responsible for the organization which produced the disaster. Under his control, practically every principle of safety in the air was abandoned.'

But despite dissension among the designers, fears by Air Ministry inspectors and the alarm of the Cardington team itself, the great man would not be swayed. Lord Thomson had other reasons for pressing ahead with his personal flight to India. He wanted to make a magnificent impression when the airship arrived at Karachi. His ambition was to become Viceroy of India and he hoped that the spectacle would help him achieve that aim. And he had to fly straight away because he did not want to miss the Imperial Conference to be held in London in mid-October.

A fellow VIP booked on the flight was not so sanguine. Air Vice-Marshal Sir Sefton Brancker, the monocled director of civil aviation, was extremely sceptical, having been privy to reports on the R101's trials. He had learned that when the airship dived at Hendon it had virtually broken its back. He knew that hydrogen constantly poured from holes caused by the gas bags chafing against each other and the superstructure. But when he voiced his concerns, Thomson told him: 'If you are afraid to go, then don't.' Sadly, Sir Sefton accepted the challenge.

Lift-off from the Royal Airship Works, Cardington, was to be on the evening of 4 October. It was wet and miserable. At 6.30 pm Thomson and his valet stepped aboard. There were four other passengers, plus 48 crew.

STORM CONDITIONS

The leaky airship was so grossly overweight that it had to drop 4 tons of water-ballast to get away. At 8 pm, over London, it received a new weather forecast by radio, predicting a 40 mph headwind over northern France, with low cloud and driving rain. The senior crew member, Major G.H. Scott, grew alarmed. He had successfully captained the R100 to Canada and back, and he knew of the deficiencies of the R101. Yet he had decided to come along 'for the ride'. Knowing that the R101 had never flown in anything but good weather conditions, Scott discussed the radio report with Thomson. What the two men said will never be known, but the airship flew on.

As the rain lashed down on the 777-foot-long airship, the weight of tons of water slowed it down and made it even more unstable. It rolled and pitched and was flying dangerously low, but inside the vast hull, crewmen went about their business while the passengers slept.

The twin-berth cabins formed the upper deck of a two-floor module sealed off from the roar of the engines and the beating of the weather. On the lower deck was the lounge, 60 feet long and more than 30 feet wide, with wicker settees, chairs and tables, and potted plants disguising the supporting pillars. Outside the lounge ran promenade decks with panoramic observation windows. Also on the lower deck were the ornate dining room, a smoking room and kitchens.

CRASH DIVE

Stairs led down to the control room, slung under the hull, which was the closest point to the ground. As the craft crossed the Channel, the watch noticed the surging seas perilously close beneath them. An officer grabbed the controls and brought the airship back to 1,000 feet.

The winds increased as the R101 crossed the French coast. Observers at Poix airfield estimated her height at only 300 feet. At 2 o'clock in the morning, the R101

Above: R101 dropping ballast as it struggles to rise. Without the stabilizing weight it rolled and tilted precariously.

> **INSIDE THE VAST HULL, CREWMEN WENT ABOUT THEIR BUSINESS WHILE THE PASSENGERS SLEPT.**

was over Beauvais in northern France. It had travelled only 200 miles in more than seven hours.

Radio operator Arthur Disley had just turned in after tapping out this message back to Britain: 'After an excellent supper, our distinguished passengers smoked a final cigar and have now gone to rest after the excitement of their leave-taking.' Disley awoke later in his berth and realized something was wrong.

The nose of the R101 had suddenly dipped.

Engineers John Binks and Albert Bell were chatting in one of the gangways. Both fell with a bump. Foreman engineer Henry Leech, alone in the smoking room, slid off the settee. His glass and soda syphon clattered from the table. The R101 righted

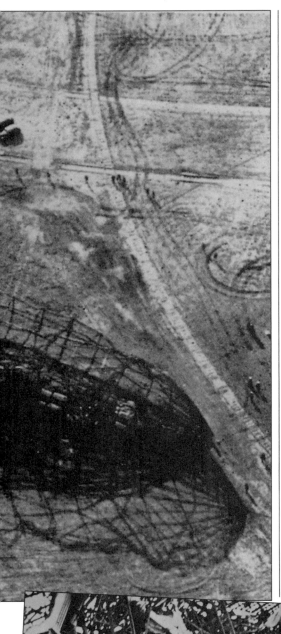

itself and again roared forward against the wind and rain. In the smoking room, Leech picked up the glasses and the soda syphon. They were unbroken. He replaced them on the table and lounged back on the settee.

Down below in Beauvais, several citizens were leaning out of their windows watching the strange airship sail by. It passed over the centre of the town, about 200 yards above the ground. It was rolling and dipping.

In the control car, the watch had just changed. The navigator looked at his altimeter – and was horrified to see that, although it recorded 1,000 feet above sea level, the airship was almost at ground level. The gentle hills around Beauvais were higher than he had thought. The engines were put at half speed and the release of water-ballast was ordered. Rigger Alf Church was walking to the crew area at the end of his term of duty when he heard an officer shout: 'Release emergency ballast.' Church ran back to his post and jettisoned half a ton of water from the nose.

The R101 was once again flying straight and level, but very low. Suddenly the nose dipped for the second time. As the airship's telegraph rang, coxswain Oughton wrestled with the controls. The elevators did not respond. The frail fabric at the nose of the ship had split. The wind was gusting in and the hydrogen was pouring out.

Below the doomed airship, on the edge of a wood, 56-year-old Alfred Roubaille was out poaching, hoping to bag a couple

---

COVERED IN PERSPIRATION THE COXSWAIN WRESTLED FRANTICALLY WITH THE CONTROLS – BUT THE R101 WAS PLUNGING TO ITS DOOM.

Left: *The charred remains of the death ship R101.*

Below left: *Every shred of fabric on the ship itself was burned, but the RAF flag survived the blaze to flutter forlornly on the wreckage.*

Below: *Air Marshal Salmond joined other dignitaries to survey the wreckage and wonder what had gone so catastrophically wrong.*

of rabbits for his family's Sunday lunch. He plodded across the sodden ground, stopping every now and then to lay his snares. Roubaille heard a roaring of engines above, looked up – and fled to the shelter of the trees. 'The airship started to sink towards the ground,' he later recounted. 'She was moving slowly forward and pointing her nose downwards. Just as the airship was nearing the ground, a strong gust of wind blew her down hard.'

Peering at the looming earth through the window of the control room, the first

Above: *Binks, Bell and Leech in the funeral procession leaving from Beauvais town hall en route to the railway station.*

officer, Lieutenant-Commander Atherstone, realized the airship was doomed. He ordered Chief Coxswain Hunt to race through the hull and alert everyone that the ship was about to crash. 'We're down, lads,' he screamed over and over.

Radio operator Disley heard the warning and swung his legs from his bunk. Leech leapt from the smoking room settee. In the engine-gondolas suspended beneath the hull, engineers Cook, Bell, Binks and Savory watched horrified as the ground came up to meet them.

Thanks to the crewman in charge of the elevators, who died pulling at the wheel in a bid to make the craft climb, the R101 touched down lightly. One man leaped from a gondola and started running away as fast as his legs would carry him. He did not look back. Only Roubaille the poacher, from his sanctuary beneath the trees, witnessed the entire catastrophe which shook the world.

BLAZING INFERNO

The R101 was blown along the ground, then bounced 60 feet back into the air. Finally, it pancaked into the moist earth of a flat field no more than 100 yards from the poacher. For a moment, the only sound was the gush of escaping gas. Then a blinding flash lit the sky. Two further explosions quickly followed and a white-hot inferno engulfed the world's mightiest airship.

Engineer Henry Leech was still in the

THE RADIO OPERATOR WAS CLAWING AT THE FABRIC AND EVEN BITING IT WITH HIS TEETH IN HIS ATTEMPT TO ESCAPE FROM THE WHITE-HOT INFERNO.

Left: *The ill-fated R101 looked majestic in flight. But a close inspection revealed it wasn't fit to undertake a journey. One man's haste and obsession to win a race led to a series of faults and flaws which went unchecked.*

smoking room when the explosions started rocking the remains of R101. He had just got up from the settee when the blazing metal ceiling crashed down on it. Flattening himself to the floor, he crawled on all fours towards a hole that had opened in the wall and leapt through the flaming envelope of the airship. Once safely outside, he heard the cries of radio operator Arthur Disley still inside the blazing hull. He was clawing at the fabric, even attempting to bite an opening in it with his teeth. Leech ran back into the inferno to help him.

Both Leech and Disley seemed doomed. But then there was a miracle. Suddenly a fiery hole opened up in the hull and the two men flung themselves through it. They landed in wet bushes and raced to safety.

Another lucky crewman was engineer Victor Savory, who was blinded by the flash of flame that roared in through the open door of his gondola. Instead of cowering away from the heat, he bravely leapt for the opening and found himself lying on the soft soil of France.

Crewman Albert Cook also tried to get out of his gondola door but found it blocked by a girder, dripping with blazing cellulose from the hull. He dragged away the girder with his bare hands and hurled himself into the undergrowth below. He was pitifully burned. Recalling the horror later, he said: 'I lay down and gave up – but only for a moment.'

The gondola of engineers John Binks and Albert Bell also became engulfed in flames. They believed they were lost. But then came yet another miracle. A ballast tank above the gondola burst – and the water cascaded onto them, putting out the flames. They were the luckiest to be alive that dreadful night.

Poacher Roubaille could never forget his personal vision of hell: 'I heard people in the wreckage crying for help. I was a hundred yards away and the heat was awful. I ran as hard as I could away from that place.'

Of the 54 people, only six – Savory, Cook, Binks, Bell, Leech and Disley – survived. Lord Thomson of Cardington was among the 48 who died because of his blind ambition.

**BEN JOHNSON
The fastest lie on Earth**

> As Ben Johnson raced to the finishing line and a gold medal on that hot September day he knew he was breaking a world record. The next day he broke a nation's heart.

A hush fell on the Olympic stadium as the world's top athletes lined up for the race of their lives, running for the title of the fastest man on Earth. The crack of a starting pistol shattered the silence. It sent the sprinters towards the finishing line 100 metres away at a breathtaking pelt, their muscles taut and glistening with perspiration, each face a mask of concentration. One man roared off the blocks faster than his rivals. His lightning reaction helped him to finish the race ahead of the field, almost before the echo of the pistol had died.

For Canadian Ben Johnson it was the moment he had dreamed of since childhood when he sped barefoot on a dusty tropical road. Now he was the record-smashing champion of the whole world, no messing. After years of toil and training, here at last was the glory he longed for. The strains of the Canadian national anthem being played in the Olympic stadium in Seoul, South Korea, that steamy Saturday afternoon in September 1988 sounded triumphantly for the athletes of a nation, heralding a future of hope. In reality it was a knell of doom for Johnson.

As he stood on the rostrum to have the coveted gold medallion draped around his neck, Johnson could barely disguise a look of anxiety. He knew he was a cheat.

AN ATHLETIC JUNKIE

Within just a few days, the world shared his shameful secret. A test for drugs used by athletes to enhance their performance proved positive. Johnson's fame turned to infamy and he was stripped of his honours, humiliated in front of his country and the world.

The fair-play fans of field events across the globe might just have forgiven him the acutely public misdemeanour, believing him to be a pawn in the hands of unscrupulous and ambitious trainers and under pressure to be the best.

But the humbling experience of being unmasked as a fraud failed to teach him a lesson for life. Less than five years later he was snared for the same offence and he was banned from competing for life. Now Johnson's only claim to fame is as an athletic junkie who has dragged the reputation of his country and his sport through the mud.

Ben Johnson was born in Falmouth, Jamaica, at the close of 1961, one of five children. At the age of 14 he emigrated with his mum, brothers and sisters to Canada, leaving his dad in Jamaica. While his mum worked as a chambermaid in a Toronto hotel, Johnson discovered he was born to run. His pounding stride easily outstripped the other schoolboys he raced. Before long he was noticed by Charlie Francis, former world-class runner, gymnasium owner and athletics trainer, who realized the teenager possessed enough talent to take him to the top.

His first big league outing on the track, aged 16, was notable only for its singular lack of success. Johnson finished last in

Above: *Once Johnson could walk with his head held high as his country's finest athlete.*

HIS POUNDING STRIDE SOON OUTSTRIPPED THE OTHER SCHOOLBOYS – BEN HAD DISCOVERED THAT HE WAS BORN TO RUN.

Opposite: *Johnson leaves the drug control centre in Hamilton after being caught cheating by taking drugs to enhance his performance – not once, but twice.*

BURNING WITH ENVY AND FRUSTRATION, JOHNSON KNEW HE WOULD DO ANYTHING TO BEAT CARL LEWIS.

Below: *Johnson burned with ambition to beat athletic legend Carl Lewis,* pictured below.

Canada's Commonwealth Games 100-metres trial, but he continued his training with grim determination. Just a year later he won the nation's junior title as well as winning citizenship. By now he was running 100 metres in 10.79 seconds.

By 1980 he was fast enough to race in the Olympics, but Canada joined the USA in a boycott of the games brought about by the intervention of the host nation, the USSR, in Afghanistan. It left the way clear for Briton Allan Wells to win gold in the prestige 100-metres event.

But for the first time that year Johnson pitted his speed and strength against Carl Lewis, the American who had made history on the track with his astonishing times. Both competed in the Pan-American Junior Games. Lewis won the 100-metres event; Johnson trailed in sixth place. Lewis's cycle of success spawned a bitter rivalry which bubbled under the surface every time they raced against each other. Lewis was determined to retain his title of undisputed speed king while Johnson was equally driven to snatch the top slot for himself.

Each day Johnson undertook gruelling training sessions in his bid to reach the top of his sport. Each year he edged closer to his goal. In 1981 he was the best runner in his country. The following year he was second to Allan Wells in the Commonwealth Games and by 1983 he made it into the semi-finals of the world championships.

In 1984, Johnson won the bronze medal in the Los Angeles Olympics in the 100-metres event.

The 1984 Games, troubled though they were by the boycott of Iron Curtain countries, had belonged to Carl Lewis, who scored gold in the 100 metres, 200 metres, relay and long jump. Lewis was heaped with accolades, having mimicked the success of the legendary Jesse Owens at the Berlin Olympics, where the affable star was repeatedly snubbed by Hitler because he was black.

Johnson burned with frustration at running once again in the shadow of the great man. He felt sure he could beat Lewis and yearned to prove himself right.

He didn't have long to wait. He claimed victory for the first time against Carl Lewis in the athletics World Cup. Already the bogey of drugs was looming large over the sport. Johnson brushed aside any doubts about his own stance on drug taking: 'I want to be the best on my own natural ability and no drugs will pass into my body.'

ROGUE COMPETITORS

It seemed the tough physical regime he was following had paid off: Johnson was no longer having to settle for second place. He won the Commonwealth and the World Championship titles in consecutive years before the fateful race at the Seoul Olympics. In the World Championships held in Rome in 1987 he not only beat Lewis but achieved a world record of 9.83 seconds. It was the year he won all his 21 races. Again, Johnson's name was linked with drug taking. His camp firmly denied

the suggestion. Coach Charlie Francis said: 'Ben's never taken drugs and never will. Some people do not know how to lose and all they can do is make excuses.' Francis insisted Johnson's astonishing strength came from four hours spent training each day, including 90 minutes devoted to throwing weights.

Olympic officials were increasingly aware of the menace posed by drug takers. The first track competitor to be disqualified after winning a medal was Finnish 10,000-metres runner Martti Vainio in 1984. There was no indication that the problem had been eradicated: if anything, gossip and speculation pointed to widespread use of steroid drugs to increase strength and endurance and cut down recovery time. To sidestep detection, junkie competitors stopped taking the drugs a month before competition. Officials were even thought to

be in cahoots with the rogue competitors taking drugs. There was known to be huge profits in it for those who sold the banned substances. Their trade was two-fold: the drug itself, and then an agent which would mask all traces of the illegal dope.

With the prospect of athletes across the board winning only with the aid of chemicals rather than by their efforts alone, the International Olympic Committee was concerned and made testing more rigorous than ever before, banning masking agents and diuretics which can inhibit the processes used to trace drugs. All medal winners and other competitors chosen at random have to give urine samples after their event. The sample is divided into two and stored in sealed containers. One bottle is analysed and if any indications of drugs misuse are found, the second sample is tested with the athlete and a medical representative present.

Before the Johnson scandal erupted, two Bulgarian weightlifters were stripped of their honours and sent home. In addition five other positive tests were taken.

MYSTIFIED

But without doubt the findings in the tests on Johnson were the most sensational. Commentators were still revelling in the excitement and thrill of the race when rumours emerged about Johnson's test result.

A substance called stanozolol was discovered in his urine. It is an anabolic steroid which is like the male hormone testosterone and boosts muscle size, strength and power.

There was outrage among his crew. While Johnson fled Seoul and the glare of publicity, his business manager Larry Heiderbrecht said: 'Ben is obviously sick at the news and will appeal. He is shattered.'

He went on to say that Johnson was probably the most tested sportsman in the world and did not take drugs anyway. There was talk of a blunder in the laboratories, a hoaxer meddling with the sample and the certainty of an appeal.

'It is obvious that something very strange has been happening. Nobody is that stupid to take drugs a few days before a big race. It would appear that the stuff has been in his system for a short period of time.

Above: *Charlie Francis, Johnson's coach, who once said: 'Ben's never taken drugs and never will.'*

Left: *Linford Christie, Britain's record-breaking runner, was horrified to learn his rival Johnson had been a cheat.*

Above: *Johnson bursts through the line in world-record time at Seoul. But his victory was a sham.*

Right: *At the Dubin enquiry in Canada in 1989, which probed the illicit use of drugs in sport, Johnson appeared to be a reformed character.*

THE PROTESTATIONS OF INNOCENCE WERE A SHAM — LIKE THE MAN WHO MADE THEM.

'Ben makes a lot of money from the sport and there is a lot of financial incentive for someone to do something. His training bag could have been left unattended and somebody could have interfered with it. The whole of Canada has been on his back but that would not make him take drugs.'

The people of Canada were mystified. Surely the local boy made good was innocent? After all, drugs testing which had taken place in Montreal before the country's athletes flew to Seoul had failed to pick up signs of abuse.

Even fellow athletes were incredulous at the turn of events. Britain's Linford Christie came third in the race, with Carl Lewis in second place. Although now in line for the silver medal instead of the bronze, he was far from pleased.

'It has been a sad day for athletics,' he said. 'I have never had any suspicion about Ben, he must have been tested over and over again.'

But any hopes of an error were dashed, as Johnson must have known they would be. His protestations of innocence were a sham. His silence was only broken by the

smashing of a glass bottle as he threw the illicit substance which had lost him the crown he so desired against the wall of his home.

Later, Carl Lewis claimed he had noticed the sure signs of steroid use before the start of that big race. Johnson's build was stockier than usual, his reactions faster and his eyes yellow. Lewis watched in amazement as Johnson produced some almost superhuman extra pace in the final spurt to victory.

THE FASTEST MAN IN THE WORLD?

Johnson was banned from competing for two years by the International Amateur Athletic Federation and stripped of the world record he clinched at the Olympics of covering 100 metres in 9.79 seconds. A row about whether or not he should ever race again ensued. The Canadian government, which had poured its dreams and cash into the promising career of the young runner, announced Johnson would never again wear its colours. But there was a groundswell of opinion which believed Johnson deserved a second chance. He had been a well-loved national hero who evoked pride and the public's sympathy. Many were convinced he was not only a patsy in the cut-throat world of international athletics, but was also capable of being the fastest man on Earth without using drugs. In fact, Johnson got letters of support not only from Canada but from across the world, along with token gold medals from those fans who felt he deserved the prestige award. His actions as an anti-drugs campaigner in schools and youth clubs around the country also won hearts and minds.

Less than a year later, Johnson talked publicly about the events which led to his disgrace. Speaking at a £3 million inquiry into drug-taking in sport he declared with his characteristic stammer: 'I know what it is like to cheat. I want kids not to take drugs. I also want to tell their parents and families.

'If I get the chance to run again then I will prove I am the best in the world. I will be back.'

He was asked by counsel Robert Armstrong if he thought he could be the fastest man in the world without taking anabolic steroids. He replied: 'I know I can be.' There was spontaneous applause from the public gallery.

Uncomfortably he admitted the statement of innocence made immediately after Seoul was a pack of lies. He said he didn't tell the truth because: 'I was ashamed for my family, other Canadian athletes and the kids who looked up to me. I did not want to tell what the truth was. I was just in a mess.'

His honesty furthered his support by the public, who believed him to be not weak but manipulated, and he was praised for his courage in coming clean. Olympic committee president Juan Antonio Samaranch pronounced that Johnson should not be dealt with any more severely than other competitors found guilty of drugs offences.

Even arch-rival Carl Lewis spoke out against a lifetime ban. There was talk of a multi-million dollar re-match between the two giants when the two-year-ban was ended.

Above: *Juan Antonio Samaranch, president of the International Olympic Committee, knew steroid abuse in sport was probably more widespread than the watching public had realized.*

Canadian TV producer Sheldon Reisler summed it up for many when he said: 'Hell, the only guy in the world who's clean is Eddie the Eagle Edwards [the British ski-jumper who came last in the Olympics]. The world is just saying "Thank God our guy didn't get caught."'

The prospect of him becoming a rich man in the wake of his immorality was hardly mentioned. No one was worried about the lack of an apology or display of repentance or that Johnson seemed to blame his coach, doctor and anyone else but himself.

The sport reeled from the exposé, then set about healing its wounds. Regulations about testing were tightened to ensure they were accurate and penalties against the cheats were increased.

Johnson started training again with a vengeance. He was no longer subsidized by the state but he had something to prove. Trainer Charlie Francis, whose name was so closely linked with the use of steroids in athletics and who was subsequently banned from national athletics, was off the scene. When the two-year ban expired, Johnson found himself a target for the drugs testers who descended on him five times in as many

months, each time producing a negative result. It seemed he had been redeemed.

His preparation for a comeback in January 1991 was accompanied with self-righteous comments such as: 'Steroids must be abolished. They must be treated by the law like heroin, and banned. I am damned glad that I was caught when I was. I didn't feel at ease with my medal anyway.'

Observers noted that he was sleeker, clear-eyed and far more relaxed than the Ben Johnson who was hooked on drugs. But rarely do sprinters surpass their best when they are in their late 20s or early 30s as Johnson by now was. He struggled to pack more power into his 5-foot-11-inch tall frame. When he returned to competition in the Copps Coliseum in Hamilton, Ontario, something vital was missing: the winning streak. Johnson appeared to have lost the stunning start from the blocks which gave him a devastating advantage over other runners. He came in second in a 50-metres race to America's Daron Council, ironically a former narcotics agent.

There was talk of Johnson spending too much time in bars instead of training on the track. But more worryingly, the message

---

JOHNSON BLAMED HIS COACH, HIS DOCTOR AND EVERYONE BUT HIMSELF.

Below: *Johnson yearned to be the best again following his ban – but he had disappointing results in his first races.*

the result appeared to broadcast was that the only way for Johnson to be the best was to take drugs.

Johnson struggled to regain winning form. It was crucial to a man who disliked coming second but still the raw edge of speed which he had once known – albeit through a chemical reaction – eluded him.

A PHONY

At the Barcelona Olympics in 1992 Johnson steered clear of the steroids scandal which this time shamed three British competitors, including Jason Livingston – nicknamed 'Baby Ben' after the fallen athletics idol. But if he thought he would leave Spain with a repaired image he was wrong. This time it wasn't steroids – it was a temper tantrum which let him down.

As the Games drew to a close Johnson wandered into the athletes' village without the mandatory security clearance. The young Spanish volunteers tried to explain they were only doing their job for the protection of all athletes at the Games. In the row which followed, Johnson was accused of punching one of the teenagers. Afterwards, he was sent home with new disgrace heaped on his muscular shoulders. His performance was as disappointing as his behaviour.

After a year of second-rate results, the winning formula was discovered again. Critics were quick to notice it coincided with the reappearance of Charlie Francis during his training sessions. Francis insisted he was only running into Johnson because his wife, hurdler Angie Coon, was working out at the same place.

Warning bells rang, however, when Johnson pulled out of Canada's national event in February 1993 as a result of injury and was not selected for the world indoor championships in March.

The storm clouds were gathering and finally burst open when a newspaper revealed Johnson had been tested positive for a second time. A urine sample taken after an indoor meeting in Montreal in January showed a high level of testosterone. It measured a ratio of 10.3 to one when six to one is considered a positive test.

Dr Arne Ljunqvist, head of a 5-strong

commission which dealt with the test, said: 'I can see no reason and no grounds on which the results can be contested. This is a clear-cut case of testosterone doping.'

Johnson remained behind the closed doors of his £400,000 detached house on the outskirts of Toronto, refusing to talk to reporters. His spokesman declared: 'Mr Johnson denies taking any prohibited substance or engaging in any improper practice since his return to competition.' But Johnson must have realized any denial from his own lips would have sounded hollow. He knew he was to be banned for life.

Above: *Johnson with Francis, the coach who oversaw his international disgrace.*

HUMILIATED BY HIS LACK OF SUCCESS, JOHNSON'S MONSTROUS DESIRE TO WIN SMOTHERED HIS BETTER JUDGEMENT.

Over page: Johnson remains haunted by his infamy.

Once again, he had been proved to be a phony: the faith put in him by the Canadian people was misguided, the forgiveness they showed him misplaced. British athletics coach Frank Dick said: 'This is very sad for the Canadian public who had forgiven Johnson once and are now having it thrown back in their faces. The man must be crazy.'

Canada's sports minister Jean Charest said Johnson had 'perverted the playing fields and hurt the sincerity of all the thousands of athletes who participate fairly'.

The only course left for the man whose glittering career was ended twice in the same shabby way was a silent withdrawal into obscurity, aged only 31. His international notoriety was now enough to shut any door in his face. Plans to blow the lid off the world of athletics where shiny syringes were as vital as clean socks collapsed like a damp squib. It was an undistinguished end to a fiasco.

The affair soured more than just one man's life and dream of being extra special. That vision was left in tatters, like the existence of the man himself. His actions caused wholesale damage to the integrity of a sport from which it may never recover.

Other athletes found themselves struggling to convince onlookers they were not only clean of drugs but worthy of the accolades they had won. Ben Johnson not only exposed the scourge of drugs in sport but illustrated how they were a positive benefit to anyone wishing strongly enough to win. He gave the lie to the old saying 'cheats never prosper'. Honest athletes are pushing for blood testing to eliminate cheats like Johnson, who can sometimes duck detection by using drugs which disguise illegal substances. Trying to make the best of it, Frank Dick remarked: 'Ben Johnson did a great service when he was caught in Seoul. It concentrated everybody on winning this war.'

But even now no one is convinced the sport is squeaky clean. It's been left to red-faced officials to limit the damage as best they can to ensure there is a future for athletics. Johnson, the man who wanted to bring honour to the sport, ended up bringing it to its knees.

MILITARY BLUNDERS

SCHWARZKOPF'S TACTICS WERE BRILLIANTLY SIMPLE: HE HAD LEARNT THE HARD WAY THAT AN ARMY WITHOUT AIR COVER WOULD SOON BE AN ARMY DEFEATED.

Safe in their positions of power, too often military leaders throw away the lives of their solders in their lust for victory. It is not their blood which stains the desert sands bright red and makes the seas and rivers bleed with anguish.

Right above: *Stormin' Norman Schwarzkopf, Commander-in-chief of Operation Desert Storm and a superb military tactician.*

Below: *Saddam in 1980 at the height of Iraq's war with Iran. In this address to his soldiers he assured them Iran would 'surrender or die'.*

Saddam Hussein's attack on Kuwait in 1990 was one gigantic blunder. How did he ever imagine that he could defy the world, especially once it became clear war was looming? Whatever Saddam's tortured reasoning, Iraq's doomed invasion has been quickly consigned to history as one of the most spectacular military failures of the 20th century.

And yet the Gulf War, which cost so few Allied lives, could have turned out so differently. True, the final result would certainly have been victory for the American-led coalition with its dazzling array of hi-tech weaponry. But had Saddam been a true, all-round tactician, Iraq would certainly have given a far better account of herself.

As the commander of Operation Desert Storm, General Norman Schwarzkopf, put it at the end of the war: 'Saddam is neither a strategist, nor is he schooled in the operational arts, nor is he a tactician, nor is he a general, nor is he a soldier. Other than that, he's a great military man.'

Saddam's problem was that he had learnt all his war-lore from the Soviets. He regarded battles as something to be fought on the ground and, ideally, from entrenched defensive positions. 'Let them come to us' could have been his motto. Had he had a more balanced military force, those tactics would undoubtedly have brought about the deaths of many more Allied soldiers. But Saddam Hussein didn't have balance. As it turned out, he didn't really have an air force.

And it was the air war, which began on 17 January 1991, that assured the Allies victory. Time and again during his meet-the-press sessions at Allied Command HQ in Riyadh, Saudi Arabia, Schwarzkopf would stress this. As a front-line Vietnam veteran he knew the effect day after day of bombing had on an enemy's morale and psyche. He had learned one of the great lessons which emerged from World War 2 strategy: an army without air cover would soon be an army defeated.

In his summing up of Allied tactics at the end of the conflict Schwarzkopf admitted that he was worried about the balance of ground forces. At the time US intelligence (wrongly, it turned out) had

predicted a defensive force of well over half a million. The Allies' fighting troops, as opposed to logistic support, was roughly half that. Schwarzkopf knew that in modern warfare an attacking army driving against heavily entrenched positions needed a five-to-one superiority of manpower. He explained how he redressed the balance.

'What we did, of course, was start an extensive air campaign ... one of the purposes was to isolate the Kuwaiti theatre of operations by taking out all the bridges and supply lines that ran between the north and the southern part of Iraq. That was to prevent reinforcement and supply coming into the southern part of Iraq and the Kuwaiti theatre.

'We also conducted a very heavy bombing campaign, and many people questioned why. This is the reason. It was necessary to reduce those [Iraqi] forces down to a strength that made them weaker, particularly along the front-line barrier that we had to go through.'

He went on: 'I think this is probably one of the most important parts of the entire briefing I can talk about. As you know, very early on we took out the Iraqi Air Force. We knew that he had very, very limited reconnaissance means. Therefore, when we took out his air force, for all intents and purposes we took out his ability to see what we were doing down here in Saudi Arabia.'

AIR BOMBARDMENT

What Schwarzkopf did was move his main ground-attack forces as far west as possible to outflank the Iraqis and meet them where their defences were weakest. The 5-week air bombardment had left Saddam's troops in no real state to fight. The first attack alone, which lasted only three hours, dropped 18,000 tons of explosives on Iraq – twice the amount that razed Dresden and roughly equal to the power of the Hiroshima atomic bomb.

So how did the Iraqi High Command allow the Allies to take control of the skies almost unchallenged by their own warplanes? It wasn't that their aircraft were a poor match. Most experts agreed that Iraq's squadrons of Soviet-built MiG-29 fighters were technically superior – even to America's awesome F-15 Eagles. As for Britain's Tornado interceptors, it would, as one RAF man put it, 'have been like putting up a robin to fight a kestrel'.

Neither was it down to training. Most Iraqi airmen had been taught alongside the

Below: *Tracer fire lights up the night sky during the opening of the Allied air attack on Baghdad. But where was Saddam's air force?*

Above: Aftermath of an air raid. With total control of the skies Allied bombers rained destruction on Baghdad.

THE RAF TORNADOS HAD THE HEAVIEST LOSSES – BUT THEY WERE THE PILOTS FORCED TO TAKE THE GREATEST RISKS.

---

very people they were now being asked to shoot out of the sky. They were as competent and intelligent as their adversaries. There was just one important difference – they didn't have the will to fight. Instead of wreaking havoc among the incoming Allied fighters they rarely even engaged them in combat.

Part of the problem was that these airmen were never really trusted by Saddam and he had little interest in either the concept of air battles or the tactical importance of supremacy in the skies. He knew where he stood with ground troops, men who had lived their lives under his leadership, who readily bought the Ba'ath Party line and who had not been tainted with Western ideals. Fliers were a different breed. Their foreign training had given them a fresh outlook on life and they were not the type to obey orders blindly without thought for themselves. Sure enough, when the chance came, they were off.

Ten days into the war the first reports began filtering through of Iraqi planes landing in Iran. The Americans claimed 24 had gone, the Iranians said only seven. Whatever the truth, the trend had been set and more and more were soon fleeing across the border. By 29 January Israel's defence minister Moshe Arens said all 25 of Iraq's Soviet-designed Sukhoi-24 bombers were in Iran. And a few days later

it was claimed more than 150 of Saddam's most modern fixed-wing aircraft were parked up inside the territory of his detested neighbour.

The first wave were clearly defectors. Iran's UN ambassador talked of pilots arriving in his country 'to save their lives and their aircraft' and judging by the way four planes crashed before reaching the border, their fuel tanks empty, it seems Iraqi pilots were prepared to risk a great deal to avoid a scrap with the Allies. Later, Iraqi officials claimed Iran had offered Saddam the use of neutral airfields to protect his air force from total destruction.

The theory has never quite rung true. For a start Saddam is known to have placed airplanes in the centres of towns and villages, knowing the Allies would not risk civilian casualties. Why should he then entrust billions of pounds' worth of hardware to an old enemy he fought for eight long years? And when Iraqi deputy prime minister Sadoun Hammadi was sent to Tehran to make enquiries about the missing air force he was told bluntly that Saddam should have asked permission for his warplanes to enter Iranian air space. As he failed to do this, Iran had a duty to impound them.

Back in Iraq the night skies still echoed to the sound of incoming bombers. RAF Tornados took some of the heaviest losses – seven planes went down during the war – but this was partly connected to their very high-risk end of the operation. Their job was to come in low – at barely 80 feet – and pepper Iraqi airfields with a cocktail of bombs and delayed-action anti-personnel mines. Iraqi gunners may have got three of them; the other four went down because of various technical failures.

On the whole Saddam's anti-aircraft gunners put up a pretty feeble show. They didn't dare turn on their own radar because attacking planes picked up a 'lock-on' instantly and immediately fired off their own HARM missiles which travelled down the incoming radar beam to the AA battery which originated it. As a result many batteries switched off their radar-guidance systems and ended up firing blind into the night sky.

On 30 January, General Schwarzkopf confirmed that he had total control of the skies above Iraq. The operation had taken exactly two weeks and it had gone better than anyone could have dreamed possible. Senior Allied officers made great play of their so-called 'smart' bombs which could be guided onto their target through their own internal sensors. One piece of video tape showed an Iraqi lorry driver motoring across a bridge seconds before a massive bomb smashed it in two. The 'luckiest man in Iraq' was how the briefer described him to Western TV viewers.

If the Allies' public relations policy was going reasonably well, Iraq's was in tatters. Saddam might have hoped to try and lure at least some world opinion onto his side, but if that was his plan he had a funny way of going about it. Exhibiting captured Allied airmen on his national TV caused a wave of revulsion around the globe and merely stiffened the West's resolve to teach him a lesson. In strictly political terms it was a blunder to rival his half-hearted commitment to air defence.

The two British airmen who appeared on Iraqi TV were John Peters and Adrian Nichol, whose Tornado was shot down over the Kuwaiti border on the first day of the war. Peters's face was badly knocked about – he had been beaten by his captors – and he seemed to be contorted in his seat. He was able to answer few questions except to confirm he had been shot down by a missile. Nichol, a burly-looking man with the Union Jack flag clearly outlined on his bottle-green uniform, went a little further.

Questioner: What was your mission?
Nichol: To attack an Iraqi airfield.
Questioner: How were you shot down?
Nichol: I was shot down by an Iraqi system. I do not know what it was.
Questioner: What do you think about the war?
Nichol: I think this war should be stopped so we can go home. I do not agree with this war on Iraq.
Other pilots, among them Americans and Italians, were exhibited in a similar way. It did not go down well with the folks back home. Suddenly a huge weight of pressure was off the Allied political leadership as the pictures caused a massive swing of public opinion against Iraq. Now the voices crying for an end to the war in Britain and America were out on a limb. Saddam had attempted a high-risk gamble, presumably

Above: *Flight Lieutenant Adrian Nichol as he appeared on TV under interrogation. It was another blunder by Saddam, in that the British and American viewers saw their 'boys' being humiliated and demanded vengeance.*

to boost the morale of his own countrymen, and had ended by digging himself even deeper into the mire.

By early February, Iraq's much-vaunted tank battalions were being picked off in the manner of a duckshoot. Aircraft such as the A10 tankbuster found them easy meat while the Americans' Apache attack helicopters inspired such fear that even the sight of them in the sky caused some Iraqis to desert their posts. One story which found its way back to Allied ground troops, before the assault to liberate Kuwait, came from an Iraqi prisoner-of-war. He revealed how 12 tanks were drawn up together inside Kuwait when one commander spotted an incoming Apache on the horizon. He radioed to all his crews to stay put – intelligence reports showed the helicopter needed to be much closer before it was in range.

Seconds later six of the tanks were simultaneously blown to smithereens in the Apache's first withering salvo. The survivors in the other tanks didn't wait for an explanation from their commander. They fled their posts in time to watch the helicopter finish the job.

THE FINAL CASUALTY?

When the final 'Big Push' arrived – the launching of a ground attack on 24 February – General Schwarzkopf was again

IN THE FIRST WITHERING SALVO OF FIRE THE SIX TANKS WERE BLOWN TO SMITHEREENS – THE TERRIFIED SURVIVORS FLED FOR THEIR LIVES.

Above: *Saddam with his 'human shield' of European hostages. He believed sending these TV pictures to the West would help his public relations campaign. Nothing could have been further from the truth.*

able to turn the Iraqis' stubborn military dogma against them. Saddam had assumed from the outset that the assault on Kuwait would come from the sea. He stationed ten Iraqi divisions along the coast and planted thousands of mines along the length of the shore. When his generals reported in early February that the Allied fleet, headed by the vintage battleships *Wisconsin* and *Missouri*, was bombarding Iraqi positions he saw this as evidence that his early assumptions were right.

The dawn of 24 February seemed to confirm it. Egyptian, Saudi and Syrian troops, backed by the US marines, advanced into southern Kuwait while the US 1st Cavalry moved in from the south-west. The Iraqis' 3rd Corps assumed this was the main thrust and moved to intercept. They could not have been wider of the mark.

In fact the attack was coming from the west, spearheaded by heavily armoured American and British divisions. The Iraqis could never have known that such a vast body of men had moved into a totally new attack position within a few weeks. When last their air reconnaissance had checked, virtually the entire Allied camp was concentrated on Kuwait's southern flank.

After that, of course, they lost their air force. They had no eyes.

The ground war was won, comfortably, inside 72 hours. Many of the advancing Allied regiments found their outflanked enemy dug in and facing the wrong way. The Iraqi army, trumpeted weeks earlier by Saddam as the world's fourth biggest, was blown away like leaves before a hurricane.

In the years since the Gulf War many have argued that Schwarzkopf's campaign was a failure in that it failed to knock Saddam from power. Yet that was never the general's brief. His political masters were able to give him only one command and that was to free Kuwait. Any officially backed assassination attempt would have thrown the United Nations into total turmoil.

But if Saddam survived, it was a shaky survival. His two glaring blunders of the war – failing to mount an air defence and failing to guard his western flank properly – had humiliated him in front of his generals. Only the fear he managed to inspire in his High Command helped him avoid a coup.

There was a third blunder. Halfway through the conflict Saddam decided on a half-cocked attempt to drag in the rest of the Arab world. He fired a series of Scud missiles against Israel and succeeded in terrorizing the civilian population. It seemed certain that Israel would lose patience and strike back. Only enormous pressure from the Bush administration in America persuaded her not to.

But the Israelis have long memories. Their secret service, the Mossad, is regarded as the most effective and efficient in the world. There can be little doubt that Saddam Hussein remains high on their list of scores to be settled.

He could yet be the final casualty of the Gulf War.

THE FALL OF SINGAPORE

It was heralded as an island fortress which would never succumb to invading armies, but thanks to blundering British commanders, a tenacious foe and the epidemic of chaos and fear, Singapore fell into the hands of the Japanese with chilling speed.

The embarrassing defeat was a devastating blow to the Allies, who saw yet another prized jewel snatched from under their noses. More than that, there were horrendous casualties among the civilian and military populations. Seventy thousand British and Australian troops were forced to surrender. In February 1942 the city of Singapore was reduced to blazing rubble.

Churchill called it 'the worst disaster and largest capitulation in British history'.

But only afterwards was the extent of the military mismanagement of the campaign to keep Singapore revealed. The Japanese commander, General Tomoyuki Yamashita, declared: 'My attack on Singapore was a bluff. I had 30,000 men and was outnumbered more than three to one. I knew that if I had been made to fight longer for Singapore I would have been beaten. That was why the surrender had to be immediate. I was extremely frightened that the British would discover our numerical weakness and lack of supplies and force me into disastrous street fighting. But they never did. My bluff worked.'

Singapore lies at the south of the Malaysian peninsula and was acquired for the East India Company by Sir Stamford Raffles in 1819 from the Sultan of Johore. Although just 20 miles long and 10 miles wide, it went on to become a busy trading post and naval base for the British in southeast Asia.

It was two months after Pearl Harbor – when the might of the American navy was crippled in dock by a Japanese air onslaught – that the battle for Singapore got under way. A sizeable force of Allied troops had been chased down the Malay Peninsula and into Singapore by the beginning of February. Inexplicably, the island remained poorly defended, despite

> SINGAPORE DID NOT FALL BECAUSE OF JAPANESE MILITARY MIGHT; SINGAPORE FELL BECAUSE OF BRITISH MILITARY INCOMPETENCE.

Left: *Iraqi tanks roll through the streets of Kuwait. They were part of a huge army left defenceless by Saddam's pathetic air cover.*

FEARING THAT THE JAPANESE SOLDIERS WOULD GO ON A VICTORIOUS DRUNKEN RAMPAGE, THE GOVERNOR OF SINGAPORE ORDERED ALL THE ALCOHOL ON THE ISLAND TO BE DESTROYED.

the expansionist, imperial policies of the Japanese so forcefully advertised in Hawaii.

Only in January 1942 did British war leader Winston Churchill learn about the lamentable state of Singapore's defences. Immediately he ordered the island to be fortified to the hilt. 'Not only must the defence of Singapore Island be maintained by every means but the whole island must be fought for until every single unit and every single strongpoint has been separately destroyed. Finally, the city of Singapore must be converted into a citadel and defended to the death. No surrender can be contemplated,' he told war leaders. Wise words, but they came too late to change the destiny of the island.

Yamashita had his sights set on Australia and was keen to steamroller ahead before the morale of his men dipped or they ran short of supplies. He began with a wave of air strikes which devastated the weakening Allied forces on the ground. The British commanders, General Wavell and General Arthur Percival, were at odds through most of the brief campaign to keep the island secure. Wavell thought the attack would come from the north-west. Percival believed the invasion would be in the north-east and posted his best troops there. On 8 February Wavell was proved to have been the better tactician.

When the Japanese landed, the Australian defenders of the area could have surprised them with a blaze of spotlights and pinned them to the beach. But the order to switch on the lights never arrived after communication links were broken. As the enemy marched in, the Australians fell back and a counter-attack never came.

It was the first of many landings. Determined Japanese soldiers took to small boats and dinghies to cross the Johore Strait which divided their island goal from the conquered mainland. Some even swam the short, shallow distance. The defenders of Singapore were in disarray, hit by falling spirits, an active fifth column of Japanese residents on Singapore and the hopeless lines of communication.

It was the last, vital factor that spelled the inevitability of defeat for the Allies. For when the Australians were at last experiencing success in fending off the waves of Japanese soldiers on one shoreline, they were ordered to pull back. It allowed the enemy to flood in unopposed. Subsequent attempts at a counter-offensive by the Allies were bound to fail. By now the troops were utterly downhearted and beleaguered as much by the inadequacy of their own commanders as by the formidable warriors from the land of the rising sun.

In Singapore city there was mayhem. Streams of refugees had flooded in and sought shelter and food where they could. Buildings were still blazing from previous air attacks, dead bodies lay uncollected in the streets. Water supplies were falling fast and the risk of serious disease loomed. There was a frenzied scrabble to board boats leaving the besieged island. The governor of Singapore ordered all liquor to be destroyed so that Japanese soldiers could not go on a victorious drunken rampage when they arrived. Oil storage tanks were set on fire by the British themselves, anxious this valuable commodity should not fall into the hands of the advancing enemy. The intense furnace produced black rain which fell over the crumbling city.

By 15 February, seven short days after the island's defences were first breached, Singapore fell. A package was air-dropped to Percival's headquarters, falling to the ground in a flutter of red and white ribbon. Inside was a message from Yamashita advising him to surrender. It ended with the sinister sentence: 'If you continue resistance, it will be difficult to bear with patience from a humanitarian point of view.'

Percival felt he had no choice. He met the slight victor at the island's Ford assembly plant to sign away the vital outpost. The dream was shattered. Britain could no longer boast that she would successfully defend her colonies, no matter where they were in the world. The brutality of the Japanese invaders against captured British and Australian forces is well recorded, and bitterness about the slavery, torture and terrible conditions the men had to endure is still evident even today. Singapore stayed in the hands of the Japanese until their leader Emperor Hirohito was himself forced to surrender, in August 1945.

THE MASSACRE OF A GENERATION

World War 1 was littered with blunders, each costing countless thousands of lives. The conflict started with an assassination which led to miffed national leaders on both sides embarking on a course of protectionism and revenge. The commanders who held sway were old men with a theoretical rather than practical knowledge of warfare: it was the era when the military man judged most successful was the one who didn't lose his nerve in the face of mounting casualties. Any officer foolish enough to advocate withdrawal to save lives would risk the wrath of his political paymasters and would surely lose his job. So it came about that dogged men who prolonged the slaughter by staying put – even if that meant a mounting death toll and no advance – won the day.

In fact, there was comparatively little troop movement in World War 1. Across Europe, the sides met in head-on confrontation, found themselves equally matched and dug in defensively for a long, drawn-out war of attrition. Trench warfare was both demoralizing and degrading for fighting soldiers, who had to endure the most appalling conditions. The most they died for was a few feet of land.

Offensives in which men were sent over the top into no man's land were largely unsuccessful but were repeated time and again by the military leaders. Both British and German soldiers had the occasional triumph in breaking through the lines of defence, but once it was achieved there was no further plan in existence to capitalize on the gain. As men and officers hesitated, the enemy rallied and the gap was closed once more in their faces. Stalemate resumed. British officers were so incompetent that on at least one occasion they released gas when there was no wind and gassed their own men.

The terrible bloodshed of this military mismanagement left Flanders awash with the dead and wounded. Names like the Somme, Verdun, Passchendaele and Ypres will always be linked with aimless slaughter which claimed the flower of a generation. And for four years the killing went on, without a change in tactics to stem the flow of massacres. Nowhere was the pointless sacrifice of young men at the hands of their blundering leaders more starkly apparent than during the Gallipoli campaign of 1915.

Turkey came into the war specifically to take a swipe at its old imperial enemies, Great Britain and Russia. It lost about

> **FOR FOUR YEARS THE POINTLESS SLAUGHTER OF THE YOUTH OF TWO NATIONS CONTINUED, WITHOUT A CHANGE IN MILITARY TACTICS.**

Above: *Churchill strides to his office at the outbreak of World War 1. He was then First Lord of the Admiralty.*

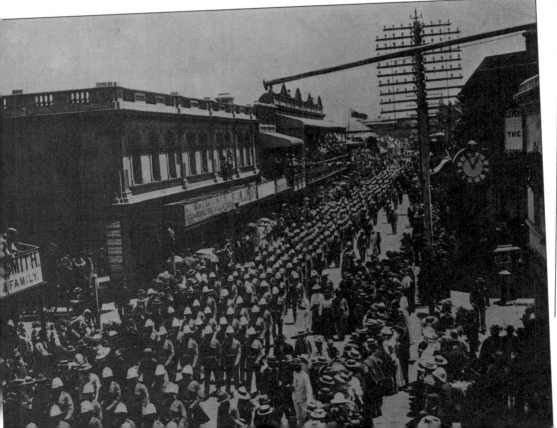

Left: *Australian troops march down the High Street at Freemantle to prepare for embarkation.*

70,000 out of a 100,000-strong army when it attacked Russian troops in the Caucasus, mainly through bitter weather conditions. Regardless of their victory, the Russians appealed to London for a diversion to relieve the pressure on its forces from the armies of the sprawling Ottoman Empire.

GALLIPOLI – A SEA OF BLOOD

The plan to strike at Turkey through the Dardanelle Straits – with an eventual goal of capital Constantinople – was inspired. The waterway which linked the Mediterranean with the Black Sea was clearly vital strategically. Gallipoli was the strand of land on one side of it. With comparative ease, the campaign should have opened up a second front for the German forces, a back door by which to tear into Kaiser Wilhelm II's troops. It was championed by the First Lord of the Admiralty, Winston Churchill.

There was a hopeful start for the British navy, who sailed into the Dardanelles in February 1915, blasted away at the outer fortifications and encountered little resistance. British marines even landed on the Gallipoli peninsula without difficulty.

But the British failed to capitalize on the element of surprise and withdrew the warships into the Aegean, having all but announced their intentions to the Turks. It gave the enemy six valuable weeks to re-arm and reinforce its scanty troops there. There was even the opportunity to mine the straits which had hitherto been a clear passage.

In March the attacking British ships sailed once again on Turkey, this time penetrating the narrow straits. Disastrously, two British battleships and one French were sunk by mines. Churchill was still determined to forge ahead with the operation despite the setback.

In the early hours of 25 April 1915 the largest amphibious force the world had ever known headed for the Gallipoli beaches. In charge was the gentlemanly Sir Ian Hamilton, without a proper map and with no information about the state of Turkish defences more recent than 1906.

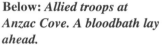

Below: *Allied troops at Anzac Cove. A bloodbath lay ahead.*

His position throughout the bloody and lengthy battles to come was to cruise the sea nearby in a large, safe ship. None of his men was warned about the terrain he would be facing, or had landed on a hostile coast like this before.

There were to be various landing points and a further diversionary skirmish staged by the French at Kum Kale on the other side of the Dardanelles. This, it transpired, was to be the single success of the expedition. The 1,500 Australians and New Zealanders who before dawn tumbled out of small boats onto the beach in the first assault were no more than barely trained reservists. In the gloom they realized for the first time there were sheer cliffs ahead of them instead of sloping beaches. Even as they were landing, a hail of bullets rained down, killing many men before they even made it to the beach. Then the guts of the survivors won the day. In the face of an onslaught from enemy fire and then a wave of Turkish fighters who appeared on the beach, the colonial troops fixed bayonets and forced the Turks back up the hill from which they had come. The site of the landing was known thereafter as Anzac Cove, by way of tribute to their courage.

British troops then emerged at Cape Helles from the bowels of a workaday collier boat which appeared to Turkish eyes to run aground by accident, but when they saw the soldiers swarming out of the disabled craft, the Turkish fighters were quick to respond and wiped out about nine-

tenths of the 2,000-strong invading force. The pilot of a spotter plane which flew over the beach that morning described the sea as 'a horrible sight, absolutely red with blood'.

Close by, a further 2,000 men landed on another beach without a shot being fired. They climbed the cliffs and explored the scrubland at the top as they awaited orders. Their officers asked permission to advance. They were poised to mount an attack on the forces pinning down their comrades just a short distance away. Permission was refused. They spent the day in limbo exposed in the open until Turkish troops pounced on them. The surprise engagement forced the British men back down the cliffs and to the water's edge where, in the absence of any direction from their commanders, they evacuated.

Left: General Sir Ian Hamilton. He led the largest amphibious force the world had ever seen onto the beaches of Gallipoli, yet he had no intelligence regarding the Turkish defences that was less than nine years old – not even a proper map.

Columns of troops did successfully breach the Turkish defences but lacked direction to make their gains effective. By midday on 26 April about 30,000 men had landed on the Gallipoli peninsula with little or no gain. General Sir William Birdwood, in charge of the Anzacs now besieged in hopeless conditions on the narrow shale beach beneath the Turkish-controlled heights, implored Hamilton to pull them out. But spurred on by the success of an

Above: *Troops landing at Gallipoli. They faced impossible terrain ahead and the Anzac commander begged Hamilton to pull the men out.*

Above: *British troops in camp on the Gallipoli peninsula.*

AT THE END OF THE ATTACK
10,000 TURKS WERE
DEAD OR DYING IN
NO MAN'S LAND.

Australian submarine in the Dardanelle Straits, Hamilton refused the plea with the advice: 'there is nothing for it but to dig yourselves right in and stick it out'.

Thus the now familiar trench warfare came to the Mediterranean with conditions every bit as foul as those in France and Belgium. There were few medical supplies and ammunition stocks were low. At Anzac Cove, the men were rationed to two bullets a day. Reinforcements were sent to the British and Australasian forces, just as they were to the Turkish side – now under the leadership of Mustapha Kemal, a future leader of the country.

On 18 May there took place the bloodiest conflict of the campaign with the Anzac Cove men being subjected to the most ferocious assault they had experienced. The Turks tried to overwhelm the Anzac trenches – to be met with volleys of bullets. At the end of the attack, 10,000 Turks were dead or dying in no man's land. It was more than the hardened fighters could bear. On 20 May they raised a Red Cross flag above the front line. It was shot into tatters. But moments later a young

Right: *These men of the 2nd Royal Naval Brigade were among the few troops who got to practice their assault landings. Here they are shown emerging from a trench in a mock attack on the island of Imbros.*

Turkish soldier emerged from the trenches, stumbled over to the Anzacs and, in faltering French, apologized for the killings. After he retreated, Red Crescent flags (the Eastern equivalent of the Red Cross) were raised by the Turks. It paved the way for an informal meeting of commanders who were later able to negotiate a cease-fire. On 24 May each side began the grim task of burying its dead in mass graves.

The truce was to end at 4.30 pm. Half an hour beforehand, the opposing soldiers met and exchanged gifts of cigarettes, fruit and mementoes. After some small talk, they shook hands, parted and returned to their respective trenches. Moments later the shooting started once more.

SCOT-FREE

Frustrated at the stalemate, politicians in London demanded another assault on Gallipoli. This time it was to come at Suvla Bay. Around 20,000 men overran the beach, making short work of the 1,000 Turks there to defend it. In charge, General Stopford, Lieutenant Governor of the Tower, was delighted. He congratulated his men before settling down for his afternoon

nap. The soldiers were allowed to swim and frolic in the sea. By the time Stopford was ready to advance the following day, the Turks had reassembled a strong army which stood in his way. Once more it was deadlock.

In October General Sir Charles Monro, who had replaced the ineffectual Hamilton, urged that the Gallipoli campaign be abandoned. Lord Kitchener, the British war figurehead, visited the scenes of suffering and reluctantly admitted there was no alternative but withdrawal. His influence and credibility were diminished in London, however, and still politicians wrangled. It was the appointment of Sir William Robertson which decided the matter. The general, who had risen through the ranks, was respected by war-time prime minister Herbert Henry Asquith; he favoured France as the theatre of war. He declared the government should end the sideshow in Gallipoli.

In December 1915 the bulk of the troops was evacuated, with complete success. Not a shot was fired.

In eight months the British and Australasian forces, some 500,000 strong, had notched up 252,000 casualties and gained nothing. For the Turks the dead and wounded numbered 251,000.

The fiasco reflected badly on Winston Churchill, innovator of the plan, who could scarcely believe how badly it had been executed. He resigned in fury and frustration. But the commanders responsible for the carnage throughout the war escaped without even a reprimand.

Above: *British troops in Gallipoli had little idea what they were fighting for. Only later did they discover the hopelessness of their cause.*

ROBERT MAXWELL
Robbing the poor to feed the rich

In World War 2 Robert Maxwell won the Military Cross for bravery and was honoured as a hero. After his death thousands of pensioners cursed him as a crook.

On Guy Fawkes Night 1991 Captain Gus Rankin, master of the luxury yacht *Lady Ghislaine*, radioed an emergency message that sent shockwaves through the world's corridors of power. The Publisher was missing, feared dead, off the Canary Islands. He had apparently slipped into the water while the vessel was cruising, and drowned.

Robert Maxwell had been best known as a self-important, publicity-seeking bully. Above all, he was obsessively vain. However, predictably, when any well-known figure dies the fulsome tributes come flooding in and Maxwell's passing proved no exception.

Former prime minister Margaret Thatcher spoke of the valuable information on Eastern Europe he would pass to her, her predecessor Edward Heath praised Maxwell's unstinting support for the European ideal, Neil Kinnock talked of his backing for the Labour Party in glowing terms, while John Major observed that Maxwell would not want the world to grieve at his death but marvel at his extraordinary life. Even Mikhail Gorbachev chipped in with a piece of gibberish acknowledging Maxwell's enormous contribution to understanding between nations in mass-media management.

Gorbachev's words, as it turned out, could hardly have been further from the truth. For as the Maxwell family prepared for the great man's burial on the Mount of Olives in Israel, bankers, accountants and financiers quietly began to assess their exposure to Maxwell's business borrowings. They did not like what they saw. The bonfire of the vanities was about to begin.

A HOUSE OF CARDS

Within days the first hint of a monumental financial scandal was starting to creep out. Many in the City, together with most of the better-informed financial journalists, had known for years that the flagship company, Maxwell Communications Corporation, was heavily borrowed with comparatively few hard assets. It was a house of cards. Maxwell's death would bring it tumbling down.

Much of the empire was so complicated, with a worldwide web of interlinked companies and trusts, that no one except Maxwell himself understood how it worked. He had been careful to shelter much of his business away from prying eyes in discreet havens such as Liechtenstein and the Cayman Islands, where enquiries about financial matters – official or otherwise – tended to hit brick walls. Whenever he raided the coffers of his companies, cash left unspent would end up offshore.

Above: *Family mourners await the funeral on Israel's Mount of Olives. Lifting the coffin was a feat in itself.*

Opposite: *Maxwell, a self-important, publicity-mad bully. Only he understood the complexities of his world-wide business empire.*

Below left: *With Margaret Thatcher. He passed her valuable information on Eastern European countries.*

Below: *Maxwell House, HQ of Maxwell Communications Corporation.*

PENSIONERS WOKE UP TO DISCOVER THAT THE FUNDS THAT THEY HAD DEPENDED ON FOR THEIR OLD AGE HAD BEEN FRITTERED AWAY.

Below: Mirror *pensioners on the march after finding that their nest-eggs had been plundered.*

But one criminal fact already shone out like a warning beacon. Maxwell had clearly plundered millions from the pension fund of his favourite company, Mirror Group Newspapers. The estimates varied but the £400 million the experts calculated seemed about right. Word spread like lightning and politicians and the media turned on Maxwell with a vengeance. Even his own paper, the *Daily Mirror*, denounced him with righteous indignation as a fraud and a crook.

The vitriol was undeniably justified. Thousands of *Mirror* employees and pensioners literally woke up one morning to discover their pot of cash, which for some had taken 40 years to build up, had been frittered away by Maxwell in an attempt to keep his companies afloat during the cold recessionary years of the 1980s.

They guessed – and they were probably right – that the money went on a futile share support operation to try to prop up the London Stock Exchange price of MCC. The reason was simple: Maxwell used shares from his businesses as collateral to borrow more cash from the banks. The banks were happy as long as the businesses flourished but when share prices began plummeting so did the value of their security. In the months before his death they were getting more and more edgy and pressure mounted on Chairman Robert.

So why did those in the know stay silent? What happened to the great British tradition of a free, fearless press? Why wasn't the charlatan exposed?

Firstly, because he was notoriously litigious. Writs from Maxwell, it was said, could fly out faster than his presses could print. He seemed to relish the prospect of cowing his enemies in the courts and legal costs were irrelevant to him. In the knowledge that Britain's laws of libel were among the most oppressive in the world, and with the recession slicing into their profits, the newspapermen stayed ominously silent.

If the merest hint of a rumour defamatory of Maxwell came to his attention he would instruct his lawyers to send a curt note to every editor in Fleet Street. They would run the story at their peril.

But it wasn't only legal bluster that restrained the papers. Before his death and subsequent unmasking, Maxwell was seen as the Man Who Got Things Done. He was a World War 2 hero, champion of the world's starving, a former Labour MP and an entrepreneur who genuinely could count many of the world's monarchs, emperors, dictators, presidents and prime ministers as his close confidante. In short, he was hot on influence. His friends in high places could always oblige with a quiet word in the ear of a journalist who was sniffing a bit too close to a Maxwell scoop.

Below: *With Prince Charles and Prince William.*

Left: *Lieutenant Robert Maxwell MC leads his men during the Victory Parade through Berlin in September 1945.*

'THE BOUNCING CZECH'

And John Major was right about his extraordinary past. Almost from the day he was born, 10 June 1923, a Czechoslovakian of Jewish parents, his life was one long roller-coaster. Not for nothing was he nicknamed the 'Bouncing Czech'.

Maxwell was born Jan Ludwig Hoch in one of the poorest parts of Czechoslovakia. At 5 years old he assured his father, a farm labourer: 'When I'm older I will own a cow and a field and make my own living.' The peasants who had to mount a daily fight against starvation laughed out loud at such a ridiculous suggestion.

It seemed even less likely the following year when young Jan caught diphtheria – then an often fatal disease. There were fears that he would never fully recover; never become strong enough to earn a living on his own. As he would do so often in his life, he contemptuously swept aside the doubters and got on with fulfilling his dreams.

At 12 he walked an incredible 400 miles from his home village of Solotvino to the city of Bratislava to look for work. Later, he laughed off the achievement, saying: 'If I were a woman I would always be pregnant. I never can say no to a challenge.'

His war record bore out that claim. He started out as a Czech soldier in Central Europe where the Nazi atrocities he encountered left him with a burning hatred of Hitler. At one stage he tried to join the French Foreign Legion, lying about his age in order to qualify, but as Hitler's hordes swept across Europe, he found himself evacuated by the Royal Navy and ended up in Liverpool. From now on his determination to defeat the Nazis took a new edge. All his family, apart from two sisters, had become victims of the Holocaust.

Maxwell wangled his way into the British Army as Private J.L. Hoch, serial number 12079140. He fought with enormous skill and courage and was decorated with the Military Cross – one of the highest honours in the army – after leading his platoon against a German pillbox in Brussels in 1944. Later he would waste no opportunity to retell his war stories. One of his Mirror Group editors revealed: 'He told me of one time at the end of the war when he was in France. He went into a barn and found a German soldier who was about .15. He told Maxwell to put up his arms and surrender. Maxwell told him to drop his gun in German. The boy did. I asked Maxwell what he did then. "I shot him, of course, you bloody fool," he replied, smiling.'

The war over, he set about building a career in publishing. Wary of any lingering Jewish hatred in Europe, he adopted the very British-sounding name of Robert Maxwell. He spoke English superbly (he had mastered nine languages by his death) and used his British contacts, such as they were, to the full. But it was only after establishing a niche in scientific publishing and distribution in

Opposite bottom right: *A youthful Maxwell in pensive mood as he waits to take his seat as MP for Buckingham.*

Below: *In happier times, Maxwell waves to his investors at a meeting of Pergamum shareholders.*

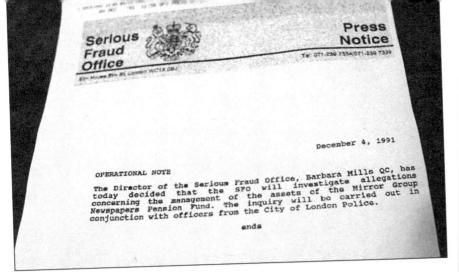

Above: The Serious Fraud Office announces it is beginning a full investigation into Maxwell's various dealings.

HE TOLD THE STARVING PEOPLE THAT HE WOULD SAVE THEM. IT WAS JUST ANOTHER OF HIS LIES.

Germany that he spotted the hole in the market which would make his name.

Convinced that cheap scientific textbooks were in demand he used his £300 war gratuity to set up Pergamon Press. The company prospered into a £6 million multi-national enterprise and for most of the fifties and sixties Maxwell's wealth and reputation grew steadily higher. Then, in 1969, the bubble burst. Maxwell had agreed to sell Pergamon to a New York financier, who then tried to wriggle out of the deal by claiming there were irregularities in the accounts. The American was right. In a bloody internal battle Maxwell was sacked by his own board and vilified in a government investigation. The Department of Trade concluded he was not a fit person to run a public company.

Yet within five years he had bounced back. He regained control of Pergamon and began expanding his horizons with a vengeance. By the beginning of the eighties he controlled the British Printing Corporation and prepared to set up the single biggest European printing group. Cash for the deal came largely from the National Westminster, and with typical Maxwell nerve he called the bank's chairman with a plan to print all their cheque books. 'After all,' he boomed, 'you and I have a mutual interest in doing business together.'

In 1984 he seized control of Mirror Group Newspapers and immediately began restructuring an organization dogged by inept management practices. Because print unions then dictated their own manpower levels, MGN had been paying printers whether there was a job for them or not. As a result some 'inkies' would clock on for a shift under the name Mickey Mouse, or some equally absurd pseudonym. Then they'd trot off to do another job secure in the knowledge that no one at the newspaper would be checking to see where they were.

BONFIRE OF VANITIES

The print unions were then perhaps the most powerful in Britain. In Maxwell, though, they met their match. He modernized the presses and introduced new technology and full colour printing. Sackings were frequent but the paper slowly began to look better and better. The only embarrassing snag for its journalists was their chairman's desire to have stories constantly appearing about his own wonderful deeds.

The classic example was his decision to launch a mercy mission for the starving of Ethiopia in 1984. He persuaded British Airways' Lord King to lend him a Tristar to carry supplies, a readers' appeal fund was launched and the paper carried columns and columns of stories about the way Maxwell was opening doors which had long stayed closed through British government bureaucracy. One former employee recalled a typical early morning meeting at which Maxwell would issue orders in the manner of a general stalking his war room.

'Get me Lord Sainsbury on the phone at home. And the chairman of Boots. And those people who promised us the milk powder. I don't give a damn if this is Sunday morning. Tell them it's a matter of life and death.'

His arrival in Addis Ababa was like a scene from a Carry On film. Maxwell strode into the airport sweeping aside immigration officials and flashing withering stares at anyone in uniform who dared to enter into his presence. Behind him a so-called welcoming party trotted along meekly in a mixture of bafflement and excitement. Then he faced the assembled ranks of press, TV, and radio, sporting his blue John Lennon-style cap and wearing his best Churchillian demeanour.

'There have been complaints that Western aid to Ethiopia is too little, too late,' he boomed. 'Well, speaking on behalf of the British nation I dispute that.' No one ventured to ask how he obtained the authority to speak for Britain. Anyway, there wasn't time. Turning on his heels Maxwell was already heading for a group of Ethiopian government dignitaries. Grabbing the hand of the nearest minister he looked him straight in the eye and declared: 'Things are going to be very different for your country from now on. Kindly tell the president that Robert Maxwell is here.'

BULLYING

When not fighting battles abroad, Maxwell loved nothing better than a chance to torment his editors and senior executives. He would keep them waiting for hours outside his office in Maxwell House, London, while he chattered away to his subordinates around the world or called some nation's leader to offer the benefit of his advice. There were only a couple of seats and a cold water machine in the waiting room.

When they did get summoned into his lair the atmosphere would be electric. Maxwell would often pick out one individual for ritual humiliation in front of his colleagues. One personnel manager was torn to shreds because of a circular letter he had sent to all Pergamon employees. Maxwell claimed: 'My old grandmother, who could never speak a word of English, brought up in the mountains of Carpathia could write better English than this.' He then ordered the unfortunate executive to shuffle out into a side office and write down why he shouldn't be sacked. As he left Maxwell roared with glee at the effects of his bullying.

Maxwell employees were not the only ones who had to bow to his whims. He disliked going out of the office for anyone, preferring them to come to him. Visiting foreign dignitaries would find themselves transported to Maxwell House by Rolls or helicopter from Heathrow. And if a guest was particularly favoured Maxwell would send his Gulfstream jet anywhere in the world.

Occasionally such lavish entertaining turned to farce. Maxwell would simultaneously host dinner for a couple of Japanese businessmen, a buffet lunch for a US trade delegation, a reception for a party of Hungarian newspapermen and plan his own quiet lunch in his study. He would tour from room to room, engaging in conversation, charming any women present, espousing his views on the world but always making an excuse to move on. And, of course, none of his guests was ever aware of the existence of others.

His family (he and his wife Betty had seven children) learned to their cost that business was never separated from home life. The two sons with closest links to the business, Kevin and Ian, were expected to be at work for 7.30 am and could expect a huge

dressing down if they were late. They rarely escaped home before a full 12 hours at their desks.

John Pole, Maxwell's head of security since 1986, said: 'He would go home to celebrate Christmas and be bored by Boxing Day. The family would gather for what they thought was going to be a holiday only to find they were going to work, but in a different country. He treated them like employees. Gradually they needed to look to other things to maintain sanity and some family life of their own.'

Top: *Maxwell and his wife Betty, pictured in 1974.*

Above: *Sons Kevin and Ian found themselves embroiled in the SFO investigation.*

Above: *Maxwell in one of his definitive pompous poses. Editors at the Mirror Group hated his thirst for self-publicity.*

Right: *His yacht the* **Lady Ghislaine,** *on which Maxwell spent his last minutes alive. It was among the most luxurious ever built and kept the publisher in touch with his minions via fax machines and satellite phones.*

Vanity was one of Maxwell's biggest vices. He needed to impress – especially women – and he hated the thought that his good looks and once enviable build had gone. Such fears caused him to suffer from bizarre eating disorders. He would suffer from uncontrollable binges, stuffing sandwiches into his mouth at the rate of five or six a time, and then a week later attempt to sustain a hopeless diet of coffee and soup. It did little to affect his usual bulk of 310 lb.

His hair was another obsession. He used to employ a former Savoy Hotel hairdresser, George Wheeler, to colour it for him every

two weeks. Maxwell and the crimper would lock themselves away for two hours while the dyes were applied to both hair and eyebrows. Everything was done in secret. No one was supposed to know it happened.

It was the same with his powder puff. Maxwell convinced himself his nose was too shiny so he took powder everywhere with him to counter the effect. If he ever forgot his puff before an important meeting it would throw him into a minor panic. Everything and everyone would have to wait while he went to fetch it. One of his editors, the *Mirror*'s Mike Molloy, recalled: 'Maxwell was theatre, he was looking for an image.'

Only on the *Lady Ghislaine*, named after his favourite daughter, could Maxwell hope to unwind amid the trappings of absolute luxury and forget about crafting that image. He loved nothing better than to sunbathe on his private deck alone, smothering his bloated mass in suncream and sleeping. The yacht was his fortress, his haven, yet at the flick of a switch he could be talking to his minions anywhere in the world by fax or radiophone. The dummy pages of the *Mirror* would regularly be faxed to him for approval.

According to the paper's former foreign editor, Nicholas Davies, who became as close to Maxwell as any newspaperman, sailing on the *Lady Ghislaine* did nothing to quell his bullying habits. Davies recalls: 'On one occasion, after a very good lunch, he phoned his chief of staff, Peter Jay, in Holborn only to find he was out to lunch.

When Jay returned his call, Maxwell turned up the heat demanding to know why he had the temerity to leave the office without permission when the chairman was abroad.

'He demanded Jay write an explanation immediately giving reasons for his absence and fax it to him on the yacht. When he received Jay's long explanatory note Maxwell read it, roaring with laughter, at what he saw as a huge joke. Then he phoned Jay back and tore into him again, pretending to be furious.'

Jay, who eventually resigned to pursue a career as economics editor with the BBC, would later tell of the 'whirling chaos' that surrounded Maxwell's operations. It was this lack of structure that meant no one but Maxwell knew the whole truth about his affairs. At times he must have struggled himself.

Jay said: 'He was not just disorderly, he actively abhorred order. The key to the man was that he had the lowest threshold of boredom. He would come in and say: "What shall I do?" He'd get an idea and start ringing people. They would turn up and wait to be told what to do, by which time he would be on to something else ... from grotesque schemes for transforming the world to fantastic rows about running newspapers.'

In a note to his successor Jay acidly observed: 'The job is essentially administration, a process of which the chairman is deeply suspicious and profoundly uncomprehending.'

PARANOID

Even when he was aboard the *Lady Ghislaine*, though, Maxwell could never truly relax. In his last years he became increasingly paranoid about the risk of attack, seeing himself as particularly vulnerable while on the yacht. He had one of his early captains, Englishman Mike Insull, buy an armoury equipped with guns for every member of crew. They were sent on courses to learn how to use them in the event of a boarding by raiders. But the guns were never referred to by name. Maxwell called them vegetables, and at the start of a voyage would sometimes sidle up to Insull and ask 'How many carrots and potatoes have you brought on this trip?'

Inevitably, after such a bizarre death, there was talk that Maxwell did not just slip into the sea by accident. Some remain convinced

he committed suicide, broken by the knowledge that his entire business empire was only weeks away from crashing around his ears. Others talk of an Arab assassin hired to wipe out a man they considered an agent for the Mossad, the Israeli secret service. Another, even more outlandish, claim is that he was rubbed out by the Mafia for trying to break into their lucrative stranglehold on US newspapers. Finally, it is rumoured the remains of the Soviet KGB had decided to settle an old score.

Of the four, the suicide theory, argue old Maxwell acquaintances, is the hardest to accept. Nicholas Davies tells how only once in the years he knew Maxwell did he hear him refer directly to suicide. Davies had been summoned to his boss's London apartment to talk over the debut of the

OUTLANDISH CLAIMS CIRCULATED AFTER HIS DEATH: ARAB ASSASSINS, THE KGB AND THE MAFIA WERE ACCUSED OF HIS MURDER.

European, his new weekly broadsheet paper. Maxwell appeared dispirited and had a heavy cold. He lounged on his bed in a white towelling robe making dismissive remarks about the paper. Then he walked to the window overlooking the city and began talking, half to himself.

'Sometimes I don't know why I go on. Everything I try, people turn against me ... I've got no friends, no one I can talk to ... no one to share my life with ... Sometimes I think I should just end it all, throw myself out of the window. I sometimes feel I can't go on.'

It was one of the few occasions anyone ever heard Maxwell admit to the failure of

Above: *Ever the extrovert, Maxwell cracks jokes with fellow party guests Liz Taylor and Malcolm Forbes. He loved nothing better than rubbing shoulders with world leaders or film stars.*

'IF YOU THINK YOU CAN PUSH US INTO AN AGREEMENT YOU'LL END UP IN THE EAST RIVER WITH YOUR THROATS SLIT.' HE WAS DEADLY SERIOUS.

his personal life. Perhaps he now knew his business empire was teetering on the edge of ruin as well. Had he stared into the abyss and realized what lay ahead? In his own mind, had he made a decision to end his life? If so, he picked the most theatrical way out possible. Disappearing from a yacht as it cruised the waters of the Canaries would, he

his death, the respected US Pulitzer Prize-winning author, Seymour Hersh, made extraordinary allegations in his book *The Samson Option*. Maxwell, he said, had for years been a Mossad agent who specialized in negotiating arms deals for Israel. But why should Maxwell bother with Mossad when he was on first-name terms with their own masters in the Israeli cabinet? And why, if Arab terrorists were responsible, did no credible organization claim responsibility?

The KGB conspiracy theory is neat and just about believable, but with Russia in a state of enormous upheaval at the time surely Red spy controllers had more important issues to tackle than killing a fat entrepreneur out on a sailing jaunt? It is said that for years Maxwell had been laundering US dollars for the Russians, taking a cut for his trouble and tucking away the proceeds in his Maxwell Foundation trust in Liechtenstein. He had also looked after the wealth of some senior Communist party figures who wanted to get their money out of the country in the face of an imminent counter-revolution.

With Russia on the brink of civil war, so the theory goes, KGB spymasters decided it was time to call in their debts. They reckoned Maxwell had made millions on the back of their cash, playing the foreign exchange markets with his natural gambler's instincts. The amounts were said to run into tens of millions of dollars and when Maxwell failed to take up the KGB's 'invitation' to pay their dividend there was talk of double-crossing. It was then that the KGB decided to show they could still flex their muscles and an agent somehow sneaked aboard the *Lady Ghislaine* to tip Maxwell over the side.

Above: *The auction of fittings from Maxwell's London penthouse was billed as the sale of the century.*

Below: *Kevin Maxwell leaving court.*

knew, guarantee even more column inches on the story of his demise.

The Arab attack theory is intriguing and if it sounds fanciful it should be taken in context with the rest of Maxwell's life. Everything that happened to him had the whiff of pure fiction. Just two weeks before

MURDER BY THE MOB?

Finally, of course, there's the mob theory. In February 1991 Maxwell had taken over the New York *Daily News* in a blaze of publicity. With a beaming face, and sporting a *Daily News* baseball cap, he gleefully held up the front page of his new baby bearing the headline: 'Roll 'em – hats off to Maxwell as News gets bigger & better than ever'.

Not everyone was happy. There were persistent rumours that for years the *News*'s distribution network had been in the hands of an organized crime syndicate. Maxwell, however, knew the Mafia men were on the

run following a police crackdown. He reckoned the only barrier to introducing new technology and making the paper profitable was the intransigent unions.

Maxwell took one of his top aides into negotiations with the unions. Scotsman Ian Watson, then a senior executive with the *European*, was tasked with trying to persuade them to accept redundancies and economies. Watson later revealed: 'After seven of the ten print unions had agreed to the cutbacks, I went to see the leaders of the remaining three, who were holding out. I remember most vividly the conversation I had with one union official. He said to me, in a broad Brooklyn accent, "Are you a New Yorker? Do you know New Yorkers? Do you understand them? If you think you can push us into an agreement you'll end up in the East River with your throats slit. All of you."' Watson said later: 'He wasn't playacting. He was deadly serious.'

Maxwell took no chances. Firstly, he asked the Manhattan district attorney's office to conduct an inquiry into the organized crime allegations. Secondly, he decided he ought to get personal protection – those who met him whenever he was in New York said he seemed to be more and more preoccupied. So it was that only days before his death he held a meeting with the head of America's most respected private security firm, Jules Kroll of Kroll Associates.

Maxwell's full conversations with Kroll have never been made public, but those close to him, such as Nicholas Davies, believe Maxwell made it clear that people were out to kill him and destroy his businesses. He named names – business rivals, known enemies and political adversaries. At the end of their two-hour talk Kroll told him to set down a memo listing the bizarre events which had led him to draw this conclusion. He never did pen that memo for within a week he had drowned.

There is, of course, the other possibility, the theory that doesn't make headlines or attract TV documentary makers. This holds that Maxwell got drunk (as he often did, especially on the yacht where Dom Perignon was always available on ice) and took a walk round the decks in the early hours because he felt unwell. Certainly his crew recall him radioing through to complain about the air conditioning. Did he just slip over a low rail close to the waterline, as some have

suggested? If so, his cries for help would fall on deaf ears. None of the crew would have been on deck at the time and the speed of the yacht would have quickly carried her away from the drowning Maxwell's spluttering cries.

Whatever the truth, it matters little to the 30,000 *Mirror* pensioners who have endured agonies wondering how they will attain the retirement life-style they planned so carefully. Legal arguments about the Maxwell empire seem certain to rage on well into the next millennium. As for Maxwell himself, a hundred epitaphs could never tell his story of courage, meteoric rise, fraud and ultimate failure. All you can say is that he died as he lived … bizarrely, mysteriously … and with the newspapers chasing close behind.

Above: *A literary lunch at London's Dorchester Hotel in 1969. Already Maxwell is looking distinctly flabby – his weight became an obsession in later life.*

MAXWELL VOICED HIS FEARS TO THE HEAD OF A POWERFUL PRIVATE SECURITY FIRM; A WEEK LATER HE WAS DEAD.

THE RACE TO THE POLES

> The quest for glory has driven men across frozen wastes to the very ends of the Earth, risking all on a gamble. Some win, and have riches and honours heaped upon them. And some lose ...

For years it had been the Holy Grail of seafarers: to find a shorter voyage from western Europe to the Orient, and to open a new trade link through the Arctic with all the profits that it entailed.

The search for a North West Passage had ended in failure many times, yet to explorers like Sir John Franklin that record served only as an added spur. If any nation was to find this elusive route it should, he felt, be his native Britain. Wasn't she the greatest naval power on Earth? Didn't her seamen have unrivalled experience? And, surely, her ships were the best?

On 19 May 1845 Sir John's expedition set sail with two ships, the *Erebus* and the *Terror*. Both had proved themselves more than capable of coping with icy seas (they had been used on an earlier jaunt by James Clark Ross to the South Pole) and they were stocked with enough carefully preserved provisions to last a good three years.

The Franklin party left in a fanfare of publicity with newspapers recording intimate details of the dangerous journey ahead. Nobody believed the voyage would be easy, but in the highest ranks of the Admiralty, and government itself, there was a quiet confidence that Sir John would somehow navigate his way through the labyrinth of straits, narrow channels and rocky gulfs known to lie in his way.

AN OMINOUS SILENCE

After two years, however, with no word from either *Erebus* or *Terror*, public opinion began to show signs of concern. Of course, the crews couldn't yet be out of food or water but all the same it seemed an ominous silence. Throughout the bitter British winter of 1847–48 tension grew. The government had to be seen to be doing something in the face of mounting pressure, and after enlisting the help of the Hudson's Bay Company, who in turn alerted roaming bands of Eskimos out on the Arctic wastes, they offered a reward of £20,000 which they hoped would help track Franklin down.

It didn't. By the summer of 1848 plans for a full-scale British search and rescue mission were well under way. Two vessels would scour known North West Passage sea lanes around the Bering Strait, while a land party would head north from Canada. Another group, headed by the acclaimed explorer James Ross, would push into the Arctic region from the east.

That winter Ross and his crew landed on Somerset Island – thought to have been a

Above: *Sir John Franklin. His attempt to navigate the North West Passage turned into a disaster.*

THE SHIPS SET SAIL IN A FANFARE OF PUBLICITY, CONFIDENT OF SUCCESS, NEVER SUSPECTING THAT THEY WERE VOYAGING INTO THE ICY WATERS OF DEATH.

Opposite: *Robert Falcon Scott, a ruthless taskmaster and disciplinarian – yet he would hide when a sled dog had to be destroyed, leaving the job to his men.*

Above: *Franklin at Bear Lake. He believed passionately that British ships should be the first through the North West Passage.*

THE MUTILATED STATE OF THE BODIES INDICATED THAT THE DYING MEN HAD TRIED TO SURVIVE BY EATING HUMAN FLESH.

possible staging post for Franklin – and covered 200 miles looking for him. They drew a blank and when they returned to England empty-handed it was seen by many as a certain sign of the Franklin party's death. Yet the Admiralty was nothing if not persistent and the following year a wave of 15 new search parties, carrying hundreds of would-be rescuers, set sail for the Arctic.

Among them was a nine-ship fleet commanded by Captain Horatio Austin with orders to search the Barrow Straits thoroughly. Austin came upon a god-forsaken, largely uninhabitable piece of land called Beechey Island and, true to his brief, decided to check it out. One of his officers, Captain Ommaney of HMS *Assistance*, took a search party ashore and with keen eyes carefully scanned the forbidding landscape.

Suddenly his eyes caught something odd: order amid the chaos, a symmetrical object in a sea of random rocks and scrub. When he got to it he found it was a primitive forge, a

store and what appeared to be a shooting gallery. There were hundreds of cans of meat stacked up ready to eat and, nearby, tombs bearing the names of three of Franklin's men. But what fate had befallen the others?

In 1853 Dr John Rae, an official with the Hudson's Bay Company, provided at least part of the answer. He had set out to cover the area around the Gulf of Boothia, an area where Eskimos were known to congregate as they waited to send hunting parties out onto the Arctic ice. Sure enough the Eskimos handed him a gigantic clue. Some other Eskimos, they said, had reported meeting a demoralized party of 40 white men who were travelling south to a point about 150 miles from where Rae now stood.

CANNIBALISM

The strangers had abandoned two large ships and claimed they were heading for the Back River. Many in their party appeared to be suffering from exhaustion and scurvy ... but at least Rae now knew there might be some survivors. Some Eskimos even claimed to have boarded the *Erebus* and the *Terror* off the coast of King William Island. Others offered grimmer news: they had stumbled upon the graves of some 30 men close to the Back River. Many of the bodies had lain huddled together in tents; others were found sheltering under a boat.

It must have been an appalling way to die, for as Rae noted after visiting the doomed camp: 'From the mutilated state of many of the bodies, and the contents of the kettles, it is evident

Right: *Austin's* Expedition, *one of the many ships sent to search for Franklin. The three largest from the left are* Assistance, Resolute *and* Pioneer. Intrepid *is slightly to the left of* Assistance.

that our wretched countrymen had been driven to the last dread alternative as a means of sustaining life.' It was a wordy way to say that Franklin's dying men had become cannibals.

Rae's report to the British government cleared up at least part of the mystery, even though he freely admitted: 'None of the Eskimos with whom I had communication saw the white men either while living or after death, nor had they ever been at the place where the corpses were found, but had their information from natives who had been there.' Despite this the government handed over half the reward money in recognition of Rae's fearless investigations. It then declared the search over, mainly on the grounds that the cost of finding 100 men (possibly scattered widely across the Arctic) was impractical. Lady Franklin's plea for a new seafarer to take up the challenge was firmly rejected.

It made little difference to her. She was not a woman easily dissuaded by anyone and with the man she loved now missing for more than seven years she set herself on raising the money for a privately funded expedition. Influential friends rallied round and on 1 July 1857 a compact steamer called the *Fox* slipped her moorings at Aberdeen and under the command of one Leopold McClintock – a veteran of previous searches – headed for the Arctic.

After stopping to take on sledge dogs and an Eskimo interpreter in Greenland the *Fox* made for Lancaster Sound. The aim was to find a suitable mooring point from which to launch a land-based search. Unfortunately massive quantities of drift ice left the ship totally immobile and she was forced to drift aimlessly with the current for an agonizing 242 days … in the wrong direction. It was not until 1 March 1859 that McClintock unearthed his first solid clue as to the fate of Franklin's men.

He was leading a small land party across the Boothia Peninsula when they met a group of Eskimo hunters. With help from his interpreter McClintock learned that years earlier a large ship had been crushed by ice off King William Island. All the crew had escaped, they believed, but then headed for a great river where they succumbed to the cold

It seemed to confirm Rae's discoveries and McClintock made haste back to his ship. His destination now was King William Island and the Back River and he divided his men into two with the intention of searching as thoroughly as possible.

On the island yet more hard clues emerged. Some Eskimos showed off items of silverware stamped with the crests of Franklin and his brother officers. Yet when McClintock at last reached the waters of the Back River he was disappointed. There were no signs of any crude settlement; no trace of white men whatsoever.

Above left: *The boat around which 30 of Franklin's men fought – and lost – their battle for survival. Some had resorted to cannibalism.*

Above: *An artist's impression of how Franklin's men would have struggled to cross the polar ice-fields.*

Above: *Lieutenant Hobson's party breaks open the cairn at Point Victory. Inside were records telling them how* **Terror** *and* **Erebus** *had been abandoned after two years locked in ice.*

Right: *Roald Amundsen. He walked away from a medical career to become an explorer.*

THE FINAL CLUES

The party crossed back to King William Island and headed up the west coast in an attempt to link up with the *Fox*'s other search party. Then, at last, they got the break they had been praying for. A weather-battered skeleton still dressed in the tatty remnants of European clothes was found lying on a snow-covered beach. On the body McClintock found a small pocket book containing a handful of letters – but still no formal record of the expedition's fate.

A little further on the searchers found two more skeletons, this time lying in a 28-foot-long boat which seemed to have once come from a ship. There were a couple of watches, two guns, spare clothing and tea and chocolate ... but still no paper records. In a further baffling twist, the boat faced north. Franklin's men could have been expected to flee south from the wrecks of their ships. Did the two unfortunates in the boat make a last desperate bid to turn back for the safety of the *Erebus* and *Terror*? If so, they had badly over-estimated their chances.

Instinct told McClintock to head north. His own log describes succinctly what happened next.

'A few miles beyond Cape Herschel the land becomes very low; many islets and shingle ridges lie far off the coast; and as we advanced we met hummocks of unusually heavy ice ... we were approaching a spot where a revelation of intense interest was awaiting.

'About 12 miles from Cape Herschel I found a small cairn built by Hobson's search party [Lieutenant Hobson was one of the *Fox*'s senior officers] and containing a note for me.'

Hobson it was who, on 6 May 1859, finally uncovered the secret of Franklin's doomed party. At Point Victory, on the north-west coast of King William Island, he found a large cairn surrounded by piles of equipment such as stoves, pickaxes, canvas shovels and instruments. There was also a rusty old cylinder which appeared to have been opened and then re-soldered. Inside they found two independently dated notices.

One log told how the *Terror* and *Erebus* had finally been abandoned on 22 April 1848 after more than two years trapped in the ice. Signed Captain F.R.M. Crozier, it ended with the postscript: 'start tomorrow, 26th, for Back's Great River'.

McClintock's men may have found the

last traces of the ill-fated Franklin expedition but they failed to answer the most important questions of all. Where did Franklin himself die? Why didn't his men join the Eskimos and learn their survival skills? And why had he been forced away from Back River? The answers remain largely conjecture.

The tragedy of Franklin's failure had, by now, been largely forgotten back home in Britain. It had certainly not dissuaded other explorers from pursuing the dream of conquering the elusive North West Passage.

A GLITTERING CHALLENGE

Foremost among them was a young Norwegian called Roald Amundsen. He was born in 1872, 13 years after the last hopes of finding Franklin had expired, yet throughout his boyhood he had nurtured an ambition to succeed where the Englishman had failed.

Although he had been channelled into a medical career the 21-year-old Amundsen decided to follow the instincts of his heart rather than his head. He threw up his studies to prepare for a career as an explorer, starting as a seaman aboard an Arctic merchantman and later serving as first mate aboard the *Belgica*, the first vessel to winter in the Antarctic.

On returning to Norway Amundsen decided to mount his own North West Passage expedition. He purchased a sturdy 72-foot ship called the *Gjoa* and during a series of voyages between 1903 and 1906 became the first man to navigate the route successfully. A glittering future now beckoned, with Amundsen a household name around the world and a hero at home. Instead of basking in the fame, the Norwegian immediately began planning his next challenge ... conquering the North Pole.

Amundsen's plans were to drift across it in a ship, a technique pioneered by his countryman Fridtjof Nansen in 1893. Nansen had noticed that wood used by Greenlanders was not from any indigenous tree population. Botanists reported that rough driftwood cast up on the shores originated from as far away as Siberia: it could only have travelled in a current which passed over the roof of the world.

Nansen's brave attempt to drift with the pack ice across the Pole had been technically a failure, though he did get to within 272 miles of the Pole. His expedition lasted more than three years and he was given up for lost in Norway after setting out from his ship, the *Fram*, with one of his young officers, Hjalmar Johansen. In the summer of 1896 the exhausted pair stumbled onto a group of desolate islands called Frans Josef Land. Miraculously they there ran into an English explorer called Frederick Jackson, who at first refused to believe what he was seeing.

Finally Jackson ventured: 'Aren't you Nansen?' The man nodded, Jackson grabbed his hand and with typical British understatement told him: 'By Jove, I am glad to see you.'

Amundsen was convinced he could make Nansen's drift theory work but sadly never got the chance. Money was tight in his government's coffers and his expedition was still in the early stages of preparation when, in September 1909, news flashed around the globe that American naval officer Robert E. Peary had conquered the North Pole.

Cannily, Amundsen hid his disappointment and announced he would continue with plans for an Arctic 'drift'. In fact his motives were almost certainly very different. He was little over a year away from one of the greatest pieces of real-life drama in the history of man's exploration of the Earth.

Above: *Nansen meets Jackson after more than three years lost in the polar wastes.*

Below: *Admiral Peary. He beat Scott and Amundsen in the race to the North Pole.*

HE WAS AN UNLIKELY HERO, BEING UNASHAMEDLY LAZY, SOMEWHAT SLOVENLY AND PRONE TO BOUTS OF EXTRAORDINARY TEMPER.

Right: *Roald Amundsen. He was first to the South Pole, through meticulous planning, wide experience and sheer single-mindedness.*

Below: Terra Nova *at anchor near Cape Evans, Antarctica.*

SCOTT OF THE ANTARCTIC

That same year the Englishman Robert Scott, already a veteran of Antarctic campaigns, announced his ambition to conquer the South Pole. He chose an old whaling ship, the *Terra Nova*, and made plans to take a party of scientists with him. They would travel on sledges pulled by Manchurian ponies (Scott had been less than impressed with the efforts of dogs on his earlier expeditions).

Scott hardly seemed the ideal character to lead such a taxing adventure. When he was a naval cadet his lecturers regarded him as unashamedly lazy, somewhat slovenly and prone to bouts of extraordinary temper. Later in his career he was marked out as a ruthless taskmaster and stickler for discipline. Yet he inspired faith and respect among his men, perhaps because despite his weak chest and comparatively puny physique he drove himself far harder than he drove them.

Scott was also something of a romantic. His day-dreaming earned him the nickname 'old mooney' and he had a habit of crying when he heard certain hymns. He hated anything he regarded as cruel and hid himself away if it was ever necessary to put down a sled dog. Though he had the heart of a lion and unrivalled willpower, his failing was to lack Amundsen's more practical, direct approach to problems.

On 1 June 1910 the *Terra Nova* set sail from the Port of London bound for New Zealand. A couple of months later Amundsen, using Nansen's proven vessel the *Fram*, also headed south with the apparent intention of rounding Cape Horn to take the Pacific route up to the North Pole. His entire crew believed the Arctic was their destination.

On 9 September at Funchal in the Madeira Islands, Amundsen dropped his bombshell. Far from heading north, he said, they would press south. Their mission was to conquer the South Pole and anyone who didn't wish to proceed was free to leave. Unsurprisingly there were no takers. Scott had not yet reached Melbourne, Australia, but when he did there was a succinctly phrased cable waiting for him. It was from Madeira and read: 'BEG LEAVE TO INFORM YOU PROCEEDING ANTARCTICA STOP AMUNDSEN'.

The news was greeted first with incredulity, then indignation by members of the British team. They had been pitched into a race for which they had never been mentally prepared, but if that was the way Amundsen wanted it, so be it.

Scott made haste for his base camp on McMurdo Sound, on the far east of the Ross Ice Shelf, but found the going through pack ice extremely slow. While waiting for the camp to be resupplied he sailed further east to spy out the lie of the land. In the Bay of Whales his nagging suspicion proved correct. Amundsen's *Fram* already lay rocking gently at anchor. And the

single-mindedness. For a start, his only aim was to reach the Pole as quickly as possible and return safely. Scott would have to make regular stops to allow his scientists to carry out their observations.

Second, the Norwegian had learned from the Eskimos how to dress lightly and warmly in loose-fitting furs to survive polar conditions. His party were better insulated and drier than Scott's men could ever hope to be in their specially constructed suits that weighed almost twice as much and stayed perpetually sodden.

Third, Amundsen's Siberian huskies

Left: *Captain Scott sets out on his last journey. He wore a specially constructed man-made suit – but it quickly became heavy and sodden.*

Norwegian had started out 60 miles nearer the Pole than he would from his base in McMurdo.

Apart from that, Amundsen had won three main advantages through meticulous planning, wide experience and sheer

were excellent performers who had been transported from Greenland under the most carefully controlled conditions possible. All the animals were fit and in perfect shape for the torturous road ahead and they were working for men who knew how to get the best out of them. Each sledge had also been intelligently reduced in weight from the planned 165 lb to a much more manageable 48 lb. Scott, meanwhile, was about to discover that his Manchurian ponies, of whom so much had been made when his expedition left London, were hopeless in extreme snow conditions.

Above: *Manchurian ponies on Scott's expedition. They proved useless in extreme conditions.*

Left: *Amundsen taking a reading with a sextant. His Eskimo-style furs proved far more practical than his rival's gear.*

Below: *Amundsen locating the exact position of the South Pole. He recalled how the Norwegian flag looked 'wonderfully well in the pure clear air'.*

THE RACE FOR GLORY

Amundsen left the Bay of Whales in October with four companions, four sledges, and 52 dogs. They covered 90 miles in the first four days and by 5 November had reached their southernmost supply point ready for the last push to the Pole. Amundsen was then able to strap on skis, attach a rope to a sledge, and have himself towed along. He later admitted: 'Yes, that was a pleasant surprise. We had never dreamed of driving on skis to the Pole.'

By this method the members of the Norwegian team found themselves only 270 miles from their target by the middle of November. Time was overwhelmingly on their side.

Scott, on the other hand, had left McMurdo Sound on 1 November and quickly ran into trouble on the Ross Ice Shelf. An Antarctic summer blizzard meant his ponies began sinking up to their necks in snow and had to be driven to their physical limits by the team. After camping for four days to wait out the storm Scott tried to push forward again. Within 15 hours his few remaining animals had to be shot and his party prepared to manhaul the sledges.

None the less the British kept going, in the clear knowledge that their duel was not only with Amundsen but also with the oncoming grip of winter. They got to their final supply point at the foot of the Beardmore Glacier well behind their planned schedule, but they still believed they could win the race. They now had the broad expanse of the glacier to move across. Amundsen, they reasoned, could not hope for such a straightforward passage.

Amundsen, indeed, had hit his first real snag. He had no choice but to negotiate a narrow ice spur he called the Axel Heiberg glacier and he found the snow so thick and crumbly that the dogs kept losing their footing. Time and again he was forced to retrace his steps to find another way up, and finally, with the way forward blocked by massive slabs of ice, he resigned himself to finding another route south. He still believed he had a good lead on Scott … and he was right.

Several hundred miles away across the unforgiving, icy wastes the British team was showing classic symptoms of fatigue.

They had just lugged their equipment 8,000 feet up the Beardmore Glacier and they remained less than half way to the South Pole.

By 7 December Amundsen had pressed ahead to latitude 88° 23' – 97 miles from the Pole – the farthest point that Irishman Sir Ernest Shackleton had reached the previous year. To commemorate the breaking of Shackleton's record Amundsen ordered the hoisting of the Norwegian national flag on one sledge. In his book *South Pole* he later recalled his thoughts.

'All the sledges had stopped and from the foremost of them the Norwegian flag was flying. It shook itself out, waved and flapped so that the silk rustled; it looked wonderfully well in the pure clear air and the shining, white surroundings ... No other moment in the whole trip affected me like this. The tears forced their way to my eyes; by no effort of will could I keep them back. Luckily, I was some way in advance of the others so that I had time to pull myself together and master my feelings before reaching my comrades.'

A week later he was just 15 miles from his goal. Amundsen recalled that he 'had the same feeling that I can remember as a little boy of the night before Christmas Eve – an intense expectation of what was going to happen'.

At 3 pm the next day the magical figure of 90° south was confirmed by the team, though just to be sure they made a 12-mile circuit of the spot, taking further sightings as they went. By general agreement it was decided to leave a tent at the South Pole with the Norwegian flag fluttering from its roof. It would be a sight to chill the heart of Robert Scott.

As Amundsen headed home, Scott's men ploughed on – growing ever wearier from the weight of their sledges. Yet on New Year's Day 1912 their leader entered an optimistic note in his log: 'Only 170 miles to the Pole and plenty of food.' Perhaps it was a touch of over-confidence that caused him on 4 December to make perhaps the greatest mistake of the entire mission.

The last dash beckoned and it had always been agreed that the make-up of this final assault party should be Scott, Captain Oates, Dr Edward Wilson, and seaman Edgar Evans. Then, seemingly on a whim, Scott added the name of Lt Birdie Bowers. It was a crazy decision. The tent would be overcrowded, a carefully worked-out routine would be thrown into chaos and the food and equipment taken for four men

Above: *Scott's party finds Amundsen's tent at the South Pole. Inside was a letter addressed to Scott, who wrote in his log: 'Great God, this is an awful place.'*

'I HAD THE SAME FEELING ... AS A LITTLE BOY ON THE NIGHT BEFORE CHRISTMAS EVE – AN INTENSE EXPECTATION OF WHAT WAS GOING TO HAPPEN.'

would now have to extend to five. Moreover, Bowers had left his skis at the bottom of the Beardmore Glacier. He would have to trudge while the others slid along.

They set out in more blizzards, which reduced the pace to just ten miles a day. At first Scott was upbeat, writing in his diary: 'It is wonderful to see that two long marches will land us at the Pole ... it ought to be a certain thing now and the only appalling possibility is the sight of the Norwegian flag forestalling ours.'

THE DEATH OF HOPE

But after 15 January his writings became gloomier. He noted: 'We started off in high spirits in the afternoon feeling that tomorrow would see us at our destination. About the second hour of that march Bowers' sharp eyes detected what he thought was a cairn ... half an hour later he detected a black speck. We marched on and found that it was a black flag tied to a sledge bearer; nearby the remains of a camp ... this told us the whole story. The Norwegians have forestalled us and are first at the Pole. It is a terrible disappointment for me and I am very sorry for my loyal companions.'

Scott at last reached his goal on 18 January 1912. He found Amundsen's tent and a letter addressed to himself. Tired and devoid of morale, the British made camp and contemplated their shattered dreams. Scott himself wrote: 'Great God, this is an awful place. Now for the run home and a desperate struggle. I wonder if we can do it.' Maybe he already realized that time had run out. The bitter Antarctic winter would soon be closing in.

On 25 January his log states: 'Only 89 miles to the next depot but it is time we cleared off this plateau ... Oates suffers from a very cold foot; Evans' fingers and

Below: *Scott* (centre) *and his men. Bitter disappointment at being beaten is etched into his face.*

nose are in a bad state and tonight Wilson is suffering tortures from his eyes ... I fear a succession of blizzards at this time of year ... not only stopping our marches but the cold, damp air takes it out of us.' As he wrote these words Amundsen was celebrating his own return to the Bay of Whales base camp. He'd gone there and back in 99 days – a journey of 1,860 miles across the most treacherous land in the world.

Despite their hardship, Scott's men found time to pursue their scientific objectives. On 7 February they arrived at the head of the Beardmore Glacier and immediately set about chipping off some of the rocks laid bare by the biting winds. They collected 35 lb before heading down to their base.

Now the problems began stacking up. First, they got lost and wasted vital rations trying to re-establish their route. Each man was down to his last meal when they stumbled upon the food depot they had been so desperately seeking. Then Edgar Evans fell and got himself concussed. He appeared dazed and rambling and, as Scott wrote, was 'absolutely changed from his normal self-reliant self'.

Later on, in the middle of a march, Evans dropped to his knees, uncovered hands bearing the ravages of frostbite, clothes dishevelled and 'a wild look in his eyes'. He died the same night. The survivors still had 430 miles to cover.

Captain Oates was the next to go. He no longer had the strength for sledge-hauling and could barely keep up because of his frostbitten feet. On 15 March he pleaded with the others to leave him behind so that they could improve their own chances. All three refused point-blank. But the following day a blizzard again swept in and the men were confined to their tent. In what was to become one of the most famous quotes in the history of exploration, the heroic Oates told his companions: 'I am going out and I may be some time'. He shuffled out into the driving snow where, somewhere, his body still lies.

Then came another setback. Oil had somehow managed to evaporate from the storage cans, which meant that the prospect of freezing to death became a distinct possibility. Two days after Oates vanished Scott, by now almost certainly in an exhausted mental state, wrote: 'We have the last half-fill of oil in our primus and a very small quantity of spirit – this alone between us and ...'

On 21 March, while just 11 miles from their final supply depot, another blizzard confined them to their tent. Scott recorded: 'Had we lived, I should have had a tale to tell of the hardihood, endurance and courage of my companions that would have stirred the heart of every Englishman. These rough notes and our dead bodies must tell the tale but surely, surely, a great rich country such as ours will see that those who are dependent on us are properly provided for.'

> **THE GALLANT OATES TRIED TO SAVE HIS COMPANIONS BY LEAVING THE TENT AND STAGGERING TO HIS DEATH IN THE ICY BLIZZARD.**

Above: *Captain Oates' supreme sacrifice. He dragged himself out into the teeth of a snowstorm, hardly able to stand on his frostbitten feet. His final words to his friends have become enshrined in the history of exploration.*

At about the same time, Scott penned a letter to Wilson's wife. It read: 'If this letter reaches you, Bill and I will have gone out together. We are very near it now and I should like you to know how splendid he was at the end – everlastingly cheerful and ready to sacrifice himself for others, never a word of blame to me for leading him into this mess.

'I can do no more to comfort you than to tell you that he died as he lived, a brave, true man – the best of comrades and the staunchest of friends. My whole heart goes out to you in pity. Yours, R. Scott'

Then, at the end of March, came the final entry in the journal. 'Every day now we have been ready to start for our depot eleven miles away, but outside the door of the tent it remains a scene of whirling drift. I do not think we can hope for any better

Above: *Scott's grave in the ice that claimed his life.*

things now. We shall stick it out to the end but we are getting weaker of course and the end cannot be far. R. Scott. For God's sake look after our people.'

The bodies were not found for eight months. Wilson and Bowers had their sleeping bags closed, Scott's was open – one arm thrown across Wilson. Reports of the scene plunged the whole of Britain into mourning.

On two counts the expedition had been truly a spectacular failure. It had failed to reach the Pole first and five of its members had met their deaths in the most appalling circumstances.

But out of that failure came a breath of triumph. For all his faults, occasional muddle-headedness and temper tantrums, Robert Scott elevated the qualities of courage and determination to heights rarely seen. He died a hero. Few men have matched him.

RUDOLPH HESS
A blunder of a peace mission

Rudolph Hess's desperate peace mission seemed too incredible to be true and the British politicians were wary. It was to be another 30 years before facts emerged that indicated that the real story might be even more amazing.

HE WAS BESOTTED BY HITLER AND DESCRIBED HIM AS 'FULL OF RARE DECENCY, FULL OF HEARTFELT GOODNESS ...'

Hitler never wanted to go to war with Chamberlain or Churchill. Despite his curt treatment of Britain's premiers, it is often recounted how he saw Russia as his main target, to provide an ample empire for the German race. The Führer would have preferred Britain as an ally rather than an enemy in his fight against the bogey of Bolshevism.

With this in mind, and with astonishing gall, his right-hand man Rudolph Hess decided to seek peace with Britain. He probably believed he had every chance of succeeding too. With the island fortress taking a heavy battering and thought to be staring into the jaws of defeat, he was guessing that the beleaguered British politicians would seize the chance an honourable end to hostilities.

In a covert expedition, Hess set off for enemy soil with the intention of seeing a Scottish duke he had previously met. This nobleman, he was confident, would introduce him to King George VI whom he felt sure shared the same repulsion as Hess himself suffered at the wholesale loss of life in the conflict.

But for a man of renowned intellect his decision was a blunder of enormous proportions. No one knows if he discussed the mad peace plan with Hitler. No one knows if he had lost his mind thanks to the grim reality of a world at war. In fact, no one even knows whether the real Rudolph Hess was incarcerated as a war criminal for 46 years in Spandau Prison, Berlin. What is sure, however, is that the night flight from Germany put an end to his glittering career and, in real terms, his life.

Walter Rudolph Richard Hess was born in Egypt on 26 April 1894, the son of a young German merchant forging a successful business in Alexandria. His abiding memories of the era spent in Egypt were of expeditions with his mother to witness nature in action in the desert beneath a scorching sun or by night under a star-lit canopy.

By 1908 he had left Africa for college at Godesberg on the Rhine and later went to a French-speaking school in Switzerland. He was being tutored in accounts and business studies in preparation for taking on his father's import and export business, not a role he relished.

ACE PILOT

So when World War 1 broke out in 1914 he volunteered to serve in the infantry, seeing action in some of the bloodiest and foulest of killing fields, including the Somme and Verdun. Despite two injuries, he fought on. It wasn't until a bullet pierced his left lung, almost killing him, that he was discharged and returned to friendly territory for convalescence. But it wasn't the end of his war. He emerged again as a fighter pilot a month before the war ended, and there was more fighting to be done in the chaos that consumed Germany after 1918. During this turbulent time he met the father-figure he yearned for, Dr Karl Haushofer, an academic who shared his views on politics and racial purity.

In 1920 he enrolled at university to study history and economics and that same year he first met and fell under the spell of Adolf Hitler. Struck by his tremendous oratory, Hess enrolled in the newly formed National Socialist Party on 1 July as member number 16.

In those early days Hess described Hitler as ' ... a character full of rare decency, full of heartfelt goodness, religious and a good Catholic. He has only one aim and for this he sacrifices himself quite unselfishly.'

Hess himself was a rather dour individual not given to laughter or joking. He did not smoke or drink and socialized only to broaden his mind by intense debate with other earnest young men looking for a new resurgence for their beloved homeland. He was certainly gullible and more than a little naïve, but stoically loyal.

When Hitler organized his uprising or *Putsch* in November 1923, Hess was at his side. They were consequently jailed for their insurrection and spent countless hours together during the 14 months they spent in a prison cell, exchanging ideas and discussing policies. Undoubtedly, Hess had a considerable input in Hitler's famous tome *Mein Kampf,* written at this time.

So the bond between Hitler and Hess was strengthening. In Hitler's subsequent climb to total power, Hess was in his shadow, working wholeheartedly for Nazism. There seemed a genuine affection between the two, shown when Hitler banned Hess from flying because he considered some of the stunts pulled off by the ace pilot too risky.

But Hess did have a distaste for wanton violence and mayhem even then. The brutality which emerged in bursts from Hitler, the leader he adored, were upsetting to him, to say the least. Most notable was the bloody purge Hitler carried out among his followers in the thirties after which Hess had to find words of explanation and comfort for distraught mothers and widows.

Hess had married his secretary Ilse Prohl but with little enthusiasm. Subsequently historians have questioned his sexuality, wondering whether or not he was gay. Some go as far as to list Albrecht Haushofer, son of the influential professor, the Duke of Hamilton and Hitler himself as Hess's partners.

It does appear the planned violent onslaught against Britain was causing Hess some anxiety. Previous peace offers to the British had fallen on deaf ears. In desperation, Hess turned to his old friend and confidant Haushofer who not only sympathized but passed on the name of a family friend in Lisbon, a Mrs Violet Roberts, who perhaps could help as an intermediary.

News that London was being pounded by the Luftwaffe and the sight of Berlin in flames convinced Hess that peace was preferable at any price. He authorized the letter to be sent to Lisbon, apparently unaware or uncaring that it might be intercepted by the British Secret Service, which it duly was.

When no reply came from Britain he sent his own letter, to which there was also no response. German morale was soaring so he knew any actions he took were unlikely to dent it. Also, he felt the Führer could easily extricate himself from the escapade which he admitted had little chance of success.

He then secured himself a plane from his flier friend Professor Willi Messerschmitt, ensuring it had sufficient capability to get him to Britain. It took some months of preparation and several abortive missions before the flight from which there would be no turning back took place. He wrote two letters to Hitler, several to his family and one to Heinrich Himmler, an adversary rather than comrade, protesting the innocence of all his men. In fact, only a couple of people did know about his plan, all of them among his staff. While others may have had their suspicions, Professor Haushofer, the man in whom he had confided many of his ambitions and woes during the previous 20 years, said he was ignorant of the peace bid. His wife Ilse, at home in bed because of illness on the day of his departure, knew nothing of his aims.

Above: *Hess with Hitler and others of the Nazi hierarchy. He was a valued confidante and advisor to the Führer, which made him an object of envy among other leading Nazis.*

Above: *Before the outbreak of World War 2, Hess helps Hitler to rally support.*

THE BLAZING PLANE CRASHED IN THE FIELD AND A LONE PARACHUTIST DRIFTED, BILLOWING DOWN TO EARTH IN THE MOONLIGHT.

TAKE-OFF

On 10 May 1941 the day dawned bright and sunny but the cloud cover Hess needed to breach Scotland's coast in safety was forecast and appeared. At last, this was the day he had waited for. Nobody thought twice about the Deputy Führer entering Augsberg airfield on an apparently workaday mission. After watching the tanks being filled and checking the guns were empty, Hess dropped into the cockpit and prepared for take-off. By 5.45 pm he was airborne, leaving Nazi Germany behind him for ever.

The circumstances of his arrival in Scotland are well documented. Shortly before 11 pm, a ploughman by the name of David McLean, of Floor's Farm, Eaglesham, near Glasgow, was deafened by a roar which shook his whole house. He rushed outside to see a plane crashed and blazing in a field and a lone parachutist billowing down to Earth in the moonlight.

At a distance, McLean called: 'Who are you? Are you German?' The reply stunned him. 'Yes, I am German. My name is Hauptmann Alfred Horn. I want to go to Dungavel House. I have an important message for the Duke of Hamilton.'

The plane had already been detected by radar as it crossed the Scottish coast. Either it was not intercepted or the weaponry used to shoot it down was defeated by the speed of the lone Messerschmitt. Royal Observer Corps staff were puzzled as to why a short range single German plane was traversing enemy airspace.

Nearby, the local home guard had also witnessed the spectacular descent of the aircraft and helped to take the pilot prisoner. Hess was unlikely to make an escape. He had badly sprained his ankle with his bumpy landing and was ensconced in McLean's comfy cottage when reinforcements arrived.

With an ancient revolver prodding his back, they left the farm for the home guard headquarters, a scout hut in Giffnock, a Glaswegian suburb. It took several hours for the wheels to grind into action. An interpreter, the Polish consul, was found. Two Royal Observer Corps officers arrived, one of whom immediately suspected the uninvited guest was Hess.

Maintaining his name was Horn and even brandishing an envelope bearing the name in a bid to convince his captors of the bogus identity, Hess asked once again to see the Duke of Hamilton.

A MISSION OF HUMANITY

Bizarrely, there was no response that night from RAF Turnhouse, under the command of the Duke of Hamilton, despite requests from the ROC men. It wasn't until 10 am the following day that the Duke turned up to interview the mystery prisoner. Hess requested a private audience with Hamilton during which he confessed for the first time that he was really Rudolph Hess and outlined the purpose of his flight. He was on a 'mission of humanity', he told Hamilton. 'The fact that I as a Reichsminister have come to this country in person is proof of my sincerity and Germany's willingness for peace.' Further, he wanted a guarantee to be able to return to Germany, whether or not his mission succeeded.

Churchill was duly briefed about the airman still known as Horn, by now held in a military hospital in Buchanan Castle at Drymen, four miles outside Glasgow.

The cigar-sucking statesman was wary. Although Hamilton and the foreign secretary Anthony Eden professed the prisoner bore a striking resemblance to Hess whom they had both met before the war, the Duke was doubtful about the story. With a string of military mishaps behind him in the opening rounds of the war, could he really be lucky enough to capture a high-ranking Nazi with such ease? Of course, the possibility of an impostor claiming to be Hess was examined, but Churchill and his colleagues were at a loss to know what game Hitler was playing, with such odd tactics. They were still pondering when German radio broadcast that Hess had gone missing in a disturbed mental state.

Later the Nazi propaganda machine churned out bulletins describing how Hess, an angel of peace, had been lured into an evil British trap. It appeared the Germans, too, were having difficulty explaining away the bizarre actions of Hess. Hitler, by all accounts, was stunned at the letter he received from Hess detailing his plans, and decided the fate of his old friend was held in the stars. Hess had promised he would not reveal the German plan to invade Russia in only a few weeks' time. Opening war on another front was a policy Hess believed to be madness, which was partly why he sought an accord with Britain. In the rambling explanation of his actions, Hess pointed out the Führer could simply deem his former deputy gone mad if any tricky questions arose. In turn, Hitler ordered that Hess be shot should he ever appear on German soil again.

Perhaps because the British military minds were so amazed at the German aviator's actions, they did not cash in on the capture of Hess in terms of morale-boosting publicity. They probably believed that the public, like themselves, would be unable to comprehend what had happened. Instead, they chose a whispering campaign designed to reach Germany only, alluding to Hess quitting Germany because he had lost confidence in the leadership and knew the war would be won by the British.

Hess was denied a piece of his aircraft as a memento, but allowed books, one of them being *Three Men in a Boat* by Jerome

Below: *Hess speaking publicly in 1937. He fervently believed in the Nazi policies of racial purity and national expansion, but disliked the party's lust for violence.*

K. Jerome. Later he requested a gun, probably planning to shoot himself, but was told the British government were short of guns at that time.

Lord Simon, the Lord Chancellor, posed as a psychiatrist in an interview with Hess in 1941. He reported that Hess had certainly come on the mission under his own steam and that Hitler knew nothing of the venture. He came to the conclusion, like many others, that Hess realized his own position in the hierarchy was being undermined despite unswerving, dog-like loyalty to his leader. It was his intention to pull off a coup with a negotiated peace that would ensure his position beside the Führer thereafter.

He also noted some worrying garbled comments from Hess which would have cast doubt on his sanity. Hess was convinced his food was being poisoned and that assassins lurked, waiting to finish him off. The British authorities were reluctant to declare Hess, codenamed Jonathan, insane because if they had there would have been various difficulties in holding him as a prisoner. He would most likely have been sent back to Germany under the rules of the Geneva Convention.

Hess was possibly expecting a grander reception and certainly better living quarters after his arrival in Britain, but the barbed wire and sentries which guarded him were in part to protect him from revenge plots. There was evidence that Polish servicemen planned to kidnap him and at the very least rough him up in retribution for the treatment their country had suffered at German hands.

He tried to commit suicide at least once during the war – he leaped over a stairwell at Mytchett Place, Surrey, where he was being held. The injuries he sustained were not life threatening. There were bouts of amnesia in which Hess claimed he could not answer any questions about himself.

JUDGEMENT AT NUREMBERG

When the war ended it was decided he was capable of standing trial at Nuremberg

Below: The *Duke of Windsor, exiled from Britain after the abdication scandal, was friendly with the Führer and visited Germany in 1937 to inspect Nazi troops.*

alongside other notorious war criminals. At this time he set out his reasoning more concisely than ever before.

'The basis of my policy … must be an understanding with England. Even today, I have not yet given up this hope. I consider this war in which for a second time within a generation the people of a noble race are decimating each other and destroying their very substance as a terrible tragedy.

'The decision to go [from Germany] was the hardest I have ever made in my life. It was rendered easier, however, when I visualized the endless rows of coffins, both in Germany and in England, with mothers in dire distress following behind. I am convinced that mothers on both sides of the Channel will have understood my action.'

Along with Admiral Donitz, Admiral Raeder, Albert Speer and others, he was sentenced to life imprisonment at Spandau Prison in West Berlin. He was known as prisoner number 7. And here he spent year upon year in solitary confinement, held while other prisoners were allowed to go free. By 1967 he was the sole inmate in the complex, being guarded by a rota of British, American, French and Russian troops. It was the Russians who were most eager to see his imprisonment continue. Without Hess, they would have been banished from this legitimate foothold in West Berlin. Not only that, they were convinced he had helped draw up plans to obliterate Russia although it was claimed in London he knew nothing of Operation Barbarossa, Hitler's ill-fated invasion of the USSR.

Unaccountably, it was 23 years before Hess agreed to see his wife Ilse and son Wolf. By August 1987 the frail 93-year-old held in Spandau was ready to die. He committed suicide by strangling himself on the flex of a lamp. The bleak prison building was demolished soon afterwards but the controversy about Hess raged on.

Hess could have been the lone diplomat he always claimed, seeking to make peace, his brain becoming addled through pressure first exerted at home in Germany and later under interrogation.

There is also the suggestion that Hess was merely an expedient pawn, that peace negotiations were well under way and Hess was assigned for the most prominent and dangerous of roles by Hitler, to secure an

armistice. For whatever reason, the British side chose to abort the peace mission, if only to satisfy the masses who had pulled together for victory in a way no one imagined possible.

It is known Hess talked to the Duke of Windsor about an end to hostilities with Britain. The misguided Duke, who abdicated the throne for the love of American divorcee Wallis Simpson, was probably convinced the British would capitulate rather than face bloodshed. Any successfully negotiated peace would perhaps have removed King George VI from the throne and reinstated the banished Duke. The intervention of the incumbent King would have possibly been enough to scupper peace plans which certainly some members of the aristocracy favoured.

IMPOSTOR!

Then there is the storm caused by Dr Hugh Thomas, a consultant in Berlin's British Military Hospital, who became convinced the Hess held behind bars was an

Above: *Churchill in characteristic pose. He was perplexed by the bizarre actions of Hess and couldn't understand why the high-ranking German had taken flight from Germany.*

'I AM CONVINCED THAT MOTHERS ON BOTH SIDES OF THE CHANNEL WILL HAVE UNDERSTOOD MY ACTION.'

impersonator. He drew his amazing conclusions after witnessing the naked body of the ageing prisoner. In 1973 he was allowed to give Hess a complete medical check-up. The Russians were insistent that no comfort was shown to prisoner number 7. Their hardened attitude nearly resulted in the death of Hess in 1969 when they failed to call in help for several days after a duodenal ulcer perforated. On humanitarian grounds, Dr Thomas was anxious to see Hess accorded decent treatment. His discovery was electrifying.

History recorded how Hess as a young man had sustained a serious lung injury among others, but his body revealed no sign of a scar. On a subsequent examination, Dr Thomas asked: 'What happened to your war wounds?' According to the doctor, Hess blanched, trembled and uttered: 'Too late, too late.'

Convinced the real Hess was not the man who had been held for all these years by the Allies, Dr Thomas looked again at the flight from Germany. The plane used could not have covered the distance between Germany and Scotland without extra fuel tanks, yet a photograph taken by Hess's adjutant revealed no fuel tanks fixed to the wings of the aircraft.

There was the mystery of why he refused to see his wife and son – perhaps for fear of being revealed as an impostor. There were also lapses in his memory which no one could account for, when he failed to recognize people the real Hess had known well. The fastidious vegetarian Hess was known to be had also been replaced by a man greedy for food who would scoff meat, fish and anything else that came his way in a sloppy, unappealing manner.

Dr Thomas's theory is that Hess died in Germany before making his flight. News that he planned a hare-brained ploy for peace filtered through to other aspiring Nazi commanders – with up to five failed attempts at making the flight, it would not be surprising. Goering is known to have hated Hess and the intimate relationship he had with Hitler. Himmler, head of the SS, yearned to replace Hitler at the top. Both wanted Hess out of the way, but killing him would have offended his all-powerful long-time friend.

So they murdered the real Hess but had to make sure that a ringer arrived in Britain

THE DISCOVERY WAS ELECTRIFYING – AND EXPLAINED WHY HESS HAD REFUSED TO SEE HIS WIFE AND SON FOR OVER 20 YEARS.

in his place to appease Hitler. Why would anyone take on such a thankless role? Many reluctant volunteers enlisted in fear of what might happen to their families if they wavered. After weeks or months of brainwashing, a lookalike might have been genuinely confused about fact and fantasy. He might accurately have guessed that any protestations at the Nuremberg trials would not have been believed.

There is even a theory that James Bond creator Ian Fleming entered into a ritual with satanist Aleister Crowley to lure Hess to Britain after the powerful deputy had been identified as a weak link in the chain of power. A biographer of Fleming says that in 1941 in Ashdown Forest, Sussex, Fleming joined Crowley and his son Amando in flowing robes chanting a spell which would woo Hess to British shores.

Official papers, however, concur with the notion that Hess worked alone and was indeed rather mentally disturbed at the time of his flight to Britain. Brigadier J. Rees, consultant psychiatrist from the army who tended Hess during his internment in Britain, wrote that he suffered from: 'periodic spells of depression and generalised nervousness ... he is suffering from insomnia and from attacks of abdominal discomfort'.

National archive material released in 1992 discounts the numerous conspiracy theories. No doubt is noted among the politicians of the day involved in the issue about the identity of the parachutist. Interviewers reported how he seemed resigned to his lonely future after deciding the mission for peace was his fate or destiny. Hess always denied Hitler had sent him. One government paper is being withheld for security reasons.

Whatever the truth, it is certain that when Hess hatched the plot to become unofficial emissary for peace, he was sealing his own miserable fate. Either he was killed in a hush-hush operation by his rivals in the Reich or he condemned himself to a life of bitter solitude lasting year upon interminable year, never to be shown mercy. While his prospects in Germany long term were perhaps less than shining, at least he would have escaped living in limbo and might have died with honour, something he would certainly have valued.

ANIMAL ANTICS

TOUCHING TALES

The terrorists thought it would be child's play to steal the world's fastest racehorse, but their naive miscalculations were to result in the ignoble destruction of the magnificent stallion.

Streaking stallion Shergar galloped to glory in fine style, winning four major races in a year. He was perhaps the greatest flat racer ever to have lived.

But one dark night he vanished from his stable, never to be seen again. The shock disappearance made headlines across the globe. What can have happened to the fantastic thoroughbred with the famous white blaze? Soon the story ranked alongside the great mysteries of the age and was spoken of in the same breath as the ghost ship *Marie Celeste* and the runaway British nobleman Lord Lucan who disappeared the night his children's nanny was murdered.

There were periodic sightings of Shergar alive and well and living in Libya, the Channel Islands and the Isle of Man. As late as 1992, bounty hunters tried to claim thousands of pounds from an insurance company on the basis that the horse lived and bred, ignoring the difficulties there would be in registering the birth of any offspring. Observers speculated about a Mafia plot or an arch-criminal taking vengeful action against the horse's wealthy owner, the Aga Khan.

But sadly it seems Shergar probably died only hours after he went missing. It seems the horse was the target of the IRA, terrorists from Northern Ireland. Detectives hired soon afterwards came to the conclusion it was a terrorist kidnap gang responsible for the snatch and that it was probably bungled.

HORSE THIEVES

In 1992 their theories were confirmed when IRA informer Sean O'Callaghan spoke out about the crime from his prison cell in Maghaberry, Belfast.

Opposite: *Shergar won the 1981 Derby in classic style. His performance was the stuff of* **Boys' Own** *fiction – 19-year-old jockey Walter Swinburn had never dared dream he would romp home ten lengths clear.*

Below: *The stable from which Shergar was snatched by IRA terrorists.*

WITH FLARING NOSTRILS THE HIGHLY STRUNG STALLION SCENTED DANGER – HE REARED UP TO STRIKE AT HIS ABDUCTORS WITH DEADLY HOOVES.

He told how on the night of 8 February 1983 a masked gang crept stealthily onto the rural Irish stud farm which was home to Shergar. It was the start of their ambitious cash-raising escapade and everything was set for an international coup.

Shergar had by this time retired from racing. His days of sprinting splendour were over now he had notched up £436,000 worth of prize money. His victory in the 1981 Epsom Derby by 10 lengths with 19-year-old Walter Swinburn in the saddle was but a memory. His winning form in the Irish Derby and the King George VI & Queen Elizabeth Diamond Stakes at Ascot in the same year had faded from the minds of all but the most ardent racegoers.

But Shergar still had his most productive cash-spinning days ahead of him. He was going to stud, visiting 50 mares a year and commanding fees of about £75,000 a time. His owner, the Aga Khan, had sold 34 shares in the wonder horse to prominent society people including Robert Sangster, Lord Derby, Stavros Niarchos and Sheikh Maktoum Al Maktoum. From silky muzzle to flicking tail, Shergar was worth £10 million. There would be a lot of influential people anxious for the safe return of Shergar once he was gone and the IRA knew it.

So under the leadership of racing fan Kevin Mallon, a fervent IRA activist recently released from a jail term for attempted murder, the gang of up to nine men moved in.

Astonishingly, there were no effective security measures for them to breach at the stud in Ballymany, County Kildare, within sight of the famous Curragh racecourse. The token measure to guard against intruders, a surveillance camera system, was faulty. It left the horse thieves ample opportunity to tow in the horsebox in which they were going to spirit away their prize.

Communicating by walkie-talkie, the gang thought the operation was a cinch – until it came to handling Shergar. While everything else may have been meticulously planned, Mallon and his cronies blundered because they had no idea how highly strung a stallion of Shergar's calibre could be. The horse could sense danger and maybe even impending doom. With flared nostrils, he reared up time and time again with an angry neigh. Here was quite a different animal from the docile creature the abductors were anticipating. By the time they were 100 miles north of the farm Shergar was in a frenzy and was injuring himself in his torment. There was no option but to shoot the poor, crazed beast.

O'Callaghan told how the body of Shergar was hurriedly buried in the Ballinamore region of County Leitrim, never again to be found amid the rocky landscape.

Meanwhile, police on both sides of the Irish border mounted a huge search. It was the biggest police hunt Eire had known. Top detectives even consulted 50 clairvoyants and psychics in the hope of recovering the horse.

Although a £2 million ransom demand was duly delivered by the kidnappers, the Aga Khan refused to pay.

It was the beginning of a string of kidnaps by the IRA, including an attempt to capture Galen Weston, the Canadian supermarket tycoon. Fooled into thinking Weston was a sitting duck at his rambling home in County Wicklow in August 1983, the gang struck again, but in fact the wealthy target was in England playing polo with the Prince of Wales. Instead, there was a band of armed police who managed to hold most of the six-member gang despite a shootout.

So now most of the kidnappers of Shergar were put behind bars although they were never brought to justice for killing the classic animal. The policeman in charge of the case, Superintendent Jim Murphy, has disclosed he knows the identities of the killers but never found enough evidence to bring them to trial.

In their wake they left an unsavoury insurance wrangle which still rumbles on today. Many of the shareholders recovered their stakes through cover-all insurance policies, but some companies refused to pay out until they received proof that Shergar was finally dead. Even the revelations by O'Callaghan failed to persuade them the horse had been killed. The fact the horse was stolen wasn't enough to secure a payout. One man, Dublin vet Stan Cosgrove, lost his house and ran into huge debt after borrowing heavily with his brother to buy a share in Shergar.

Now a six-year time limit for claims appears to exclude the unlucky few left out of pocket to the tune of £250,000 by the sad affair.

IRA BRUTALITY

Army horse Sefton was also the victim of brutal cruelty on his home turf at the hands of heartless IRA bombers.

It should have been a proud and prestigious occasion for Sefton and his troop in Hyde Park on that fateful day in 1982. Horses and men were kitted out in their finery for ceremonial duties. Little did they realize they were to be cut down by a car bomb packed with nails planted by the IRA.

Four men and seven horses died. Sefton was as close to death as a horse could get, with savage injuries inflicted after he took the full force of the blast. He suffered 38 wounds including a deep cut to his jugular vein. It seemed his life would ebb away. But one man was determined to save him: Army vet Major Noel Carding spent an hour and a half treating the bloodied gashes and, amid the scene of carnage, saved his life.

The photograph of the injuries to Sefton's face and body flashed around the world and said more about the terrible consequences of the bomb blast than a million words. Convalescing in his stable, he received hundreds of get-well gifts and cards.

Within months, Sefton proved to the world he was a fighter. He made a feted first public appearance after the blast: at the

Above: *Sefton with the Army vet who saved his life, Major Noel Carding. The horse suffered 38 separate wounds from flying nails.*

Left: *Sefton didn't take easily to the pomp and ceremony of life in the Household Cavalry.*

Above: *Sefton with Trooper Pederson. In his own way, Sefton hit back at the terrorists responsible for maiming him. He raised thousands of pounds for forces' charities.*

THE CRUEL 6-INCH NAILS CUT THE VELVETY FLESH OF THE HORSES TO RIBBONS.

---

prestige Horse of the Year Show in London, side by side with Echo, the police horse also hurt in the explosion.

Questions were asked in the House of Commons as to whether both horses should be awarded medals of honour.

With pride, the horse the IRA couldn't kill took his place back in the ranks and reassumed the royal role for which he had been trained. He worked for another two years before retiring in 1984 with 15 years' service to his credit.

Sefton had been born in Ireland in 1963 and was 3 years old when he caught the eye of a purchasing officer from the British Army charged with buying at least 50 horses a year for the cavalry. But there was no hint of the glory to come when, known simply as 5816, he was hustled onto a ferry, one of 37 horses making the arduous journey from Ireland to new pastures in England.

Sefton was ebony in colour but for his four white socks and substantial blaze – which indicated early on he was a horse with character. It is well known among horse handlers that the animals bearing white marks are the liveliest of the bunch.

This gelding also had a wicked eye that glinted with mischief and, true to the old saying, he was not the easiest horse to manage. But his abundant spirit appealed to the Army's horse experts. He was picked for duty with the Royal Horse Guards and christened Sefton after an earl from the same regiment who had served with distinction in two world wars and later became Lord Mayor of Liverpool.

It takes months to train a horse to remain calm in the face of brass bands, traffic, and rowdy people, not to mention wearing cumbersome regalia. By 1968 Sefton was put on trial to see if he was ready to go on parade. He failed the test.

Nevertheless, he was brought out looking splendid for the 1968 Trooping of the Colour before the queen. Hating every minute of the pomp and pageantry, he skittered and reared, distinguishing himself only as the worst behaved horse of the day.

It wasn't until three months later that he passed the Horse Guards' test of excellence and moved on to daily duties around some of the most majestic landmarks of London. He became a familiar sight around Whitehall, the Victoria Monument and Pall Mall.

Afterwards, he had a spell at a training school and in Germany with the North Atlantic Treaty Organization forces before returning to Wellington Barracks, central London.

He took part in the Queen's Silver Jubilee celebrations and the Royal Wedding street procession following the vows sworn at St Paul's Cathedral by Prince Charles and Lady Diana Spencer. Gradually Sefton put his skittish days behind him, becoming a veteran of the Royal Parade and even winning prizes for his demeanour.

It seemed a day just like any other when Sefton and the rest of the troop set off on 20 July 1982 from the barrack stables to the Whitehall sentry posts. But at 10.40 am a huge explosion ripped the parading pack to pieces. Using remote control, the terrorists detonated a 25 lb gelignite bomb stuffed with 30 lb of 6 in and 4 in nails which cut the velvet flesh of the horses to ribbons. Sefton had a nail in his head, a scorched eyeball, metal remains of the car in his neck, and was gushing with blood from his wounds.

Given only a fifty-fifty chance of survival, he had none the less fared better than stablemates Yeastvite, Epaulette, Rochester, Waterford, Falcon, Zara and Cedric, all of whom perished.

The wounds would take months to heal. But Sefton's indomitable spirit had captured the hearts and minds of the world. He became a symbol of survival and endurance in the face of cowardice and horror. As the outrage was followed the same day by another bomb which killed seven bandsmen in Regent's Park, feelings were running high. Each member of the royal family sent messages of sympathy to the barracks. The public rallied by donating £100,000, fruit, vegetables and some 250,000 Polo mints. Sefton became a celebrity, helping to raise thousands of pounds for forces' charitable funds.

It was an emotional moment when he finally left the Hyde Park barracks for the last time. The Band of the Blues and Royals played 'Auld Lang Syne' and the 'Black Horse' as his horsebox was marched regally out of the front gates.

His destination was the Home of Rest for Horses at Speen Farm near Princes Risborough, Buckinghamshire, where he happily accepted the adulation of visitors, especially when they showed their appreciation with a sugar lump or biscuit.

The end came for Sefton only when he became lame at the age of 30 years. Despite the efforts of vets at the Defence Animal Centre's Veterinary Hospital in Melton Mowbray, Leicestershire, he was put down in July 1993.

AGAINST THE ODDS

Everyone loves a winner and Red Rum was revered more than most victorious horses. The very name Red Rum became a byword for success in Britain as the tremendous horse stormed past the post ahead of the field three times in the country's toughest race, the Grand National.

But the affection and esteem Rummy commanded wasn't just for his astonishing abilities over the jumps and in the field. Here was a horse who made it to the top of

Above: *Sefton and his rider, Trooper Michael Pederson, launch the horse's biography. With them are* **(from left)** *celebrities Brough Scott, Anita Harris and Barbara Woodhouse.*

Above: *Red Rum on one of his regular beach gallops.*

Below: *Red Rum wins his third Grand National, in 1977.*

hurdles where he made his name. It didn't augur well when his mother was declared mad. With this dubious heritage, Rummy was bought and sold three times in quick succession. Even now, he was determined to distinguish himself. Aged just 2, he won his first race. His prize for the triumph over five furlongs was a mere £133.

But his existence was loveless and bleak until a chance meeting in a taxi cab put him on the road to stardom.

The taxi fare was Noel le Mare, the son of a missionary who started a civil engineering business with just a few pounds in his pocket. Years later his company, Norwest Holst, was a multi-million pound enterprise. But Le Mare, now in his 80s, wasn't satisfied.

Back in 1906 he had witnessed Grand National mania on the streets of Liverpool after Ascetic's Silver roared to victory. It was his dream to own a Grand National winner of his own.

The cabbie was struggling horse-trainer Ginger McCain. Down on his luck, McCain was forced behind the wheel to

his profession against all the odds: he was a back-street kid who made it to the big time. When jockeys and trainers were blind to his talents and ran him ragged, he was determined to win through. He even beat a crippling illness before clinching the title of Britain's best-loved horse.

He was bred for flat racing, not the

earn cash when three seasons as a trainer bought him only three winners. But he had enough energy and enthusiasm to impress Le Mare, who charged him to find the Grand National winner he yearned for.

In August 1972 McCain found Rummy at Doncaster Sales and paid 6,000 guineas of Le Mare's cash for him. The horse was 7 years old and had already been through five trainers. He was also suffering pedalostitis, a crumbling of the foot's main bone that was usually incurable. But at last here was someone who would cherish him and have the faith needed to bring out the best bubbling underneath in Rummy.

McCain nearly gave up when he realized the animal on which his hopes were pinned was lame, but regular gallops in the sand and sea at Southport were to provide an unexpected and enduring cure. His stable was as humble as his training ground: it was a tumbledown shack behind McCain's second-hand-car showroom. But nothing was going to hold this horse back. Excitement mounted when Red Rum won race after race. With five victories behind him, he lined up for the first time at the start of the 1973 Grand National. As usual, the course was buzzing with excitement and throbbing with anticipation. It was an

atmosphere Red Rum relished. It was a pounding, grinding race with a nail-biting finish. Crisp was ahead and looked certain to win the coveted trophy, but Red Rum had other ideas and produced astonishing

Above: *A farewell to Aintree. Red Rum makes his last appearance on the course that made his name.*

THE STRUGGLING HORSE-TRAINER SENSED THE SPIRIT IN THE CRIPPLED NAG.

Left: *In retirement Rummy was as busy as ever. Here he opens a betting shop in north London.*

speed and drive which left spectators gasping. He overtook Crisp, won the race and knocked 19 seconds off the course record. He returned in 1974 to repeat his victory, by now the nation's favourite race horse. Red Rum revelled in the gruelling course, labelled cruel by animal rights' demonstrators. The following two years saw him pipped at the post but he wasn't satisfied at the thought of bowing out as second best: he would go for the hat-trick.

In 1977 McCain was once again to be found at the centre of the hubbub at Aintree on Grand National Day. 'Everybody, it seemed, wanted me to win the National a third time. The horse had so much presence that year,' he recalled. 'He virtually owned Aintree. It was uncanny.'

Red Rum didn't let his fans down. He romped home with 25 lengths to spare. Only a foot injury stopped him competing in 1978, an old man of 13 years of age.

The fracture which put an end to his Grand National days put him out of racing for ever, but he had notched up an incredible record. He had won a quarter of all the races around the jumps he had entered. His prize money totalled a record £115,000.

When owner Le Mare died, the horse passed to Ginger McCain, the man who had made him great. Still oozing with personality and popularity, Red Rum found himself at the centre of fresh thrills. He was invited to open supermarkets and fetes and appear at bashes alongside other celebrities. Soon he was the first horse in Britain to become a company. Red Rum Ltd was even more profitable than Red Rum, the racer. Within a few years, his appearance fees had soared into the £200,000 bracket. A decade later and the amount was more than £1 million.

But Red Rum was held in special regard

Below: A terrified Misty is hauled through the streets during a Spanish fiesta in 1990.

by the British people. He was a back-street kid who made good through guts, dedication and sheer hard work. In 1991 it seemed the end of the track had finally come for Red Rum when a sudden illness threatened his life. Against all odds, Rummy fought back and once again was the winner, returning to good health, to the relief of his owner and horse lovers across the country.

BEASTS OF BURDEN

The front pages of Britain's newspapers are usually the reserve of politicians and stars involved in outrage or scandal. It's rare that any animal makes it big in the media, let alone a humble donkey.

But that's just what Blackie, the ill-treated donkey from Spain, did back in 1987.

His mournful eyes gazed from every newspaper as his woeful plight was exposed. He grabbed the headlines with an extraordinary story which would make him the most famous donkey in the world.

His tale started in the sun-baked mountain village of Villanueva de la Vera. It is only 140 miles from the cosmopolitan Spanish capital of Madrid but it might as well be in a different country.

For the village still observes ancient fiestas involving appalling cruelty to animals which leave the rest of the world wincing. Despite growing unease in Spain – where 83 per cent of the population opposes blatant torture of animals – the locals involved were prepared to risk their public image for the sake of some dubious fiesta frolics.

Blackie would spend 364 days of every year unnoticed and unloved in a field. But

Above: *Peace at last. After the horrors of fiesta time Blackie lived out his last years in the care of the Sidmouth donkey sanctuary, southern England.*

THE APPALLING CRUELTY
BEGAN AS BOTTLES OF
SPIRITS WERE FORCIBLY
POURED DOWN THE
DONKEY'S THROAT.

on Shrove Tuesday came his moment of gory glory. On that day the villagers mark the capture of an evil rapist hundreds of years ago with the Fiesta del Pero-Palo.

Traditionally, the chosen donkey is locked in the village hall with young men fired up by drink and the relentless pursuit of 'pleasure' is on. The donkey is forced to join the revelry as bottles of spirit are poured down its throat. Then comes the street parade.

The heaviest man in the village is chosen to ride the donkey, whose legs are already buckling through the effects of drink. Behind them follows a chanting, jeering mass ready to push and shove the unfortunate animal if it falters.

Shaking and scarred across his rump, Blackie survived the ordeal at least once before one horrified animal lover and a host of British newspapers intervened.

Victoria Moore, half of a cabaret act with her guitar-playing husband, read about the impending fiesta and discovered there was little she could do from her home in Southport, Lancashire, to stop the atrocity. She announced her intention to visit the village personally to see what she could achieve.

Ignoring the death threat bearing a Spanish postmark which landed on her doormat, she set off for Spain, encountering a team of determined journalists en route. She describes her first stroll through the village as like something from the film *High Noon*. 'Residents stared at me from doorways and threw bangers,' she recalls.

By this time international journalists had joined their British counterparts, complete with TV camera crews, to observe the stand-off between the locals and the animal rights campaigner. Astonished at being the focus of such widespread attention, the Spaniards allowed Blackie to trot unfettered through the town before he was sold for £280. Mrs Moore was helped by one newspaper, the *Daily Star*, in returning Blackie to Britain, where he lived out his days at the country's largest donkey sanctuary, at Sidmouth, south Devon.

Journalists from the *Daily Star* were cock-a-hoop at securing the by-now famous donkey for themselves, thus getting the edge over their bitter Fleet Street rivals, *The Sun*. Yet *The Sun* was also claiming to have the redeemed donkey in its care. The

public at home were mystified. How could both sides be claiming victory when clearly only one donkey was at stake?

It seems a business-minded local man was at the heart of the confusion. He passed off a donkey to *The Sun* for a healthy number of pesetas, pretending it was Blackie. When *Star* journalists appeared, he claimed the donkey he had sold was actually a ringer for Blackie. Yet he was prepared to sell the real Blackie to the *Star* – for a price. That was how the *Star* journalists were able to return triumphant, leaving their opponents with some difficult explanations to make. There was talk of kidnap attempts on the rescued animal by the competitive hacks who had much more to lose than just readers. At the end of the affair one journalist did change jobs, switching from *The Sun* to the *Star*.

For six years Blackie retained his top status. Visitors poured through the gates of the sanctuary to meet the wiry haired donkey with a soft white muzzle who so narrowly escaped death and degradation at the hands of tormentors in search of fun.

He died aged around 20 in the sanctuary in May 1993 after a 10-day illness in which he stopped eating. Before being put down he was given a nibble of his favourite treat, a ginger biscuit, and then quietly died, leaving his girlfriend and paddock companion Lola desolate. He was buried in a marked grave within the boundaries of the sanctuary where he had finally found peace.

Sanctuary owner Dr Elizabeth Svendsen said: 'He was very weak and had come to the end of the road. We are heartbroken. But bearing in mind his very tough life and the trauma of the fiesta in Villanueva de la Vera, he has done very well to enjoy six years of happy, well-cared-for life in the sanctuary with Lola.'

Blackie fared better than Misty, his successor. His owner was the village mayor Felix Perez. But Senor Perez signed him over to a life of barbarism when he donated the 6-year-old to the village for use in the annual fiesta. Misty survived at least three fiestas despite the best attempts of the villagers to crush him under their combined weights.

Journalist Ed Owen witnessed the fiesta in 1990. 'A crowd of drunken revellers surrounded the terrified donkey and careered uncontrollably around the village.

'I waded into the staggering mass of drunken humanity and found the donkey squashed on the cobbles, covered in sweat. Misty tried to raise his head as the heaving crowd endeavoured to lift him and remount. He was quivering as though having an epileptic fit, nostrils flared and shaking, foam dripping from his mouth.

'The poor animal was ruthlessly prodded and tugged as the raging yobs in Villanueva de la Vera forced him to rise on trembling legs.'

Misty's ordeal lasted 90 minutes, after which he had lost an estimated 50 lb in weight and his heart rate was double the norm.

Earlier in the 1980s the nightmare was too much for one of the donkeys, who died under the strain. His body was left floating in the village fountain.

Mrs Moore went on to found the charity FACE, Fight Animal Cruelty in Europe. She continues to battle for the halt of other fiestas which have sprung up around Spain following the demise of dictator Franco, who had banned them. Her efforts helped to stop the fiesta at Manganese de la Polvorosa in which live goats are thrown from the church tower. 'But the overall picture is bleak. Twenty-seven thousand bulls, cows and calves plus an unknown number of goats and chickens are tortured, raped, mutilated and killed very year in these events. There is a lot more to do.'

> **THE BEAST WAS SHAKING WITH TERROR AND FOAM WAS DRIPPING FROM HIS MOUTH.**

Below: *British animal lovers give Misty a health check before his ordeal.*

ANIMALS ON TV

Many animal stars of the screen will willingly 'die' for their art – again and again and again. Most are blissfully content with their roles and the endless titbits, but for an unfortunate few the demands made upon them can lead to tragedy.

Show a director an actor who is keen to please, obedient and never throws a tantrum – and he will show you a star.

That's why the animals who are so familiar on our TV screens today are favoured by studio bosses. Professional from the tips of their damp noses to the end of their quivering tails, animals who appear on the box or in the cinema are trained to the peak of perfection.

Never work with children or animals, the old saying goes. However, while tots might give you a hard time, the schooled pet never will – as plenty of Hollywood directors would testify.

One of them, Joe Camp, was haunted by the moving story of a boy and his dog and the adventures they had together, mainly because they reminded him so much of his own happy childhood.

He managed to secure a small budget, then set about finding the stars. He had the pick of budding actors keen to cut their teeth on the happy home-on-the-range kind of story he was backing. But the pup star – the key to the success of the film, as Camp well knew – was a harder nut to crack.

CUTE CANINES

He scoured the kennels of Hollywood and the surrounding area looking for the perfect canine. Bloodhounds were too big, terriers too small and poodles all wrong.

One day Camp arrived at the Hollywood dog home run by Frank Inn and spotted the dog of his dreams. He found Higgins, an amiable mongrel, and knew instantly that his search was over.

Trouble was, Higgins was a veteran of the animal acting business and the star of a long-running and highly successful US TV series called *Petticoat Junction* along with Eddie Albert. He was also the grand old age of 11, mature by any standard in the dog world and about to be pensioned off for retirement.

Camp was determined his search would not be in vain. Together with owner Frank Inn he decided Higgins could make a glorious comeback, this time with the name Benji. It simply meant that a young relative by the name of Hazel was brought in to do some of the more energetic stunts.

The result was an overnight sensation. Everybody wanted to see *Benji*, released in 1974, which had the hero hound saving two children from kidnappers and earning a place in their grateful parents' home. It grossed $52 million in the days when

Above: *Talk about hamming it up! Pippin shows it's snow joke when you're a star.*

Opposite: *Do I look cute or what? Pippin's appealing expressions won the hearts of millions.*

MOST ANIMAL STARS ADORE THE LIFE THEY LEAD — THEY BASK IN THE LIMELIGHT AND LOVE THE LIFE-STYLE.

blockbusters were rare if not unheard of. There were sequels in which Higgins was replaced by Benji II, a female this time but every inch as endearing as the original. The last Benji film to be made, in 1987, was *Benji the Hunted* and featured Benji III. This time the cute canine was living rough in the wild and saving threatened animals along the way.

Higgins, the grand old man of canine stars, founded an acting dynasty which went successfully transatlantic in the shape of his granddaughter, Pippin, now perhaps the best-known pooch in the business.

Pippin was given to Englishwoman Ann Head as a puppy just before she returned to Britain after a 7-year spell spent working in the USA. Ann worked alongside Frank Inn and was on the way to becoming one of the world's best-known animal trainers.

Everywhere she went, Pippin would shadow her, watching and learning as other animal stars went through their paces. And Pippin was hungry to learn.

As Ann points out, the only way a dog can be trained is to ensure it is blissfully happy.

'About 80 per cent of their ability comes from the environment they are in and 20 per cent is hereditary. My animals absolutely adore the life they lead. The secret is that they are incredibly contented and they aren't put under any pressure.'

Her animals must be not only good natured and patient, but also adaptable. They must be able to repeat a stunt a dozen or more times until the scene is perfect. Alternatively, rehearsed routines could be changed at any minute by a director seeing new angles so you must be able to teach an old dog new tricks at the drop of a hat. It takes years to tutor a dog until it reaches its peak.

'Unfortunately, 99.9 per cent of pets simply cannot cut the mustard, no matter how talented their owners believe them to be,' explains Ann, of Crowthorne, Berkshire.

Pippin is so gifted she even trotted off with two advertising industry Oscars in 1989 in Cannes, beating a 3,642-strong field of commercials from all over the world. The coveted Grand Prix awards are just a few of the honours she has achieved.

And she's no stranger to viewers of TV advertisements in Britain and Europe, while viewers as far flung as Japan and Taiwan have met Pippin through their TV screens.

Her range of skills has caused its fair share of problems for unsuspecting passers-by, however. Pippin is top dog when it comes to playing dead, and it was for this reason that she was picked to star in a police film narrated by actor Richard Briers about the dangers of telephone box vandalism. Liberal amounts of fake blood were applied and she draped herself over the arms of an actor who looked suitably sorrowful. But a passing motorist who obviously didn't see the camera poised on the other side of the road screeched to a halt and insisted on taking the apparently injured dog and devoted master to the vet's.

The kind words dried up in the driver's mouth when the blood-splattered dog miraculously revived, jumped to the floor and began wagging her tail furiously.

Now aged 11 years, Pippin has her own stunt man, grandson Higgins, aged 2 and named after his famous great-great-grandfather. In Pippin's latest starring role alongside actress Lynda Baron in a children's TV series, Higgins was used for some of the physically demanding sequences.

Below: Superdog Pippin was the animal star of the advertising industry. He even got two Oscars for his performances.

A VERY IMPORTANT PUSS

Ann Head is also in charge of today's Arthur, successor to the king of cat stars. Arthur was the cat who came to fame thanks to a knockout left hook. It was his ability to scoop cat food out of a tin with a paw that brought the rather superior white feline to prominence.

The first Arthur made his TV debut in 1966. He may have been all white but he led a most colourful life. There was even confusion over whether he was really a she by the name of Samantha. Arthur became the talk of the country after being the subject of a court case and, later, a kidnap.

Arthur was apparently a stray found roaming in Hemel Hempstead in 1964 by actor Toneye Manning and was eventually adopted by Manning's friend, actress June Clyne.

Miss Clyne was astonished when she found the cat could help himself to food once the tin was opened. It was a simply a matter of preference. Nobody appeared to have taught him, yet he chose the paw. He was, she realized, an advertising man's dream but she refused to part with her beloved pet. Instead, she was willing to give cat food manufacturers Spillers a lifetime option which would have allowed Arthur star status while remaining at home. Sadly, Miss Clyne died before negotiations were completed.

Spillers went on to acquire Arthur for a highly successful advertising campaign when he put his foot in it time and time again and soon became a Very Important Puss. With rightful ownership unclear following the untimely death of Miss Clyne, Spillers paid her mother £600 and Toneye Manning £700 to secure all rights to the cat.

But Mr Manning was unhappy and took the case to court. He had not only found Arthur but had also married Miss Clyne, he insisted, the wedding having taken place aboard a ferry in the Irish Sea.

A mighty cat fight took place with both sides laying claim to Arthur. Each won victories in the first rounds of the battle with consecutive court rulings awarding Arthur first to Mr Manning, then to Spillers.

Mr Manning told how he delivered the prized puss to the Russian Embassy for asylum. When he refused to hand Arthur

Above: *This canny trick became Arthur the cat's trademark. He went on to star in £4 million-worth of TV commercials.*

over to Spillers he was jailed for contempt of court, serving 15 days in Brixton prison.

In court, he alleged Spillers was cruel to Arthur and even extracted his teeth to ensure he would eat out of the can.

The claim was emphatically denied by Spillers, who said that although Arthur was being treated for a gum disease no extractions had taken place.

Hearing the amazing case, Mr Justice Bridge turned dentist for a few moments when Arthur paraded along the bench and bared his teeth. Later the judge dismissed the cruelty allegations and in November 1969 decided the cat belonged to Spillers fair and square.

Arthur went to a cats' home in Essex to continue his career, pampered with a diet of fresh fish, steak, chicken and rabbit and at work only nine days a year. All was well for five years and then the mog found himself splashed over the front pages again after being snatched from his comfortable cattery home. By now Arthur was 14 years old – 98 in human terms – and there were genuine fears about his health.

No one knows what went on in those

> **IT WAS ALLEGED THAT THE PETFOOD COMPANY WAS CRUEL TO ARTHUR AND EVEN YANKED OUT HIS TEETH TO FORCE HIM TO EAT FROM THE CAN.**

dark days when he was in the clutches of villains. Poor Arthur wasn't saying when he clambered over the fence of pensioner Arthur Turvey's home in Dunstable, Bedfordshire, some 40 miles from the cattery, bedraggled and hungry. When he started feeding himself, Mr Turvey instantly knew the identity of his unexpected caller. When Arthur returned home he found one small change – a security guard posted outside his cattery.

Arthur finally died peacefully in March 1976, a month before his 17th birthday.

There was a simple but moving burial. 'It is a sad loss to everyone who knew him,' said Robin Davis, product manager of Spillers Foods. 'He had so much personality. Everyone who saw him fell for his marvellous character. He could really sell the message.'

Arthur had starred in £4 million worth of commercials. If only he had been human he would have earned a handsome £100,000 for his 30 films.

Several cats were groomed to take his place. One of them, Sam, even made it to the screen. But soon he was dropped, even though he had mastered the paw performance to perfection. A spokesman for Spillers said: 'He just wasn't as good as Arthur. It is very difficult to replace a cat

Above: *Arthur became so valuable he even took to travelling around with his personal bodyguard.*

Right: *Lights. Action! The new Arthur settles into his role.*

Left: *Legendary trainer Ann Head scoured the country in search of a successor to Arthur. She at last found Arthur II in a Hertfordshire, England, animal shelter. He was so ill after being abandoned that she had to talk a vet out of putting him down.*

like that. Now we are using big cats – lions – in our advertisements.'

But a decade later Spillers thought again about the success they had known with Arthur. The search was on for a replacement for King Arthur. Ann Head was the woman charged with the job of talent scout. Little did she realize the animal she sought was close to death, languishing in the Wood Green Animal Shelter in Royston, Hertfordshire.

He had been abandoned by a family which was moving and didn't want him any more.

Ann recalls: 'I picked him up and played with him for a few minutes. He looked ghastly and had lost interest in himself but I knew he was the right cat.'

He was so poorly she even had to talk a vet out of putting him to sleep. And sure enough, with lashings of tender love and care the new Arthur made a complete recovery.

'We have built up a good relationship, he will walk into any studio with a full crew and lights and just perform because he loves it,' says Ann.

Not only that, he makes regular celebrity appearances at cat shows around the country where he will offer his regal paw to visitors.

MONKEY BUSINESS

It seems Arthur was so successful in hiking the sales of Kattomeat, the product he promoted, that the dish was renamed Arthur's in his honour. And there's no doubt that a bunch of animal stars have worked wonders for tea makers Brooke Bond, accelerating sales to the tune of £2 billion. It makes them higher grossing advertising stars than even the likes of superstars Michael Jackson and Madonna.

These animal stars were the unforgettable chimps who slurped PG Tips tea all day long, first making their memorable debut in 1956.

It was on Christmas Day and comedian Peter Sellers spoke for the chimps as they sat having tea in a country house out of dainty china cups on a table laid with silver service.

Later advertisements had them as furniture removers struggling with a piano. When the younger one pipes up: 'Dad, do you know the piano is on my foot?' his father, Mr Shifter, responds with the immortal line: 'You hum it, son, I'll play it.'

Chummy was the chimp who starred in that particular classic. And he was no neanderthal when it came to musical tastes.

Above: *The first PG Tips tea party, filmed in 1956.*

Below: *Mr Shifter.*

The crew tried to substitute a playing piano for one with doctored keys which wouldn't sound a note. Chummy would have nothing to do with it, assuming a policy of non-cooperation until the real thing was supplied.

Then there was the Tour de France cycle race commercial which ended with a worn-out racer pleading: 'Avez-vous un cuppa?' And who can forget the 007 skit which had a chimp as Bond, Brooke Bond?

Other celebrities who did the voices of the chimps include Bob Monkhouse, Su Pollard, Willie Rushton, Cilla Black and Donald Sinden.

The chimpanzees are born in family groups or join one because they have been rejected by their mothers. They are all captive born. The training starts only a few weeks before the shoot date and is fun and entertaining for them. The majority of the actions they do are an extension of their natural playfulness and inquisitiveness. Their reputation for being difficult to work with is unfounded, according to Brooke Bond executive Duncan Bogey: 'We do need to shoot a lot of film but it never takes longer than for humans – about three days.'

Their contributions to the success of the advertising is recognized by Brooke Bond with a strict code of practice that guarantees the chimpanzees long-term security in retirement. When they are pensioned off they go to private zoos to be visited regularly by their trainers.

As the years have rolled by, the outcry against using animals for human gain has intensified. Some activists claim the chimps are as outdated a means of advertising as the zoos which cage them. So far, Brooke Bond has no plans to take them off the air.

MR CHATTERBOX

While the voices of the chimps were dubbed, there was one famous animal star who managed his own lines. He was Sparkie, the biggest earning budgie in the world.

Sparkie sprang to prominence in 1958 after being entered in a budgie talking contest by his owner, Mrs Mattie Williams, of Newcastle upon Tyne. She had no idea when she was given the bird as a 6-week-old chick in 1954 that he was something special. When she taught him to say 'pretty Sparkie' in the space of just three weeks she thought he was a standard speaker. But she wasn't prepared for the massive diction he acquired, first under her tuition, then on his own. In total, he mastered 531 words, 383 sentences and eight complete nursery rhymes.

Of course, he won the BBC-run contest and was signed up immediately to advertise a well-known brand of budgie seed on the TV under the new name of 'Mr Chatterbox'. There followed a recording contract and a single was made with Sparkie illustrating the techniques for teaching budgies to talk.

He earned more than £1,000, and had his own bank account and even an income tax number.

When he was 8 years old Sparkie was discovered struggling for breath in the bottom of his cage and died soon afterwards in the loving hands of his owner, just after uttering for the last time: 'I love Mamma'.

Even after death Sparkie remained a celebrity. He was stuffed, mounted on his favourite perch and put in Newcastle's Hancocks Museum with a tape of his incredible nattering.

DYING DOLPHINS

Not all tales of star animals have such a happy ending. Flipper was the world's most famous dolphin after a TV series

captured the imagination of children everywhere.

But the pressures of being a star took its toll. The five captive mammals used for the series were starved to make them perform the necessary tricks. Kathy, the dolphin used most in front of the camera, finally decided she had suffered enough.

One day she caught the eye of her trainer and simply stopped breathing while he held her in his arms. In dolphin terms, she had committed suicide, choosing death rather than prolonged captivity.

It was an experience that scarred the trainer Ric O'Barry. Now he is devoted to releasing all caged dolphins into the wild, where their life span can be up to 40 years instead of the five years that is usual in captivity.

He explains: 'Dolphins only breathe by conscious effort and they can stop living any time they like simply by holding their breath.

'Kathy committed suicide that way, and I am sure many other captive dolphins do – though the reason is always put down as pneumonia or some other stress-related illness.

Above: *Cyril the Cyclist. His catch-phrase –* **avez-vous un cuppa?** *– became a standing joke among schoolchildren the length of Britain.*

SPARKIE'S DYING WORDS WERE FOR HIS LOVING MISTRESS.

'Flipper was both the best thing and the worst thing that ever happened to dolphins. On the one hand she made the public aware of these wonderful animals. On the other, by performing her tricks she allowed the abuse of the animals to become regarded as normal and natural.'

O'Barry went on to establish a haven for dolphins in the Turks and Caicos Islands in the British West Indies.

LASSIE – THE COMPUTER WUFF

Lassie, the wonder dog, has been a firm favourite since he loped on to the screen some 46 years ago, although this blockbusting series brought bad luck for its child star.

Lassie had the uncanny knack of keeping his masters out of trouble not only by averting physical danger but also by deflecting those moral dilemmas which strike at the heart of the young.

His first big screen debut was in 1943 in the film *Lassie Come Home,* alongside Roddy McDowall, Elsa Lanchester and Elizabeth Taylor. He was the dog who made a courageous journey to return to the sides of his loving but poor owners.

There followed a series for TV with Lassie teaming up with Tommy Rettig as loyal owner Jeff Miller. There was plenty of press speculation about the calming influence of the classy canine. But Tommy went on to suffer troubles of his own after his involvement in the series ended when he was just 15. There was a messy divorce case and a conviction for growing marijuana. A prison term for conspiracy to smuggle cocaine was overturned.

It was with some relief then, that Tommy joined the latest series playing Jeff's uncle and even penned some of the scripts.

Every screen Lassie has been trained by the Weatherwax family in the San Fernando Valley of Los Angeles. The last to win the role was the great-great-grandson of the original. Nowadays it is not just old-fashioned crooks and collapsing mine shafts that bother the smart collie. He has been taught to grapple with the intricacies of computers in his bid to keep the peace.

HER TRAINER COULDN'T FORGET THE LOOK IN HER EYES AS SHE COMMITTED SUICIDE, CHOOSING DEATH RATHER THAN CAPTIVITY.

Opposite: *Flipper was both the best thing and the worst thing that ever happened to dolphins, claimed his trainer.*

Left: *Lassie with child actor Roddy McDowall. The dog's Big Screen debut came in 1943 with* Lassie Come Home.

Below: *Lassie with his medallion from the Lucky Dog National Canine Defence League.*

THE CAT'S WHISKERS

Fairy-tales are full of stories of Pusses in Boots, but in real life the adventures of our feline friends as they work their way through ten of their nine lives sometimes defy belief.

'**E**verybody wants to be a cat,' goes the song, and millions of captivated moggy lovers would offer no argument.

Among domestic animals it's hard to think of any that enjoy a cushier life-style. Once they've latched on to a caring owner, found food and a fire, and taunted any resident dogs into submission, they can devote themselves to their greatest love – sleeping.

Yet this popular image is not entirely fair, History shows that some survive well beyond their allotted quota of nine lives and still take life's little risks in their stride.

MOGGY MASCOTS

Cats at war are the classic example. They first seem to have joined up (or rather got themselves conscripted) during the Crimean War of 1854–55.

Captured Russian soldiers would produce helpless little bundles of fur from beneath their greatcoats, kittens they had kept to nurture as best they could until they were old enough to hunt for themselves.

Sometimes the mascot's job went further. Mourka, a tom who saw service with a Russian gun crew during the terrible Battle of Stalingrad in 1942–43, found himself sent on errands across some of the most heavily shelled land in the world.

A message from the battery to HQ would be attached to his collar and Mourka would willingly set off to deliver. Once he had arrived safely – and he managed the run many times – he would be given food and fuss and after a night's rest turned out

Above: *Simon's grave at Ilford, Essex.*

Left: *The Dickin Medal awarded posthumously. Simon remains the only moggy ever to have won the animal equivalent to the VC.*

Opposite: *Simon, with one of his shipmates from HMS Amethyst.*

to find his way back to his comrades at the front.

No one knows what happened to Mourka after the war ended. It seems incredible that he could have survived given the conditions that existed in the city at that time. Yet Russian soldiers who heard of his adventures remained convinced he led a charmed life and insisted he would have lived to enjoy happier times.

Mourka may have had a tough war but

> THE CREW WHO HAD SURVIVED THE TERRIBLE ONSLAUGHT WERE AMAZED TO SEE THE BLEEDING CAT STRUGGLE OUT OF THE SHELL-SHATTERED CABIN.

his experiences pale besides those of the Royal Navy's most famous mascot, Simon.

This black-and-white ship's cat, a neutered male, was serving aboard HMS *Amethyst* when the so-called Yangtse Incident erupted in 1949. He'd been handed over as a kitten to the vessel's commanding officer, Lt Cdr Griffiths, a year earlier and was a much loved sight on the ship.

Sailors would always be passing him tasty titbits and he had the freedom of any berth. His rat-catching abilities quickly became legendary and his shipmates would pass the time on a long voyage placing bets on how many dead rats he could produce in a day.

Then the crisis at Nanking boiled up, with the feared army of Red China sweeping aside all resistance which crossed its path. The Chinese captured the Yangtse below Nanking and *Amethyst* was immediately ordered in to protect and evacuate British citizens in the area. Simon was to find himself in the midst of one of the greatest-ever naval adventures.

As the *Amethyst* steamed upriver she came under fire from Chinese batteries on both banks. The ship was struck several times and at last limped on to a sandbank in midstream. When the guns at last fell silent, 54 of her crew were lying dead, dying or seriously injured.

One of the shells had come down on the captain's quarters while Simon was inside as resident guest. The captain died instantly, but amazingly the cat struggled out of the mangled cabin with head and leg injuries and some surface burns. He crawled into a hiding place to lick his wounds and many of the ship's company believed he had quietly gone to find a place to die.

But a few days later he emerged and was soon back at his old rat-catching tricks. This cheered the crew greatly as scores of rats, flushed out by the bombardment, had begun taking over the ship and were causing an enormous health hazard.

Over the next three months Simon played a crucial part in helping keep up the morale of the men. The Chinese had apparently ruled that the ship should not be destroyed, but held prisoner until the right diplomatic conditions were in place for its release.

As the wrangling continued life aboard *Amethyst* was fast becoming unbearable. The weather had been sweltering for weeks, oil stocks were running low and food was becoming fetid. Faced with the choice of staying put to die by disease, or risking the guns, the new commander, Lt Cdr Kerans, decided to make a run for it.

With his engines and hull patched up he headed back downriver under cover of darkness to escape into the South China Sea.

When Simon and his shipmates arrived back in Hong Kong they were given a hero's welcome. The little cat's fame had, by now, been reported around the world and he was showered with presents from a personal fan club.

His story, though, ended on a note of sadness. Simon returned with *Amethyst* to Plymouth for a refit and was taken into quarantine. Three weeks later he was dead, perhaps because he had never fully recovered from the trauma of battle.

To this day Simon remains the only cat ever to have won the Dickin Medal – the animal equivalent of the Victoria Cross. It was presented to him posthumously on 13 April 1950 for his 'meritorious and distinguished service' by the Lord Mayor of Plymouth.

His remains now lie in the People's Dispensary for Sick Animals cemetery at Ilford, Essex.

FEARLESS FELINES

There are many other feline heroes of the waves but two of the most famous this century are the German puss Oscar and an American pet called Maizie.

Oscar, a year-old tabby, was one of several cats aboard *Bismarck* when the ship set sail to wreak havoc among wartime North Atlantic convoys.

When *Bismarck* was finally tracked down by the British fleet and despatched to the bottom of the sea off the French coast, Oscar was plucked out of the waves along with the rest of the German survivors. He joined the crew of the Royal Navy destroyer HMS *Cossack*.

All went well until six months later when *Cossack* was herself torpedoed and sunk. Once again Oscar survived unscathed – this time the aircraft carrier *Ark Royal* was his saviour.

His next life lasted a mere three days. *Ark Royal* was hit by a torpedo in the Mediterranean with heavy loss of life, but though Oscar's chances should have been negligible he somehow clambered on to a piece of wood and was rescued.

After a brief spell in Gibraltar he was found a place in a rest home for old sailors in Northern Ireland, where he lived out his days rather more peacefully. He is likely to remain the only puss ever to escape from three separate shipwrecks.

As for Maizie, she proved how important animals can be to the psychological welfare of humans by propping up the morale of six shipwrecked US sailors whose life raft was set adrift in the Pacific. Maizie stayed alive by eating malted milk tablets and a little water and would move around the laps of each man in turn, licking and comforting them. As one sailor admitted later: 'If Maizie hadn't been with us we might have gone nuts.'

Records show that only one 'civilian' cat has ever won a bravery medal – an attractive female tabby aptly named Faith who moved in to the rectory at St Augustine's Church, next to St Paul's Cathedral.

Just as the Blitz was beginning, with fires erupting around St Paul's, Faith gave birth to a kitten – it was named Panda. The sound of the bombs clearly distressed Faith, but she stayed and could often be seen wandering around the old building as if searching for something. One day the rector understood. He saw her grab Panda from her basket on the top floor and carry him down three flights of stairs to the basement where she'd found a recess containing a pile of old musical scores.

Three days later, on 9 September 1940, a bomb scored a direct hit on the building. Masonry crashed around, fires exploded above her, but throughout it all Faith kept faith. She stayed calm in her hidey-hole, shielding Panda between her front paws, until the noise, dust and smoke subsided. The two cats were found by the rector the next day as he sifted through the ruins, meowing pitifully from the recess where they had been covered by debris.

Both crawled out, dusty but unhurt, and Faith was later awarded a special silver medal by the People's Dispensary for Sick Animals.

Most cat owners can recount tales of how their favourite puss used up at least one of its nine lives, but who can match the performance of a stray called Bonnington (named after the famous British mountaineer Chris Bonnington)?

In February 1980 this moggy got trapped in a dead end with a snarling dog about to pounce for the kill. There was only one escape and it was a sheer climb upwards. Undeterred, Bonnington clawed her way up

THROUGHOUT THE BOMBING RAID SHE SHIELDED HER KITTEN WITH HER FRONT PAWS, AS MASONRY CRASHED DOWN ON THEM AND FIRES EXPLODED ALL AROUND.

Left: *Faith was another feline medal winner. She survived the Blitz on London.*

Below: *Patricia was hurled from the top of the 205 ft St John's Bridge in Portland, Oregon. She survived to become a celebrity.*

Above: *This puss, called Jeremy, got himself stuck at the top of a 65 ft tree in North London.*

THE CAT THOUGHT THE BRICK KILN WOULD BE A COSY PLACE TO SPEND THE WEEKEND; HE WAS RIGHT — THE TEMPERATURE REACHED 320°C.

the Bradford block of flats for more than 70 ft before cowering in a gap just below the roof. She was later rescued by an RSPCA man who concluded the pebble-dashed walls of the building had provided just enough grip for the incredible climb.

A similar drama was recorded in Bolton three years later when an inquisitive ginger tom made it to the top of a 150 ft chimney up an old access ladder. He couldn't, however, work out the way down and had to cling on in howling winds for almost a day and a half before he was spotted and rescued.

Sometimes cats with Bonnington-type tendencies don't want to be rescued. One such, called Mincho, ran up a 40 ft tree and stayed there quite happily for six years. Locals in Buenos Aires would push food up to her on the end of a pole and a friendly local milkman made daily deliveries. During her self-imposed exile she even produced three litters – presumably the local toms considered a climb up the tree was well worth their trouble.

PARACHUTING PUSSES

Mincho doesn't quite fall into the miraculous escapes category, but a ginger tom called Gros Minou certainly does … quite literally. Gros, owned by a Canadian surgeon, fell from the 20th-floor balcony of her master's Outremont penthouse, and plunged more than 200 feet into a flower bed. To the utter disbelief of her vet she survived with little more than a fractured pelvis. Within a week she was crawling again and later made a full recovery.

Other famous fallers include a tom called Pussycat who plunged 120 ft from an 11th-floor flat in London's Maida Vale in 1965. He suffered a broken leg and some internal damage but was soon back to full fitness and was later made a life member of the British Parachute Association.

Then there was perhaps the most celebrated moggy plunger of all – a pregnant puss called Patricia. She survived a fall of around 205 ft after she was hurled off the top of the St John's Bridge in Portland, Oregon, by a heartless motorist. Patricia spent several minutes in the freezing waters of the Willamett River before she was hauled out shocked and bedraggled by two fishermen who were,

appropriately enough, out to catch catfish. They must have gone home with the tallest angler's tale in history.

That night Patricia aborted two of her kittens but an exploratory operation by a vet found that although all her organs were severely bruised there was no life-threatening injury. Patricia was later adopted by local cat lovers Fritz and Mardi Jacob and went on to make numerous star guest appearances at cat shows across America.

Studies have shown that falling cats reach their maximum speed of 40 mph after about 60 ft. In theory, this should mean that if it's possible for them to survive a 200 ft fall it's also possible for them to handle 2,000 ft or more. Thankfully the theory never seems to have been put to the test.

NINE LIVES?

There are plenty of other examples of cats cheating death just as they seemed to be shuffling off this mortal coil. One of the most bizarre accounts came from Cambridgeshire, England, when a tom called Sedgewick decided to make an electricity substation part of his territory. He could hardly have made a bigger mistake.

As his paw touched a live wire he received a 33,000-volt shock which blacked out more than 40,000 homes. Yet, incredibly, a seriously singed Sedgewick recovered consciousness sufficiently to drag himself 60 ft back to the home of his owner, a Mr Ray Hammond. Mr Hammond could hardly recognize his pet – he later likened Sedgewick to a burnt-out car tyre – but after suitable care from a vet the chastened cat was soon back to his old self.

There are loads more from the feline mould which produced Sedgewick. Like the cat which once accidentally got itself shut in a brick kiln in Minerva, Ohio, one Friday evening and actually made it out alive the following Monday despite temperatures approaching 320°C.

And what about the one which got itself buried in tons of cement for more than two days? It had been looked after by labourers working on a new cultural centre in Skopje, Yugoslavia, but suddenly vanished on the day they were setting up planks to mould a new wall.

When the wood was later pulled off, the cat was found embedded in the concrete and had somehow kept breathing by squeezing its nose through a crack in the boards. The impression its body left was preserved and became a popular tourist attraction.

There are three other documented reports of cats disproving the old adage that curiosity will always make an end of them. The first dates back to 1955 when a painfully thin puss was found in a packing case full of car components at Natal in South Africa.

The case had been sealed up at the old Morris car works in Cowley, England, in August – three months earlier – and the cat had stayed alive by eating an instruction manual and licking engine oil. She was rushed to a vet but died the following day.

A happier ending was recorded in Cairo when a puss was pulled out of a diesel engine crate which had been sealed up 41 days earlier in Detroit, Michigan. She had also lived on engine grease and, though thin, it had kept her in good enough condition to give birth to four kittens. The entire family was nursed back to health and later thrived.

Then there was a tabby called Thumper which belonged to a Westminster woman. Thumper was fascinated by the workings of the lift to her home but somehow contrived to get herself stuck at the bottom of the shaft. Her owner assumed she had wandered off and got run over, until passengers in the lift detected her pitiful meows from the basement. She was rescued after more than seven weeks on a diet of oily water, but never quite recovered and eventually had to be put to sleep.

Bearing in mind that most cats hate water, the most miserable ordeal of all was endured by a 3-year-old called Peter. He was pulled out of the wreck of a ship called the *Tjoba* when it capsized and sank in the River Rhine in 1964. Peter kept going for an amazing eight days under water by keeping his head and whiskers inside a tiny air pocket.

WILDCAT STRIKES

It's this uncanny knack for survival that tends to mark cats out among most household pets. Perhaps their genetic

make-up means that, even today, they are not so very far removed from their cousins, the big cats. Given half a chance they can quickly adapt to going native.

Proof of this is emerging across the globe. Captive-bred animals such as lynxes, pumas, black panthers and jungle cats have shown they can keep themselves alive in unfamiliar country, even though it was always thought they would lack the necessary hunting skills.

Above: *One of the mysterious big cats now repopulating Britain's wilder regions. This one was shot in Scotland in 1983.*

Left: *The cast of a big cat's paw mark made after a farmer saw the animal in Devon, England. The paw measures 5 in across.*

THE BEAST OF EXMOOR
HAUNTS THE BLEAK
MOORLANDS, SLAUGHTERING
SHEEP AND EVADING
CAPTURE WITH FELINE
CUNNING.

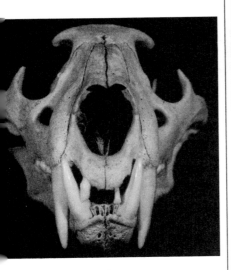

Above: *The skull of a big cat, thought to be the size of a lion, found on Dartmoor, Devon, in 1988.*

Above right: *Ship's cat from the* **Cutty Sark**, *berthed in London.*

In England, sightings of wildcats are becoming increasingly common. The so-called Beast of Exmoor, which slaughtered sheep for years on the bleak moorland which is one of England's last wildernesses, has been seen by too many witnesses (including police) to be a figment of imagination.

And in Shropshire scientists have been given even better evidence – the body of what is thought to have been a jungle cat. This animal, which is not native to Britain or Europe, was found by farmer Norman Evans in 1989 near his home. It seems to have been knocked down by a car and died of starvation because of its subsequent inability to hunt.

Forensic tests later showed it had probably been living wild for up to five years after escaping from some private collection. Despite its distinctive short, black-ringed tail, the stripes on its limbs and its terrifying inch-long fangs, it had managed to keep itself away from prying human eyes with outstanding success.

Though bigger captive-bred cats, such as panthers and pumas, can and do support themselves after escaping into the countryside, it is unlikely that they would ever get the chance to breed. Interbreeding between these animals is rare, and their offspring are almost always sterile.

That's why the future for wild jungle cats is so fascinating. They can breed successfully with feral animals, the closest relative to domestic cats, and their offspring remain fully fertile.

According to one of the world's leading experts on cat hybrids, cryptozoologist Karl Shuker, it is possible that in Britain and many other countries around the world wildcats are emerging as permanent wildlife residents.

He says: 'There is a realistic chance that interbreeding between escapee jungle cats, leopard cats, and feral domestic cats has begun in Britain's countryside.

'If this continues, eventually a self-perpetuating strain of notably large hybrids could become established here – hybrids, moreover, that possess genes from a wild non-native species unlike the hybrids produced by interbreeding between feral domestic cats and the native Scottish wildcat.

'The result would be a startling feline parallel to the cross-breeding between native red deer and naturalized Asian sika deer – and an unpredictable addition to the British ecosystem.'

Perhaps the biggest single difference between domestic cats and the escapees is the way they each regard home. Whereas the wilder feline will happily roam hundreds of miles to hunt, domestic moggies positively hate moving off their established territory.

PUSSY FOOTING IT

In past centuries it was always considered unlucky to make a cat 'do a flit' – move from one property to another. This was partly because of a cat's reputation as a witch's familiar. Perceived wisdom suggested one should avoid upsetting the animal at all costs.

Consequently there are countless stories of cats overcoming unlikely odds to return to areas they regard as home. One of the greatest feats was accomplished by a little Australian tom named Silky who was taken with his owners on a caravan holiday about 200 miles north of Brisbane. On the first night Silky was allowed out to have a wander round but he immediately vanished and a search failed to find any trace of him. Owner Ken Philips and his family hoped against hope he would turn up during the holiday but he never did and they reluctantly made the 1,481-mile trek home to Melbourne, Victoria, without him.

Nine months later, however, Silky reappeared on the doorstep of their home. He was exhausted and half-starved, but seemed to have coped with his journey well. It was only after he had settled down again for a few days that the enormous physical strain of the journey seemed to catch up with him. A week after his miracle reappearance he died.

Even more extraordinary is the story of a cream-coloured Persian cross called Sugar. His owners, a Mr and Mrs Woods, had to leave him with a helpful neighbour when they decided to retire from their house in Anderson, California, to a farm in Oklahoma.

Sugar was terrified of cars and even being carried near one threw him into a panic. Transporting him for more than 1,500 miles was unthinkable. The Woods thought they had said goodbye to their pet for ever, but one morning 13 months later a cat looking suspiciously like Sugar suddenly hopped on to Mrs Woods's back as she bent to do some weeding.

Above: *This pampered puss was left a fortune when her owner died – ensuring luxury to the end of her days.*

Left: *The best-protected cat in London. This moggy got herself adopted by the Life Guards of the Royal Household.*

> **IN AN EFFORT TO CURB HIS WANDERLUST HIS OWNER EVEN DOSED HIM WITH THE CONTRACEPTIVE PILL.**

At first she refused to believe it could be her old cat but as she stroked the 'stranger' she found his hip joint had the same peculiarity that had troubled Sugar for many years. A phone call to her former neighbour confirmed the startling fact that the cat had somehow tracked them down.

If some pussies are expert navigators, others seem to have almost been bred as marathon moggies. In 1960 a tabby called McCavity scampered from Glasgow back to his old home in Truro, Cornwall, in an incredible three weeks. That meant he covered the 500 miles at the rate of almost 24 miles a day. Sadly, the effort killed him. The day after he arrived back a neighbour found him and gave him milk but he was already too exhausted to drink it.

Three years later an even more remarkable case surfaced in South Africa. A 12-year-old tom managed to cover the 700 miles between Johannesburg and Port Elisabeth (his old home) in only ten days. Seventy miles a day sounds hard to believe but the other possibilities are even less convincing.

It wasn't as though the cat was a tug-of-love case, in which the losing owner had gone to fetch him. So how did he manage it? Hitch-hike?

Just as there are fast cats, there are slow and persistent ones. The slowest tracker on record was a lovely Siamese called Ching. She toddled off from a caravan site at Ammanford, South Wales, in 1967 to find the family home back at Stow-on-the-Wold in Gloucestershire. It took her three years, which works out at a less-than-impressive rate of 175 yards a day.

The prize for persistence, on the other hand, has to go to a Persian cross named BC who in 1979 was so irritated at being moved out of his comfortable home in Palmerston North, New Zealand, that he made it his mission in life to return. So return he did. Seventy-eight times, in fact. The journey may only have been two miles but there were at least four main roads in between and countless others where he could have fallen foul of cars.

His owner, Mrs Marjorie Cummerfield, tried everything she could think of to stop him. She once ambushed him in mid-route, but that only made him more watchful the next time he escaped. She even followed a vet's advice to give him hormone treatment in the form of the contraceptive pill. It may have done wonders for BC's hormones but it did nothing for his wanderlust.

Amazingly BC survived the perils of 20th-century transport to die peacefully of natural causes in 1983.

Mother-love is perhaps the strongest emotion of all in cats (in common with the rest of us) and there can be no better mum than a puss owned by a Manhattan family. They took her out to a summer house 100 miles away in the countryside for a few idyllic months. The plan certainly suited puss, for she quickly became pregnant, and when it was time to leave she vamooshed.

Her owners returned to New York, resigned to losing her for ever. Then, three months later, she appeared from nowhere carrying a kitten in her mouth – clearly determined that the little one should grow up in the city with a family that could be loved and trusted.

The celebration was hardly under way though when she again did a bunk, leaving the kitten behind. Two weeks passed and just as hope was again fading up she popped again ... with another kitten between her teeth. Her owners needed no more clues as to what was going on. They packed cat and kittens in the car and headed back to the sticks to find the rest of the litter to save mum the trouble of running a complete shuttle service.

Pussy-footing is OK for some, but the

Below: Lucky the cat survived nine weeks inside a crate being shipped from the UK to Texas. Here British Caledonian staff prepare to fly him home.

more discerning moggy travellers find that what's good enough for humans is good enough for them. Take air travel. One of the most extraordinary journeys ever recorded of the animal kingdom happened in the spring of 1979 when a Siamese called Wan Ton somehow hopped on to a jumbo jet from Guam in the south Pacific.

He was found in the hold of the jet by staff at London Heathrow, shivering and looking extremely sorry for himself. There was just one problem for the British authorities as they quarantined Wan Ton ready to return him to the American naval family which owned him. No plane flew from that part of the world direct to London. Somehow, Wan Ton had changed planes at Washington DC.

Another seasoned air traveller was Hamlet, a cat owned by one Paul Rackheath of Norfolk. In February 1984 he was on the official passenger list of a BA jumbo flying out of Toronto, but he obviously didn't like the menu because he escaped from his cage and vanished into the hold.

It wasn't until two months later that a startled aircraft engineer caught sight of a thin, scrawny scrap of fur behind some panelling. He pulled out Hamlet, who had apparently survived by licking condensation. Though he didn't know it, the hapless feline had flown around 600,000 miles in a little over seven weeks, including stopovers in Jamaica, Singapore, Australia and Kuwait.

Finally, there is the not quite so traumatic but every bit as uncomfortable story of Buttons, a 'lucky' black cat from Great Yarmouth, England.

He vanished one afternoon at exactly the time as his owner's next-door-neighbour set off from home to drive to Aberdeen. Being a sensible sort of motorist, the driver, a Mr Fraser Robertson, decided to pull in to a service station to check his oil. As he lifted the bonnet he instantly spied Buttons curled up around the battery and absolutely covered in thick engine grime.

As Mr Robertson observed later: 'How she survived six hours of non-stop driving I will never know.

'The engine was incredibly hot and what with the petrol fumes, the oil smoke and the noise it must have been a terrifying experience for her.'

Fortunately things got better for Buttons. She got a quick bite at the service station and was then driven on to Aberdeen with the luxury of being able to curl up on the back seat.

Best of all, one airline gave her a free flight home.

Left: *They may have nine lives but it still helps to have the Royal Society for the Prevention of Cruelty to Animals on their side.*

Below: *American puss Shandy became the only cat in the world to eat her dinner with chopsticks!*

UNDER THE SEA

The leviathans of the mysterious deeps are a symbol of nature's power and greatness, but some people will pursue even these majestic creatures and subject them to cruel ordeals in their insatiable lust for money.

For many they are the symbol of nature's greatness: the sight of whales roaming the oceans unfettered and free is a reminder that the world still has giants on the loose. Yet also they are a poignant sign of human power misused. The majestic mammals which should have been cherished have been threatened by greed.

As fishing fleets sought to spear or net whales to profit from their meat and oils, their numbers dwindled to the point of extinction. Just in time, the world woke up to its folly. Commercial whaling was banned – although controversy still rages about the issue – and the seas seemed at last a little safer for these graceful creatures.

At a time when whales had earned a special place in the hearts of wildlife lovers, one in particular captured the imagination of the West as it strove to escape from its Russian masters.

KILLER WHALES?

Brightness the beluga whale was a reluctant volunteer in the Russian Navy, one of several whales and dolphins in captivity at a Black Sea laboratory in Sebastopol, trained for dangerous missions under the waves.

Special underwater agents like Brightness have been used by America and Russia for the past 30 years. They were in action against Vietcong frogmen during America's involvement in the Vietnam conflict. So valuable were they that Russian

Opposite: *A white beluga whale, similar to Brightness, makes friends with a diver in the Black Sea.*

Below: *Brightness was eventually caught by his Russian masters, despite worldwide protests. Here he is winched unceremoniously aboard a trawler.*

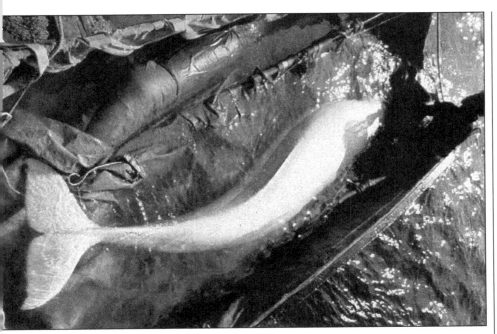

Above: *Brightness lies helpless on his makeshift stretcher – sedated for the long voyage back to captivity.*

THE FRIENDLY FUGITIVE
EVEN MANAGED BROAD
SMILES FOR THE CAMERA.

Right: *Movie director Michael Winner vowed to raise £100,000 to buy Brightness from the Russians.*

fishermen were paid a ransom for supplying live beluga whales.

Taking advantage of their amiable personality and sharp wit, scientists trained them to stick limpet mines or listening devices on submarines or ships and even kill enemy divers with a syringe attached to their noses. Diving swiftly to enormous depths and impervious to the cold, the whale seemed a perfect antidote to the menace of enemy submarines. They were even taught to distinguish different metals. But stealth alone would not save them from certain death in their explosives work. Clearly visible thanks to their bright white skins, they would be easy targets in times of war. Theirs would almost certainly be kamikaze missions.

Few people realized lovable whales and dolphins were being trained for warfare even though an estimated 100 were caged for the purpose in Russia alone. Then Brightness made a bid for freedom. It happened in November 1991 when a winter storm lashed at the Black Sea coast. The wind whipped up a sea strong enough to tear down the cages which penned Brightness and his buddy Gorgeous.

For several months Brightness enjoyed a freedom in the waves he had never known before, but it seems he missed the human companionship he had grown used to in captivity. He turned up off the Turkish coast, 500 miles from where he disappeared. Fishermen and tourists alike were treated to regular displays of his antics off the village of Gerze. He would allow admirers to pet and feed him. Soon the eyes of the world were on the frolicking, feted creature who even managed broad smiles for the cameras.

But it was the start of an international battle over his future between Russia and the West. Both sides agreed the waters of the Black Sea would become too warm for the fugitive whale to survive as the summer hotted up. Russians insisted the creature should be returned to them, claiming he was being trained for circus work. Brightness was never used for military purposes, insisted the Leningrad Scientific Research Institute, and would perish in the icy waters of the Arctic, his natural habitat. In fact, he depended on the close human contact he had grown to know and had been wasting away while he was at sea, it was claimed.

In Britain, scorn was poured on the news that Brightness was anything other than a pawn in the Cold War games played by the superpowers. Claims that he was being prepared for a life as a circus attraction led to an outcry. Furious campaigners claimed the only place fit for the whale was the open sea. Britain's Whale and Dolphin Conservation Society hurriedly assembled a team of experts to assess the best course of action. An airlift to the Arctic was on the cards. 'We have no doubt it could survive there', declared director Sean Whyte.

But as the freedom fighters were

mobilizing their forces, the Russians acted. For an hour Brightness ducked and dived, thwarting their attempts at capture. But finally the 900 lb creature was lassoed around the tail by a diver and hauled aboard a specially adapted trawler to be carted back unceremoniously in a heavyweight sling. Before the 120-mile journey back to Russian territory and a two-day journey to the Sebastopol base, he was sedated. For once, Brightness – whose Russian name Tishka means 'laughing man' – had lost the by-now familiar beam. Instead, the 7-year-old whale looked glum and despairing.

Politicians declined to intervene because of the sensitive nature of the issue, but the row refused to go away. Revelations that 13 ft long Brightness was to star in a travelling marine show touring the holiday hotspots in a floating cage further outraged conservationists. Dr Boris Zhurid, director of the Aquamarine Dolphinarium in Sebastopol, described how the sea-borne cage comprising three swimming pools was to be pulled by a tug.

There was no comfort, either, for those who sought freedom for Brightness in the knowledge that an American oceanarium keen to begin breeding beluga whales in captivity was prepared to pay £100,000 to the hard-up Russians and import Brightness as a celebrity to its 170,000 sq ft pool, already home to two belugas and four dolphins.

British star Paul McCartney, TV writer Carla Lane and film producer Michael Winner pledged to raise £100,000 so they could buy the whale and release him back into the wild. But their attempts failed.

Just two months after he was harnessed off Turkey, Brightness was performing in a show, doing tricks such as singing, waving his fins and fetching balls.

But the clowning, grinning animal who had so beguiled the world was gone, his spirit numbed by the cheerless monotony of life in the ring.

Thanks to pressure from Turkey, the Russians were ready to release Brightness into the waters where he first tasted freedom, to recuperate. British rescuers then negotiated a way of freeing Brightness and fellow captive Yegor after a lengthy rehabilitation process. There was jubilation among the conservationists who wanted him free.

However, between them, nature and the

whale who refused to be caged had other ideas. History repeated itself when a violent storm wrecked the netting which held Brightness. One dolphin was killed and another, along with Yegor the whale, was seriously hurt. Despite an alert put out along the coastline, Brightness disappeared, choosing the depths of the Black Sea to swim in and only coming up occasionally for air. Soviet news agency TASS offered a £400 reward for the creature, describing him as a state asset. There were fears he could have been killed by pollution or even starved to death.

Above: *Brightness makes his triumphant return to the Black Sea port of Gerze, Turkey, in April 1993.*

THE ESKIMOS COULD NOT
BEAR TO SEE SUCH NOBLE
CREATURES BLOODIED AND
BATTERED AS THEY TRIED TO
FORCE A PATH THROUGH THE
FROZEN SEAS.

It was four months before Brightness was spotted, in April 1993, safe and well and making himself at home once again in the waters off the Turkish coast. He came up to give free shows, to the delight of the Turkish crowds which gathered. But bitterly aware of his previous encounters, he refused to stay long enough to be caught. As far as anyone knows, Brightness is still enjoying freedom, somewhere under the waves in the Black Sea.

A CAGE OF ICE

It was the plight of whales in peril which focused the attention of the world in 1988. This time Russia and America were united in their efforts to free three whales trapped by ice in the Arctic.

The trio of Californian greys had become trapped after lingering too long in the sea at Barrow, Alaska, before migrating south in the face of unusually cold weather. The winter ice closed in relentlessly around them.

It was the Eskimos living in the darkened, snowy wastes of the north who first realized the appalling predicament of the whales. They witnessed the increasingly desperate animals becoming bashed and bloodied as they tried to force a path through the unyielding crust of ice that caged them.

The Eskimos live by hunting whales, but even they could not bear to see the grand animals die such a cruel death, being suffocated by snow.

In rotas, they used picks and saws to make life-saving air holes in the 2 ft thick ice, each one closer to the sea, now some five miles distant. Each whale was given a pet name: they were Pouto, Siku and Kannick, meaning Ice Hole, Ice and Snowflake. To keep one 20 ft by 24 ft breathing hole open meant men working in relays for a week. Their endeavours were screened on American TV and the nation watched with bated breath to see if the animals would make it.

Soon oil workers, members of Greenpeace, national guardsmen and biologists joined the army intent on freeing the whales. Each day the open sea was getting further away as the big winter freeze got a grip.

In temperatures of minus 13°C during the day and with winds peaking at 30 mph, the volunteers were clad in special heavy-duty parkas, insulated trousers, vacuum-lined boots and even facemasks to protect them against the biting cold. Their reward was a bond which sprang up between beast and man, based on trust and a shared hope. It was enough to make grown men endure until they were on the point of collapse.

One of the whales was 30 ft long and thought to be about 6 years old. The others were smaller, probably aged only about 2.

Right: *Californian grey whales battle for survival after being cut off by advancing ice north of Alaska. Volunteers worked around the clock to keep their air holes open. The whales were freed ... but no one knows whether they survived to reach breeding grounds.*

It was clear that more high-tech methods would be needed if the whales were to stand any chance at all. Initial hopes lay in an effective ice-crushing hovercraft barge which would pulverize the ice and open an escape route for the whales. Normally used for transporting supplies to oil drilling sites, it was based 200 miles away and time was crucial. A giant helicopter was ready to hoist the 185-ton machine to the scene.

But jagged icebergs posed a threat to the air cushion on which the ice cutter travelled before it even approached Barrow. The whales had been trapped for more than two weeks before the steel-tipped concrete block began punching holes at 75 yd spaces towards the trapped animals.

For one it was already too late. The smallest of the three lost his struggle for life. To the consternation of the army of rescuers, he failed to surface one morning and the whale the American-speaking observers had called Bone was pronounced lost. He was severely weakened after the skin on his snout had been worn away against the ice, exposing the bone beneath. The remaining two, known as Crossbeak and Bonnet to the Americans, continued their bleak course from air hole to air hole.

Other dangers were now threatening. Hungry polar bears had picked up the scent of whales in trouble. Several were closing in for a kill, having already claimed the life of a whale trapped further down the coast. If they decided to attack, there was little the onlookers could do. There arose the spectre of the whales, the centre of media attention from all over the world, being eaten alive as the cameras rolled.

Then there was the question of cost. The rescue operation was gobbling up money to the tune of some $1 million. Critics began braving the public obsession with the freedom of the whales. Could not the money have been better spent on the nation's homeless or sick?

Scientists weighed in with their doubts as well. Exhausted as they were by their fight against the ice, the whales were surely unlikely to survive the trip down to the warmer waters of Mexico where others of their kind were beginning to mate. There were sharks to contend with off the shores of British Columbia, too.

Fortunately for the trapped whales, America's President Reagan and President Gorbachev from the USSR didn't agree. Distracted though he was with a presidential election at home, President Reagan, like most of his country, found the battle for survival off the northern tip of his territory compelling.

And he seized on an offer by the Soviet president of two ice breakers to churn up a path for the whales. The Soviets could already boast of some success in freeing whales. In 1985 they lured nearly 1,000 white whales from beneath ice in the Bering Sea, playing classical music underwater to soothe the petrified creatures.

Only 40 died and the Russians were confident they could repeat their achievement. Finally, following the ship *Vladimir Arseniev*, the two whales reached seas free of the icy shackles which had harnessed them for three weeks.

Below: *Dolphins love to play alongside boats, leaping to catch the odd morsel of food. Though gentle to human beings, they can turn into raging fighters when confronted by sharks.*

Above: *Pacific bottlenose dolphins at play.*

WOULD THE WHALES REACH THE SAFETY OF WARMER WATERS – OR WOULD THEY PERISH?

Below: *Fungie the dolphin frolics with divers.*

distress of the whales. They realized that with the world backing the whales, it would be too devastating for the countless well-wishers if the whales didn't make it. As for the previous three weeks, hope was all everybody had.

Blue whales are the largest mammals to have inhabited the Earth. They have been recorded with lengths of up to 108 ft and weights of up to an astonishing 131 tons. Swimming at speed, they can reach 14 knots. Even baby blues are a force to be reckoned with: they can measure 25 ft on arrival with a weight of more than 7 tons. In 1932 the tongue of an 89 ft long whale weighed in at a mind-boggling 3 tons 3 cwt.

A message was flashed simultaneously to Presidents Reagan and Gorbachev. It was hailed as a meaningful accord between the two superpowers with a history of antagonism. The US president sent a message of personal thanks to everyone involved in the feat. 'It's an inspiring endeavour. The human persistence and determination of many individuals on behalf of these whales shows mankind's concern for the environment.'

No one knows the eventual fate of the whales: whether they reached the safety of warmer waters or died in the fight to get there.

Scientists in the frontline of the rescue could easily have monitored their progress by attaching radio transmitters to them but decided against it. It wasn't just that they were concerned that it would add to the

THE DANCE OF THE DOLPHINS

With their might and grandeur, whales are surely the rulers under the waves, but they have to go a long way to pip the dolphin in the popularity stakes. Perhaps it is the dolphins' cheeky, toothy grin or a warmth which radiates out of the coldest of waters. Above all, they appear to revel in human companionship.

Naturalist Sir David Attenborough explains: 'They have a justifiable reputation for helping man. Possibly it is because we are approximately the same size and they feel they are helping others of their own kind.'

Next to humans, dolphins have the largest and most complex brains in the animal kingdom.

Above all, they love to help children, perhaps sensing they are the least able to

help themselves. That's why they are used in Miami in therapy for autistic children.

In 1988 three children were rescued by a caring dolphin after they were thrown from a blazing ferry by their father into the sea off Java. The gentle creature used his nose to guide them to a waiting life raft.

Surfer Adam Maguire was quite literally saved from the jaws of death by dolphins after he was attacked by a shark off the coast of New South Wales, Australia.

The 17-year-old had been larking about with some pals and a school of dolphins when a 13 ft killer shark struck. As it tried to take a bite out of the schoolboy, three gallant dolphins intervened. They butted and bashed the attacker until it gave up and swam off.

Afterwards Adam, from Ballina, Brisbane, said: 'We were out and there was a school of dolphins around. We were just mucking around with them. They were catching waves with us.

'Then I saw what appeared to be a dolphin charging towards me. But 5 metres away I realized it was a shark. By then it was too late and I was knocked off my board. Then the shark came back again and bit me.

'I just tried to push it away and then I saw it swim off. As it left, I saw three dolphins chasing it away.'

Two shipwrecked sailors were nudged to safety through shark-infested waters off Indonesia by a school of dolphins. A Dutch helicopter pilot also owes his life to a sea-borne saviour. After he crashed in the sea in the Far East a dolphin pushed his life raft for nine days until they reached land.

The argument that dolphins are better friends to mankind than even a dog has been disputed by scientists who reckon they would probably act to save themselves and their young rather than any human victim.

Yet Dr Horace Dobbs, a former scientist at Harwell, Oxfordshire, found himself reassessing his views on dolphins after he saw one swim beneath his 13-year-old son in waters off the Isle of Man and provide a ride around the bay. The experience prompted him to write a book, *Dance to a Dolphin's Song*, and convinced him that swimming with the animals was a cure for depression. 'I felt I had to know more about creatures with such a closeness to man. The best way to teach a dog is to reward him with food but dolphins aren't interested in bribery. They are motivated by love. If a trainer turns his back on a dolphin it feels badly rejected.'

Ask any of the residents around Dingle Bay in Ireland and they will give dolphins a glowing reference. That's where Fungi the dolphin has set up home, to the delight of residents and tourists alike. They cram themselves into small boats and head out to sea to watch his playful antics. Ted Kennedy Junior, son of Senator Teddy Kennedy, was one of thousands who travelled across the world and Ireland to be captivated by the flip-flap frolics in the water.

Fungi became the star of several films, including a documentary called *The Dolphin's Gift*, narrated by actor John Hurt.

Likewise, on the bleak north-east coast of Britain, Jimmy the dolphin made himself at home in the harbour of Amble to the

Above: *A school of southern right whale dolphins assemble off the Chilean coast. The mammal's close relationship with mankind is the stuff of legend – yet there are still fishermen who cruelly hunt them to obtain the 'aphrodisiac' dorsal fin.*

THIS BARBAROUS PRACTICE LEAVES THE DOLPHIN BLEEDING TO DEATH AND SPIRALLING OUT OF CONTROL INTO THE DEPTHS OF THE OCEAN.

Right: *This killer shark caught off Miami in 1972 had preyed on swimmers in local waters. Its razor-like teeth enabled it to kill in seconds.*

Below: *A great white shark, the model for the monster in the hit movie* Jaws.

surprise and joy of the locals. Flatteringly, he appears to stay because he wants to, not because he needs to.

Sadly, however, there are people who will happily line their own pockets at the expense of even the closest animal ally.

Dolphins are slaughtered wholesale by unscrupulous tuna fishermen when they become trapped in mammoth drag nets which are trawled through the seas.

Even more appallingly, a trade in dolphin fins has sparked a barbarous practice. It began when *Science* magazine branded dolphins as 'promiscuous as Errol Flynn'. Apparently, desperate Japanese men believed crushed dorsal fin from the sexually active creature would be a cure-all for their own sexual inadequacies.

It has prompted greedy fishermen off the Japanese and Australian coasts to haul dolphins aboard their boats, hack off the desired fin and ditch the body back into the sea, alive, bleeding profusely and spiralling out of control into the depths of the ocean.

There are rich pickings for fishermen, who can sell the fin for £1,000 a time. Although they risk imprisonment and a hefty fine, there's little chance of them ever being caught.

It was this horrible fate that befell Charlie, a friendly dolphin from the waters of Shark Bay, Western Australia. After being speared by a fishing hook, Charlie beached himself, hoping for some human aid. It came and cheerful Charlie repaid the kindness of the passing fisherman by driving fish into his net. He was a firm favourite with all the local people, particularly the children. But this trusting and loyal creature was killed by the ruthless fin fishermen.

In his honour, a dolphin sanctuary was formed and is home to scores of dolphins who will happily play and prance in the water with visiting families.

People can enter the water safe in the knowledge that the dolphins will see off any marauding shark, one of the most feared creatures on Earth.

THE JAWS OF DEATH

Sharks have always posed a threat in the water, but the 1975 film *Jaws* – masterly in its suspense although criticized for its unrealistic monster model – moulded the paranoia of a generation.

And it may be that just such a beast existed after a spate of attacks along America's east coast in July 1916, thought to be the work of one rogue creature. Four people died and another was injured at a time when it was widely believed sharks did not attack bathers in the safer northern waters – while perhaps large mackerel or turtles might. In the first attack, the shark was so tenacious it clamped onto its victim's leg in as little as 18 in of water.

Four days later and 35 miles farther north another man died. Within the week, two more people died and another was savagely injured after the shark entered a sheltered creek 20 miles from the open sea. President Woodrow Wilson summoned his advisors in a bid to curb the menace while shark hunters took to the water.

It was only days before a great white measuring 8.5 ft was hooked; its stomach contained a mass of flesh and bone. When the attacks ended, it was assumed this was the shark responsible for all the killings.

Possibly the worst shark attack in recent years came in June 1993 when a 34-year-old British woman was eaten alive by a 16 ft long shark during a dive.

The 2-ton great white shark – the same breed which terrorized the resort in *Jaws* – attacked moments after Therese Cartwright went into the water with two other divers, intending to study seal pups in a colony off the coast of Tasmania, Australia.

The shark probably mistook Mrs Cartwright, aged 34, for one of the seals it normally feasts on. Mrs Cartwright was mother to quadruplets born in 1987 following fertility treatment and also to an 11-month-old son. They were in an escort boat with her husband Ian when the shark attacked. The family had left their native Kent for a new life in Australia and midwife Mrs Cartwright was on the point of qualifying for a Master's degree.

In the same week bride Debbie Ford watched as her husband was eaten alive by an 18 ft great white shark. The couple had been married for only three weeks.

Victim John Ford was diving off the New South Wales resort of Byron Bay when the monster loomed. Fishermen gave chase but the shark was so powerful it dragged a trawler 4 miles out to sea before breaking out of its nets. Experts deemed it unlikely that the same fish was responsible for both deaths.

There have been 491 shark attacks around the Australian coastline since the first was recorded in 1792, 182 of them being fatal.

That is an average of two a year.

But even the awesome great white is suffering at human hands. Although they are not a protected species, there are thought to be as few as 2,000 remaining worldwide. Despite their menace, biologists want the numbers conserved because of their important role in the ecosystem.

The largest of the sharks is the rare whale shark. It is a peaceable enough fish but it averages 50 ft in length and weighs 15 tons. One baby examined by scientists had a liver weighing 600 lb and 3,000 teeth in each of its jaws. The whale shark also has the unnerving habit of scratching its back on the bottom of boats, with quite frightening consequences.

Sometimes even a shark meets its match, however. Kelly Rafferty, a 38-year-old fisherman, fell overboard in shark-filled waters off Cairns, Australia, in May 1992. But Kelly wasn't about to become breakfast for any passing fish. He described his 9-mile swim to safety. 'I slapped a 12 ft tiger shark out of the road, got some stingers out of my feet and punched a 4 ft Java shark on the way to shore.' Doctors who treated him in hospital said afterwards he was in good condition despite the ordeal.

Above: *A shark ends its fight for survival as fishermen in South Australian waters haul it aboard their boat.*

EACH OF ITS POWERFUL JAWS CONTAINS 3,000 VICIOUS TEETH.

THE STARS AND
ANIMAL RIGHTS

Imprisoned by fame themselves, it is hardly surprising that many celebrities use their wealth and power to fight for the rights of animals who have no voice.

In the hype-ridden world of showbiz the animal kingdom is, for many stars, the only way truly to escape. Famous faces queue up to defend species at risk with a passion matched only on stage or in front of a camera.

Perhaps it's because the stars get tired of the human hassle – the terms of a new film deal, agents upping their cut or some schmuck trying to sell gossip to the papers.

Whatever the reason, animals suffering abuse get some powerful voices on their side.

And for those lucky enough to be picked as pets of the stars there are luxuries many humans can only dream of.

MONKEY BUSINESS

Take Bubbles the chimp, for instance. Life started as badly as it possibly could for him in the research laboratory of an American company.

Yet just as it seemed he might end up as one more grim statistic of science, along came salvation in the shape of one of the world's best-known singers, Michael Jackson.

Michael rescued Bubbles and gave him a new life about as far removed as possible from his job as a living, breathing experiment. There began a love affair as intense as any Hollywood has ever seen.

For six years Bubbles never left Michael's side. He toured with the Jackson entourage, staying in £2,000-a-night hotel suites and living off the finest food.

He even slept next to his master's bed.

Michael would kit him out in the latest designer clothes to make sure he never looked underdressed at the constant round of parties.

And Bubbles, real name *Anthropopithecus*, was once even said to have bathed in Perrier water because Jackson thought it would be purer for his fur.

When Bubbles wasn't on tour he could enjoy the freedom of Michael's Santa Ynez ranch under the care of his personal animal bodyguard Miko Brando, son of Marlon.

Michael, of course, would try to visit daily to play and talk or collect him for

another personal appearance at some star-studded bash. Sadly, however, that close relationship had to end.

Male chimps are known to have terrible tempers. At 160 lb, Bubbles easily had the muscle-power to kill a man.

Reluctantly Michael agreed his favourite pet would have to retire to a private zoo at Sylmar, Los Angeles. And although Bubbles lost a little of his freedom, love, care and the company of other chimps helped him to settle in quickly.

Bubbles's friendship with Michael is typical of relationships that many stars enjoy with the animal kingdom.

Famous actors and singers will tell time and again how they trust animals more than humans, and talk of the need to stand up for creatures defenceless against the ravages of mankind.

Opposite: *Liz Taylor and her former husband Richard Burton had a weakness for cute, hairy dogs.*

Above: *Michael Jackson with his pet chimp Bubbles and friend. Bubbles got used to the luxury of £2,000-a-night hotels.*

ONCE SHE LAVISHED HER CARE AND ATTENTION ON MEN; NOW HER LOVE IS GIVEN TO STRAY CATS AND DOGS.

BRIGITTE'S BATTLE

Take Brigitte Bardot, once Hollywood's biggest sex bomb.

She now lives the life of a recluse, surrounded by the animals she has rescued, in her St Tropez villa La Madrague.

'It was a choice I was perfectly happy with,' she says.

'Since then I have dedicated my life, and a very large part of my wealth, to the protection of animals.

'I prefer the company of animals to that of people because they never disappoint you. Someone once said that man's best friends never hurt us until they die.

'I've had a great love of animals all my life. I can't explain why. I've always felt closer to them than to people. I can't give you a reason for that either. It's just the way it is.'

Brigitte, who has 21 dogs, 20 cats, horses, goats, sheep and a donkey called Mimosa, says she never turns away a stray animal in need.

She has taken in old horses saved from the abattoir and ensured that huntsmen seeking foxes or wild boar know that if they venture onto her land they will be treated as trespassers.

Trappers using legholds now declared illegal in most of Europe have come in for a particularly hard Bardot tongue-lashing.

She has even fronted her own TV series – *Hunting and Hunters* – in which she took on one of the most powerful lobbies in France, the farmers.

Brigitte pointed out that a staggering 73 per cent of French people thought hunters abused their rights. She quoted 66 per cent support for her dream of making them face much tougher rules covering the way they operate.

But her biggest campaign to date is an attempt to have all of France's estimated 35 million stray cats and dogs sterilized, a move she argues would drastically reduce the miseries suffered by strays.

Such is her passion that she has willed her £2 million home to her Bardot Foundation for the Protection of Animals.

The actress, star of *And God Created Woman*, has a pessimistic view of the future.

She speaks of the world getting worse for both people and animals – a phenomenon she calls 'the decline of the end of the millenium'.

She adds: 'Too many people who are in a position to change things are indifferent.

'Existing laws are not implemented. Poachers are devastating wildlife, destroying everything for money. Laboratories use animals in vivisection experiments that are like something out of a science fiction horror film.

'I'm a vegetarian. I only wear clothes made from cotton or wool. I don't buy any cosmetics tested on animals.

'Learning to respect animal life would teach us to respect the lives of the weakest humans, who are suffering in the same intolerable way.'

MODEL ON THE CATWALK

If the prospect of caring for 20 cats is daunting, pity Celia Hammond, one of the most celebrated models ever to stare from the cover of *Vogue*.

She gave up the glamour and glitz of her 1960s career to devote herself to rescuing strays – a full-time job she now describes as 'the most important thing in my life'.

Now she has 250 in the catteries of her home in east Sussex, southern England, with dozens more sick or injured animals

Below: Actress Brigitte Bardot with some of the stray dogs that have become the focus of her animal welfare campaign.

allowed to roam the rooms of her house.

Her obsession – she readily admits it is one – started when a photographer friend gave her three kittens, Rosie, Dozy and Sophie.

Gradually she took more and more interest in the welfare of strays, somehow working her rescue missions into the demanding life of a top model.

She says: 'It got to the point where it became more important than my work.

'I was not turning up to jobs and pretending I was ill when really I was out rescuing strays.'

Celia's ultimate goal – like Bardot's in France – is to tackle the root cause of homeless cats and dogs in Britain by equipping spaying clinics capable of operating at very low costs.

In the meantime she does her bit by making night trips to London four times per week to track down and rescue strays.

Most she finds trapped in rundown or derelict buildings or in the dock wastelands east of the City.

'The obsession isn't about being surrounded with cats,' she says.

'To be honest, I'd be quite happy to be with one cat, or even no cats.

'The obsession is to solve the problem of there being two and a half million stray cats and dogs in Britain at the moment. I want to do something about that by preventing them from breeding.'

Celia says she'd love to spend more time on her social life, or indulging her hobby of prowling round auction rooms and antique shops.

But she admits: 'If I did I would torture myself about all the animals that were suffering because I had taken the day off.'

There does seem to be something about cats that inspires almost total devotion from showbusiness types. You'd think ordinary toms and tabbies were hard enough work, yet for some the challenge comes much bigger. Big cats in fact.

THE BIG CATS

Virginia McKenna, known to millions as the star of the tear-jerker *Born Free*, is perhaps the best-known devotee.

During her 11 months filming that classic she and husband Bill Travers found themselves drawn closer and closer into the

lives of the proud beasts working alongside them.

It was an experience which changed her life and made her decide to wage a personal war against conditions captive animals have to endure.

In 1983 an elephant she'd worked with on a movie titled *An Elephant Called Slowly* was given a new home at London Zoo. The animal later sickened and eventually had to be put to sleep.

For Virginia it was a massive emotional blow and she vowed to launch her own charity dedicated to investigate the treatment of caged animals.

Today Zoo Check is one of the most

Above: *Former* Vogue *cover girl Celia Hammond* (right) *with fellow model Sue Gunn. Celia began taking in cats in the early 1980s – now she has 250.*

Above: *Born free: Virginia McKenna and Bill Travers with their beloved lion, Elsa.*

THE FILM CHANGED HER LIFE AND SHE DECIDED TO FIGHT HER OWN PERSONAL WAR.

powerful voices in the entire animal rights lobby.

Virginia says: 'People should only have access to zoos if they don't cause suffering to animals.

'For example, it's totally unacceptable to have polar bears in zoos. They're so deprived by the way they're kept.

'I'm also very against keeping elephants in captivity. In the wild they have a complex life-style that is impossible to duplicate in a zoo or circus.'

She now spends most of her time on the charity's workload after taking a decision not to return to the theatre. She describes her acting career as a 'wonderful innings' but insists animal welfare is now more important.

'Having seen so many animals in zoos in so many countries, and given the terrible images of their plight that I carry about with me always, I know I must do something for them.

'That's what my heart says.

'I know some scientists, the boffins, might say: "She's just a nutty actress."

'I may be a bit nutty but I feel quite rational.'

Another Hollywood star brought to the animal rights cause through films is Tippi Hedren, star of Hitchcock's *The Birds* and mother of Melanie Griffith.

She was shooting (cameras, not guns) in Africa in the late 1960s when she and ex-husband Noel Marshall found themselves entranced by lions.

They started their own temporary sanctuary, made the film *Roar* with their 'pets' and then bought a ranch near Los Angeles to give the animals a permanent reserve.

Tippi says: 'Many of the animals were very old, and didn't last long.

'We now have great cats which include African lions, American mountain lions, Bengali and Siberian tigers, black-spotted leopards and cougars, two African elephants and my pot-bellied pig, Sir Winston Churchill.

'The great cats have mystique, they're magnificent and they have a frightening quality about them.

'We try to understand them. We know what makes them happy, what makes them angry. That's very important as they are volatile animals, quite capable of destroying you. One did attack me and had my head in its mouth.

'But they're very special. They accept each other just as they are.'

She describes herself as 'the luckiest lady in the world' to live with such exotic species around her. And, she freely admits, they dictate almost everything she does.

One of the tigers, named Natasha, is so jealous of Tippi's time she will never let her do anything other than offer her full attention.

That means taking a newspaper or magazine out of the actress's hand and, if necessary, tearing it to shreds.

But with big cats around, Tippi is tolerant.

She says: 'People should understand that every single animal, every critter on the Earth has a personality which is magical. They are thinking, feeling beings and they have every right to a dignified life.'

Tippi has ploughed every penny of her savings into her reserve. And with a staff of 15 to pay, it's not a cheap hobby.

'I've probably taken on more than I can handle,' she admits.

'But I still take great joy in hearing the lions roaring.'

ANIMAL WELFARE

Famous names who have the animal welfare 'obsession' recognize that unless they're careful, their own living can be jeopardized.

Loretta Swit – Hot Lips Houlihan in the comedy series *M*A*S*H* – jokes: 'I can't remember a time when I wasn't interested in animal welfare.

'It's really my second career, though my agent would say: "No, it's her first." '

As tough-talking Major Houlihan Loretta strikes a blow for women's equality with almost every order she blasts out. Off screen, her one-woman campaign for animals is fought with every bit as much intensity.

She says: 'Wildlife is my great love but it's not just a question of loving animals.

'The whole world loves animals. The people who own and love animals also hunt, wear fur coats, eat meat, wear leather, have crocodile belts.

> **THE GREAT CAT RIPPED THE NEWSPAPER FROM THE ACTRESS'S HAND AND TORE IT TO SHREDS.**

Below: *When Tippi Hendren puts the cat out for the night she needs to have her wits about her. Here she and husband Noel Marshall pet one of their Siberian tigers.*

Right: *Loretta Swit with a young seal. 'It's the world I care about,' she says.*

Below: *Loretta with a friendly turtle.*

'I don't do any of these things and I actually fight for animals.

'I've got dirt under my nails and been bitten by mosquitos tagging sea turtles and counting their eggs so I could raise money for a beach in Florida where the turtles come every year and lay their eggs. If the land gets developed they will die.'

She is furious with those who say she's 'crazy' about animals.

'That's not it at all. I'm not just an animal lover. It's the world I care about – the rainforest and the fact that we lose one species every four hours.'

Loretta supports around 14 separate animal welfare groups, including Beauty Without Cruelty and the US Humane Society. She agrees with Bardot and Celia Hammond that one of the great scandals of our modern civilization is the number of strays on the streets.

The figure of five million animals a year put down in the USA horrifies her – especially as the country's puppy 'farms' keep turning out more and more.

She said: 'We're all animals. Some of us run around on two legs, some on four, some swim, some fly.

'And this is the only place we all have.'

Other big names in the animal rights business include Dustin Hoffman, Jack Nicholson, Tom Cruise, Barbra Streisand,

Joanna Lumley and Live Aid mastermind Bob Geldof.

Joanna is one of the co-founders of the international Elefriends campaign, set up to persuade consumers not to buy ivory.

She was appalled to discover how the animals are slaughtered by poachers toting Russian-made submachine guns, who then saw off the tusks for sale abroad.

Joanna says: 'People have stopped wearing furs because they now know about the cruelty and damage.

'We want to do the same for elephants. If people know what is involved they will stop buying ivory.

'Elephants live like we do. They are infinitely kind. They are not predators.

'They look after their own.'

But if famous names generally carry clout in the cause of animals, one husband-and-wife team is the undisputed champion.

Ex-Beatle Paul McCartney and his American-born wife Linda are ready to take on all comers in their support for animal rights.

That includes big multi-national companies who have spent years crafting their public image.

One US car maker with a record of conducting animal experiments was banned from taking advertising space on McCartney's 1993 world tour.

McCartney threatened to make his own TV and radio adverts telling the world the nature of the experiments. Jubilant campaigners immediately rang the company telling them: 'McCartney is getting involved.

'Do you really want to take on Paul McCartney?'

The company quickly issued a statement making clear it 'no longer had any animal trauma research activity'.

McCartney, who has sold 38 million records since the Beatles split up, is not one to hold back on his adopted cause.

He and Linda are both vegetarians, sworn to 'never eat anything with a face', and have carried out scores of high-profile campaigns to publicize their beliefs.

On one occasion the couple bought and freed lobsters destined for the dinner table. They have also forced fox hunters off their land, threatening legal action against anybody who defies them.

Paul regularly attacks the barbaric slaughter of whales. 'Keep the sea blue, not red' is one of his favourite slogans.

He also made a personal plea to US President Ronald Reagan to save tiny long-tailed Macaques monkeys from medical experiments. Thirty of them were used, more than half of which died.

On his record 'Looking For Changes' – described as McCartney's most powerful protest song to date – he portrays shocking images of life in a research laboratory.

One line goes: 'I saw a rabbit with its eyes full of tears, the lab that owned her had been doing it for years.'

Another reads: 'I saw a monkey that was learning to choke, a guy beside him gave him cigarettes to smoke.'

The McCartneys have been vegetarian since 1973, when Linda and Paul sat down to a leg of roast lamb … and then noticed some live ones gambolling about in a field outside.

Linda is now trying to re-educate the palates of the Western world with her own

Above: *Paul McCartney is a leading voice in animal rights campaigning. Major companies with a questionable record of experimentation on captive creatures think twice before taking him on.*

Above: *Carla Lane at home.*
'Animals have pure and
innocent souls and
humans haven't,' she says.

brand of meatless meals. She's made a good start, with 50 million of the meals sold.

She says: 'I'm desperate about vegetarianism. We're all talking about a peaceful world and yet you can legally take a cow, a pig, a sheep and murder it.

'Now I think animals should have a little more dignity. I just don't believe in the word "slaughterhouse".

'It's an evil thing, like I think Hitler was an evil man, but we moved the people out and the chickens in.

'I just try and plant a seed. I do kiss people who eat meat. I have a lot of friends and relatives who eat meat and they're lovely people.'

Her tactics are to combine high-profile stunts – such as her letter to Australian prime minister and pig farmer Paul Keating – and the art of gentle persuasion, namely her vegetarian cookbook.

Of Keating Linda says: 'He's a pig farmer and I believe if you're going to lead a country you have to be a great person.

'So I sent him and his wife my cookbook and just mentioned that they might think and grow, that there might be a better way. I've probably bristled him, I'm sure they think "how dare she, more money than sense".'

The cookbook, she insists, isn't for vegetarians. It's to help convert long-standing meat eaters.

'I did it to say to the truck driver "You can eat great, I can make it easy for your wife".

'You can make a stew out of a veggie

burger, no gristle, no pain, no death, no fat.

'People ask where I get my strength if I don't eat flesh. I say, where do the elephant, the gorilla, the bull get their strength?

'They don't eat meat.'

One of Linda and Paul's closest allies is British playwright Carla Lane, author of hit TV comedies such as *The Liver Birds*, *Butterflies*, *Bread* and *Luv*.

She has carved out a hugely successful and lucrative career. Yet she has sworn to leave every penny of her wealth to the creatures she cares for at her £1.5 million sanctuary in the heart of the Sussex countryside.

That's good news for the likes of a one-winged heron, 800 birds, a blind hamster, a limping pheasant, 20 goats, 10 dogs, 15 cats and a field full of mud-caked ponies.

Carla, who runs the Animal Line organization – a telephone helpline for anyone looking after sick creatures – with Linda McCartney says: 'People might think I'm crazy.

'But animals have pure and innocent souls, and humans haven't.

'I have talked to my sons, Carl and Nigel, and told them that neither they nor their children will get any money – it will all go on the sanctuary.

'But they said "Mum, if that's what you're happy doing, it's fine with us." '

Carla's attempt to find havens for her animal friends extends to a tiny island off the north-west coast of Wales. She bought it in 1991 after hearing that the wildlife which lived there was dying.

She says: 'I went to see it two weeks after I bought it.

'All the animals had died. Others swam away. But one little deer swam back and gave birth on the island.

'When the baby was 4 months old we took it back to the mainland. We did the same the following year. And now there is a little herd of deer running amok somewhere around Abersoch.

'On the island itself we've got lots of little black rabbits which originated in the 12th century there. And we've got every bird you can possibly think of, and lots of lovely wild flowers.

'I've got a little croft on the island, but I never stay there because it's very steep and I'm very frightened of heights. I'm also frightened of water.

'How I came to buy an island I'll never know.'

> **'KEEP THE SEA BLUE, NOT RED.'**

Below: *Linda McCartney and Carla. Their Animal Line organization is aimed at giving practical advice to anyone caring for sick creatures.*

The British Homing World's
PIGEON RACING GAZETTE

NOVEMBER 1993

No. 11. Vol 49.

Price £1.20p

Peter Bennett

"Hillside Vend"

First Open N...

BIRDS OF A FEATHER

Birds of all feathers have captivated the human race for centuries with their lovely songs, their brilliant plumage and their fantastic powers of flight, but at times the relationship between people and their birds has had a deeper significance ...

In countryside and cities, on mountain ranges and throughout suburban towns, you never have to look far to 'watch the birdie'. The sound of a warbling song and the sight of a small feathered bundle hopping about without a care is one of the wonders of nature that each of us can enjoy, no matter where we live. And from the soaring flight of the magnificent eagle to the tiny, fluttering lark, birds have been a source of fascination for people throughout the centuries.

Legend has it that Icarus lost his life in his bid to mimic the flight of a bird, and no aircraft has yet managed to master the graceful skyward movements and aerobatic skills displayed by our feathered friends.

Even now these captivating creatures are the centre of interest for many, and that interest can sometimes border on obsession.

PIGEON POST

To the untrained eye pigeons may seem to proliferate in our capitals. To many they are simply a nuisance, but an expert will soon spot the aristocrat of the breed, a racer.

The world's most valuable pigeon cost £110,000 in 1992. British breeder Michael Massarella parted with the cash for Invincible Spirit, a pigeon who earned his colours by beating 27,000 other birds in the Barcelona International, one of the prestige races on the pigeon fanciers' calendar. He completed the 719-mile course in a mere 21 hours.

When it came to getting the bird from its base in Holland, however, the new owner decided against nature's way and in favour of new technology. Luxuriating in a first class seat, the pigeon was served a breakfast of maize, lettuce and mineral water in his posh travelling box.

After touchdown at Gatwick airport he was ferried by chauffeur-driven Rolls-Royce to his new home at Louella Pigeon World near Loughborough, Leicestershire, for a new life as a super stud.

For Mr Massarella there were no qualms about parting with the vast sum for a pigeon. At the time he said: 'We are absolutely delighted with him. We hope he will have many happy and productive years with us.'

It is not the first time he has shelled out big money for a cooing wonder. In 1988 he paid £77,000 for Champion Smaragd, then the world's most pricey pigeon. Pigeons like these can achieve breathtaking speeds. In 1914 a racing pigeon travelling over an 80-mile course in Northern Ireland flew at 93.55 mph.

But pigeon racing isn't only about skill

Above: Icarus tumbles from heaven after his wax wings are melted by the Sun. For thousands of years man has been captivated by the secret of flight.

Opposite: The Pigeon Racing Gazette – the pigeon fancier's Bible. Sums of up to £110,000 are paid for the right bird.

and speed. As with all things, luck plays its part. Scratch the wonder pigeon found that out.

He was one of 3,500 birds who set off on a race from the heart of France to their base in Britain, some 700 miles away. A cloak of thick fog over the English Channel together with some unseasonal storms sent the birds' homing mechanisms haywire and most of them ended up in Belgium. Scratch was the only bird to make it home to Yorkshire in time.

His astonishing success won him all 25 prizes which had been up for grabs – two trophies and a total of £600.

Above: *The Roman emperor Honorius was among the earliest pigeon fanciers.*

Right: *Not all pigeon lofts are wood shacks. This architectural masterpiece is in Cappadocia, Turkey.*

'I knew Scratch was good,' commented owner Alan Embleton, aged 15. 'But I never expected him to do this well.'

Eventually 29 other birds turned up but they were too late to be considered for the competition, held in July 1992.

Yorkshire pigeon official Peter Kerr was baffled. 'Thousands of pounds worth of prize-winning birds have disappeared off the face of the Earth.'

Sadly it is never easy for racing pigeons, who not only have extreme weather conditions to contend with but also high-sided lorries, birds of prey – and the neighbourhood moggies.

Fate dealt a cruel blow to prize pigeon Percy in the same month. Still puffing after finishing a race from France he was crunched by a cat called Sylvester. Dismayed owner Pat Lees, aged 55, said: 'I'd been waiting hours for him to turn up when this fat cat jumped out and grabbed him in its teeth.'

It took an hour and a half to snatch poor Percy from the jaws of the ginger tom, by which time he had died. But there was enough time to clock him in and win a posthumous third prize in the race.

When pigeon fancier Ken Warkup found a cat dining out on one of his prize birds he decided to take revenge. Unfortunately not only did the cat scupper one of his birds, it also landed him in court.

Enraged Ken stuffed the cat called Sam in a sack and dumped him in a field 12 miles away from home in Bridlington, Yorkshire. However, the cat was not to be outdone and found his own way home five months later looking rather sorry for himself. When Ken was quizzed by an officer from the Royal Society for the Prevention of Cruelty to Animals, he confessed.

Left: *This woodcut of 1523 shows men of a besieged city summoning help with carrier pigeons.*

Below: *A carrier pigeon with message case attached to its leg. The birds have even ferried ransom demands.*

In March 1992 he told magistrates: 'I've bred pigeons for 24 years and some of them are worth a lot of money. I don't want them ending up as cat meat.' After admitting a cruelty charge he was given a 12-month conditional discharge.

With their amazing ability to find a way home, it is not surprising that an enterprising villain seized on pigeon post as a way to cash in on crime. Taiwan police were left in a flap when the owners of stolen cars were told to cough up for the return of their missing motor.

The hapless victims were directed to a local park to find a bamboo bird cage and instructed to attach the ransom money in a pouch to the neck of the pigeon inside. When the bird was released, there was little the surveillance team could do other than watch helplessly through binoculars as the pigeon made a dash for home, soon lost from sight among buildings and trees.

It seems likely the person profiting from his pigeons was an armchair crook who didn't even bother to steal the car in the

first place. He simply seized on the names and numbers of genuine victims from the local newspapers. Police were convinced he was pulling off a hoax because none of the vehicles turned up despite the payments made by the owners.

Smart as he or she may have been, however, the money made out of the scam was only corn. The bird was unable to carry large amounts of cash because it would have been hampered by the weight.

Of course, it is not just in the present that people have discovered the uses of pigeons. Among the earliest domesticated birds, they were held sacred as long ago as 4500 BC in Mesopotamia and they were used to carry the results in the original Olympic Games to outlying villages. In 1150 the first pigeon post was set up by the sultan of Baghdad.

Initally brought to Britain by the

Top: *'Cher Ami' – saviour of US troops.*

Above: *GI Joe with the Dickin Medal.*

THE PLUCKY BIRD TOOK TO THE AIR AGAIN, DESPITE FOUR BULLET WOUNDS; THE SOLDIERS' LIVES DEPENDED ON HIM REACHING HIS DESTINATION.

Crusaders, pigeons were once the reserve of royalty, nobility and the clergy, and until two centuries ago usually ended up on the menu.

Then their uses, particularly in times of conflict, became clear.

The most famed homing bird of World War 1 was a cock named Cher Ami who was given the Croix de Guerre, a top French military honour. One of 500,000 birds brought to war-torn France by the American Expeditionary Force, he served with the infantry. On 4 October 1918, his battalion was being shelled by not only

enemy German guns but also American positions, in error.

With defeat and annihilation in prospect, the pigeon was sent back to base bearing the message: 'Our own artillery is dropping a barrage directly on us ... for heaven's sake stop it.'

But Cher Ami was unable to dodge the enemy fire. He was felled almost instantly by a bullet and plunged to the ground. In despair, an American yelled: 'Cher Ami, go home.' With that the plucky pigeon once again took to the air, suffered three more bullet wounds which destroyed his breast bone, right leg and one of his eyes, and flew an incredible 24 miles in 25 minutes to the division headquarters. The battalion was saved, thanks to this doughty winged messenger, who was taken back home to the US and survived until June 1919. After his death he was stuffed and put on display in Washington's Smithsonian Institute.

During World War 2 no fewer than 31 birds were awarded the Dickin Medal for bravery.

One of them, Mary, survived an attack by a hawk, enemy fire, a 1000 lb bomb which exploded outside her loft in Exeter and later, a gash which ran the length of her body. Still she refused to give up the fight for life and for her country.

Another, GI Joe, an American pigeon, carried a swift message to Air Command when they were about to bomb an enemy position telling them that their target had been taken by the Allies. A few moments later and countless soldiers would have been slaughtered by their own comrades.

The multi-talented pigeon has also been found to be an excellent quality inspector, turfing out plastic nuts and other components with defects in a British car factory production line, all for the reward of some grain. A Russian scientist discovered pigeons could classify up to 4,000 ball bearings an hour.

ROYAL RAVENS

The British royal family's interests lie not so much in pigeons but in ravens. Folklore says the Crown and Empire will fall if the sleek black ravens which make their home at the Tower of London disappear.

Just to be on the safe side, the raven

population which freely roams the grounds of the Tower by day has clipped wings to be sure they don't flee under cover of darkness. They are so tame they are whistled into bed by the Beefeaters.

Although the species has bred successfully in London for centuries, it is rare for the birds at the Tower to hatch eggs, probably because the mating ritual involves some airborne antics. Many there today were brought from sanctuaries as orphans from nests elsewhere. So it was with some excitement that fledglings were welcomed at the Tower in 1989, the first to be born there in 300 years.

A nesting box well away from the gaze of gawping tourists had been provided and five eggs duly appeared, thanks to Charlie and Rhys, two of eight birds permanently on the site. Due to overcrowding, the young ones were taken off to sanctuaries around the country, still the property of the queen and liable to be summoned at a moment's notice if duty calls.

A deputy governor, Colonel John Wynn, explains: 'Charles II wanted to get rid of hundreds that were around during his reign.

Left: *Charles II. He was advised against wiping out the hundreds of ravens in London. Was this the origin of the Tower legend?*

It is said that he was advised to keep some of the birds. The legend that the Crown and Empire will fall if the Tower loses its ravens may date from this incident.

'They are enormously popular with our visitors, particularly the children. Among the attractions, they come behind the Crown

Below: *A raven at the Tower of London. If the birds leave, according to legend, the monarchy will fall.*

THE JUDGE ORDERED THE ROWDY ROOSTER TO KEEP ITS BEAK SHUT UNTIL BREAKFAST TIME.

Jewels and equal with the instruments of torture, which is pretty high up.'

HENPECKED

When it comes to pets it is more likely that hens or ducks will rule the roost. Sometimes the bond between people and their feathered friends gets to be no yolk, as Cathy Brooks discovered. For Cathy, aged 28, isn't the only woman in her husband's life. She must vie for his affections with a hand-reared hen called Kiki and is one of Britain's few hen-pecked wives.

Husband Keith, aged 47, is so attached to the 7-year-old white hen Kiki that he lets her live a life of luxury in their three-bedroomed home in Canterbury, Kent, where she spends the night in her own chair in the kitchen and joins the family for meals at the dinner table.

Cathy says: 'Kiki was on the scene before I came along and Keith is very attached to her. He says she's almost human. I think she's just a bird that makes a mess on the carpet and goes for

your dinner when you are eating.'

Keith hatched out Kiki in an incubator. 'There was an immediate parental bonding and now she's absolutely one of the family.'

Kiki might be a bird with plenty of personality but she is a mere shadow of some of her bigger cousins bred in the USA. The largest chicken ever recorded was a 22 lb rooster called Weirdo in California. Born as a result of cross-breeding, he was also unusually aggressive and killed two cats, crippled a dog and ripped through a wire fence to maul another giant rooster. There was certainly no doubt cast on his sexuality.

But there have been cases of chickens changing sex and even cockerels laying eggs. The sex change is the result of a hormone imbalance which might rectify itself given time. To the disbelief of experts worldwide, Sri Lankan housewife Swarna Kulasiri reported that her lone cock in a 100-strong poultry run had begun to lay an egg a day. So perplexed was she by the amazing feat, she isolated the bird, which

Below: *Britain's most vocal cockerel, Corky, with his original owner Margery Johns. He would wake up at 3.30 am.*

Above: *Yagamo, 'the arrowed duck'. He became a huge crowd puller in Tokyo until he was captured in early 1993 to have the arrow removed. Vets found the plucky bird had also been wounded by shotgun pellets.*

retained its large comb and cock-a-doodle-do crow, and watched with her own eyes as he produced a large, brown egg.

While they may be able to switch sex, there seems little a cockerel can do about its morning call. British justice said differently when it pronounced a cockerel must keep its beak shut until breakfast time because of the disturbance he caused to neighbours.

Corky, the early riser, was the bird at the heart of a neighbourhood dispute which was eventually waged in court.

His owner, Margery Johns, of Hartland, north Devon, was fond of the 4-year-old rowdy rooster who serviced 14 hens at her home. But neighbour John Ritchings and his wife Lindsey were plagued by Corky's crowing, which they claimed began as early as 3.30 am. Former personnel director Mr Ritchings started keeping data on the cock-a-doodle-doos on his computer.

First he had a relocation order slapped on Corky, which had the bird ousted from his henhouse to a distant greenhouse. Then, when a noise prosecution against Mrs Johns and her bird brought by the local council failed, Mr Ritchings sought another court order, this time to stop Corky from disturbing the peace.

At Taunton County Court in March 1993, Mr Ritchings explained: 'The cock would wake us as early as 3.30 in the morning, most of the time with a quick burst. There would then be a peaceable period, another quick burst, another peaceful period and then at 5 or 7 am the crowing became almost continuous and it became very difficult to get any sleep.

'When nothing was done about the problem I began making a computerized database in which I made notes of the exact minute of Corky's crows and the effect it had on my sleep pattern.'

THE ANGLERS WERE HOPING FOR A NIBBLE – BUT ALL THEY GOT WAS A NASTY PECK.

Noise pollution inspector Christopher Utting agreed the crowing was too loud after becoming an early bird himself to measure the nuisance. But other villagers who had never complained about the fowl noise thought differently, believing townies were trying to remould the centuries-old traditions of the rural areas. A coachload travelled 60 miles to support Mrs Johns and Corky, claiming she had every right to keep farm animals in the countryside with all their attendant noises.

Judge Malcolm Cotterill didn't agree, however. He made a gagging order against Corky between the hours of midnight and 7 am. Mrs Johns – who said she might as well try to stop the traffic noise as prevent Corky from doing what came naturally – even tried soundproofing her henhouse. All to no avail. She was landed with costs amounting to some £20,000.

Judge Cotterill then made an appeal for calm in the tiny village. 'I regret the fact this case has been elevated to a crusade on behalf of oppressed chickens,' he announced.

Afterwards, Mrs Johns said: 'I feel there is an important principle involved. Country life is country life and to complain about a cockerel crowing is the thin end of the wedge.

'A mile away from us there is a farmer whose cows are being monitored for the noise they make. They're talking about smells now. They want to deodorize farmyards. Well, I would much rather smell cow muck than a London bus but you don't get country bumpkins moving to London and demanding that they stop the buses, do you?'

Corky was saved from exile by the offer of a new home from a farm-turned-tourist attraction in the vicinity where he could crow at all hours.

LUCKY DUCKS

Ducks, somewhat quieter creatures altogether, have also earned a special place in people's hearts, none more so than Donald, the lady duck mascot of the 2nd Gordon Highlanders who was captured during active service in World War 2 and held in a Japanese prisoner of war camp in Thailand. Usually all animals belonging to prisoners were destroyed, but duck master Corporal William Gray told the guards that Donald was a sacred bird, worshipped every morning by the company, as was common practice between men and ducks throughout their native Scotland.

By way of reward Donald during 18 months in captivity laid 163 eggs which were dished up to ailing internees. She returned to Scotland with Corporal Gray and spent the rest of her days in Forgue, Aberdeenshire.

The longest living ducks on record were a pair owned by Gladys Blackbeard of Cape Province, South Africa. Given to her by a soldier in 1917, they lived to celebrate their 49th birthday in June 1966. Ducks are normally dead at half that grand old age.

Perhaps the luckiest duck of all was Yagamo of Japan. The pintail duck was shot through the middle with a bow but survived even though the 30 cm pink carbon-fibre arrow which impaled his back protruded from his stomach. He walked and flew with ease and there was no sign of blood.

First spotted in January 1993, he was soon the centre of attraction for crowds of concerned on-lookers and a host of TV cameras and reporters. Yagamo – which means 'the arrowed duck' – wasn't struck on being a star.

He tried to elude the throngs by flying between ponds in the capital, Tokyo, until pleas for peace from zoo officials trying to catch the duck in order to remove the arrow had some effect. On 12 February he was netted and taken to Ueno Zoo where the arrow was taken out. X-rays revealed the bird also had two shotgun pellets lodged in its body but surgeons decided to leave them because of the danger of a prolonged operation. Eleven days after the operation Yagamo was released into the wild once more, ready to join the annual spring migration to Siberia.

RARE BIRDS

Canary Jimmy was not so lucky and succumbed to death back in 1920, but his owner, cobbler Edidio Rusomanno, fulfilled a promise to give his much loved pet a fabulous send-off. Jimmy's body was put in a fine white casket and carried by a hearse followed by two coaches and a 15-piece band to its final resting place in a local New Jersey park. Edidio wept in front of the 10,000 people who turned up for the event before returning to a slap-up feast at his shop.

Another pet bird, the budgerigar, has won the affection of dedicated owners everywhere, thanks to its curious ability to mimic language. Budgies originated in Australia but came to Britain back in 1840 with returning naturalist John Gould. Now there are probably more caged budgies than there are wild ones.

One of the world's longest surviving budgies was a hen called Charlie who died at her London home in June 1977 after living for more than 29 years. One of the strangest was Jenny, a budgie owned by June Lowton, of Nottingham, who refused to roost on her perch like others of her kind but snoozed flat out on the bottom of the cage with her feet stuck in the air, looking much as a dead budgie would.

Willy, a fly-by-night budgie, was the subject of one of the greatest fishermen's tales ever told. Three anglers spent hours waiting for a nibble as they bobbed about in the English Channel in the summer of 1991. In fact, they ended up getting a nasty peck.

Just as it seemed they were going to return home empty handed they caught – a budgie. The worn-out bird flopped down in the sea beside their boat and was netted by

Below: *Goldie the golden eagle. After his escape from Regent's Park Zoo in 1965 he stayed on the run for two weeks. He survived on food scraps and the odd juicy London duck!*

THE MIGHTY OWL
TERRORIZED LOCAL
RESIDENTS AND EVEN
DIVEBOMBED A
ROTTWEILER.

Below: *Ostriches can deliver a kick capable of killing ... they are also no mean soccer players.*

the three men, their only catch of the trip. He rewarded them for the free ride to terra firma with a series of sharp nips.

One of the men, Geoff Lowley, said: 'Our wives were expecting some nice plaice or skate for supper but they thought it was hilarious when all we came back with was a budgie.'

It's thought the bird escaped from a passing ship. Geoff adopted the little scrap, took him to his home in Torbay, Devon, and christened him Willy. Sadly, a photographer who came to snap the by-now famous flying catch propped open the door of the cage – and Willy proved he was the bird they could not tame by flying off into the sunset, never to be seen again.

A barred warbler caused just as much of a surprise when it turned up in Britain one December day. The ornithological rarity touched down in South Woodham Ferrers, Essex, in 1992 when it should, in fact, have been in Kenya escaping the winter chill of its East European home. Soon, avid bird-watchers – or twitchers as they are known – from all over the country gathered at the spot, but the warbler's first days in frosty Britain were also to be its last.

Local birdwatcher Ray Trevett explained: 'The county bird recorder came down and confirmed the sighting. Soon there were about 25 people here with cameras and binoculars. It was all fluffed up and survived two nights of heavy frost. It was hopping around happily.

'This large black cat had been patrolling around. Suddenly we noticed the bird wasn't in its tree. The cat appeared with the bird in its mouth. It scampered off and by the time we found the bird it had been decapitated.

'When I broke the news to the birdwatchers they were very upset. It was a major twitch.'

Another rare sight in British skies is the golden eagle. Once familiar over the country's mountain ranges, this magnificent bird of prey was blamed by farmers for early lamb deaths and was hunted, poisoned or trapped until numbers plummeted to crisis point. Only a carefully planned programme ensured its survival.

But residents of London who never would have dreamed an eagle would be swooping in the capital's skies had an unexpected treat in March 1965 when Goldie the golden eagle fled from his home in Regent's Park Zoo.

Crowds turned out to see the tawny hawk-like bird, some 3 ft tall, perched in tree tops above the park, causing traffic chaos. Goldie, meanwhile, was revelling in his newfound freedom, stretching his wings at will after being penned in for most of his seven years.

When keepers were unable to tempt him back, they confessed he could survive for years in the park, picking off ducks from the pond when he was hungry. Mostly, people were delighted he had escaped from the confines of the cage where he had been kept in captivity. In fact, he was recaptured after a fortnight, only to make a second bid for freedom some nine months later.

Thor, the European eagle owl, also caused a stir, this time in Nottingham in 1991 when he bowled over a man in the street. Thor fled his aviary home in Derbyshire when it was damaged in a storm.

The 2 ft tall bird with a wing span of 4 ft flattened woodyard worker Michael Barke, aged 23, as he made his way to work. Afterwards Mr Barke said: 'I was walking down the road when it came out of nowhere – it just went for me and headbutted me, I'm still shaking.'

During his brief spell of freedom before recapture, Thor alarmed local residents by peering in their windows at night. The mighty owl, the world's largest species, also divebombed a hefty Rottweiler dog.

The largest known bird in the world is the ostrich, which can reach 8 ft in height and weigh up to 300 lb. At a canter, the flightless bird can reach 30 mph and will deliver a hefty kick by way of attack. So imagine the surprise of brothers Nathan and Daniel Pedley when just such a bird joined in their game of football in the leafy and suburban environs of Stokenchurch, Buckinghamshire, in November 1989. The runaway bird – a rhea, which looks like an ostrich – niftily side-stepped the soccer-mad boys and pursuing police with some impressive dribbling skills. 'Unfortunately it was flattened later in a tackle by a car on the M40,' commented a police spokesman.

But mystery surrounds the allegation that a possibly larger breed, thought to be extinct, is actually surviving in New Zealand. Biologists thought that lanky moas died out at least 400 years ago.

Yet in January 1993 hotel owner and hiker Paddy Freaney and two companions saw a 6 ft tall bird with reddish-brown and grey feathers almost to its knees, a long neck and large feet hiding in a bush. As the creature fled across a stream, Freaney fired off a shot on his camera and also took photos of what he claimed were footprints.

At first the country's Department of Conservation was intrigued by the claims and the inconclusive photograph and considered a probe. But claims that Freaney was a publicity-seeking hoaxer persuaded them to ditch their plans. There

were allegations and counter-allegations about the authenticity of the photos and the witnesses. Even news that two German tourists had seen what they believed to be moas in the same region eight months prior to the incident failed to convince the authorities.

In fact, there have been alleged sightings of the distinctive bird throughout New Zealand's South Island during the past 100 years. Freaney responded to the government's lack of interest by launching his own investigation. It looks as if it is another enduring mystery of Yeti-sized proportions for humanity to ponder.

Above: *Goldie the golden eagle arrives safely back in the arms of his keeper. Yet just two weeks later he made another bid for freedom.*

SHAGGY DOG STORIES

Since the first dog came in from the wild night, tempted by the warmth of the campfire and the smell of roasting meat, the dog's loyalty, love and bravery has proved time and time again that he is indeed man's very best friend.

They're both hunter and bodyguard, sometimes lifesavers ... and always friends to the end.

Since their prehistoric ancestors *Tomarctus* first roamed the Earth some 15 million years ago, dogs have emerged as one of our most successful species.

That's partly because they carved out an early understanding with the dominant animal – man – so ensuring that while other beasts got left out in the cold, they had the chance of a bit of fire and a few scraps of meat.

In return those first 'pampered' pooches offered a whole range of services for their keep. The most basic was to give warning of an intruder's approach but their intelligence and obedience later marked them out as superb trackers and farm hands.

The relationship has developed to become unique in the animal kingdom. In terms of sheer devotion, bravery and love, no two other species come closer.

FAITHFUL FRIENDS

Take the Scottish terrier Greyfriars Bobby. In the mid-18th century he was the ever-present partner of a Midlothian landowner by the name of Gray and every market day they would stroll into Edinburgh to buy feed and pick up the weekly shopping.

Then, suddenly, Mr Gray was taken ill and died during one of the journeys. He was later buried in the nearby Greyfriars cemetery. In all the drama the fate of poor Bobby went unnoticed.

The morning after the funeral Bobby was found sitting on his master's grave. The churchwarden at first chased him away but after he persistently refused to leave his post, and when the rain and chilly weather left the lonely animal shivering, the warden took pity and tried to feed him.

Bobby quickly made it clear that sweet buns were the only food he fancied, and as word spread among the locals of his extraordinary loyalty he found there was never any shortage of snacks.

Some people tried to adopt him, but he never would stay, always preferring the grave of the only man he loved. So the people clubbed together to build him a small kennel there. Such was his celebrity status that the lord provost of Edinburgh presented him with his own collar, inscribed 'Greyfriars Bobby'.

Opposite: *Greyfriars Bobby.*

Below: *The world's first scuba-diving dog, Mutley, with his American owner Gene Alba. Mutley also liked skiing and motorbike rides.*

THE FAITHFUL FIDO NEVER GAVE UP HOPE THAT ONE DAY THE MASTER HE LONGED TO SEE WOULD RETURN.

Below: *Rally, the radio-controlled police dog, was trained from the age of 3 months to recognize commands over a walkie-talkie. Japanese police use him on mountain rescue work.*

Bobby at last joined his old master in 1872 and of course there could be no argument about where he should be buried. He even had a statue erected on the streets he'd known so well.

Amazingly, such devotion is not particularly unusual. During the war a little Italian mongrel called Fido was left desolate when his master died in a bombing raid in Florence. The pair of them had lived in a village just outside the town and every evening at the same time it was Fido's habit to trot down and meet the bus.

Even when it was clear to everyone else that the dog's master had died, Fido never gave up hope. For an incredible 15 years he continued to lope down to the bus stop to check the faces of the returning commuters in case he recognized the one he longed to see.

In 1958 the villagers of Borgo San Lorenzo put up a memorial to their favourite mongrel and decided the mayor should give him a specially struck gold medal. But just as the beaming burgher prepared to hang it round Fido's neck, the dog raced off.

For a few moments there was alarm and puzzlement among the crowd. Had they scared the little dog? Why was he so desperate to run away? Then someone checked a watch and realized the obvious.

It was time for the bus.

Japan has a similar story of a dog called Hachiko who would walk with his owner to the railway station every day. But one evening his master, a lecturer at Tokyo University, died of a heart attack at work.

Hachiko may have pined, but he never gave up hope. Every day until his death in 1935 he went to the station at his usual time to meet the incoming train.

By then he was almost a national hero, with schools across the nation receiving mini-replicas of him. His face even adorned a postage stamp.

PUPPY-LOVE

The love-bond is something bitches with pups know all about. One of the saddest stories illustrating this is told in Northern Ireland where a retriever gave birth to an unwanted litter. The owner destroyed them

at birth, put them in a weighted sack and drove to a lake some 15 miles away, where he hurled the lifeless bodies into the middle.

The bitch was not allowed out of the house for two weeks but on the day the door was opened for her she dashed off and vanished. The man tracked her down 48 hours later to the same lake, where she was swimming around the spot where her puppies lay. She was close to death herself – physically drained by the effort of constant swimming – and her owner was so appalled at what he'd put her through that he vowed he would never again put down another puppy.

There are happier accounts of mother-love in dogs, however. In the spring of 1977 a mongrel called Beauty and her pup found themselves trapped after exploring a deserted house in Worcestershire, central England. For three days the two dogs were left without any food or water and Beauty finally made the decision it was down to her to save herself and her puppy.

Incredibly she squeezed into the bottom of a 45 ft chimney and slowly and painfully wriggled her way up to the top, where she emerged barking loudly enough to bring passers-by running.

On seeing the soot-covered dog it was clear she was raising the alarm and emergency services were called to break into the house. Beauty and her pup were reunited, much to the joy of themselves and their owners. They had apparently begun their adventure after squeezing through a hole in their fence at home.

If Beauty's feat was remarkable, the rescue performed by one bitch with new-born pups was nothing short of a miracle of nature. According to a story in the former *Bath Journal* her heartless owner decided the runt of her four pups should be destroyed. The pitiful animal was hurled into a bucket of water and held down with a mop for a few minutes. The body was then chucked into the ashes box of a fire.

The following morning a dumbstruck servant discovered the bitch still had four, very much alive, puppies. At first he thought another had simply arrived late … then he checked the ashes box and discovered the dead pup's body was missing.

Incredibly its mum had scrabbled through the cinders and placed the little one back with its brothers and sisters. Milk, warmth and love had done the rest.

Above: *Eyes for the blind; guide dog training is one of the most effective ways to help blind people lead a normal life. Gentle Labradors are the perfect breed.*

GASSED, SHOT AND BATTERED, THE DOG COWERED IN THE SHED, TOO TERRIFIED TO EVEN WHIMPER.

HOUNDED

It's hard to believe man's best friend gets treated in this way and when cases of cruelty hit the headlines the public's outrage knows no bounds. If the guilty parties are featured in the press they can usually rest assured that whatever they did to a dog, around ten million dog lovers are queuing up to do it to them.

The classic example of such sentiments happened in July 1973 when a lovable young beagle cross named Dumpy was unfortunate enough to be seen by the local dog catcher roaming the streets of Salem, Ohio. He was grabbed and bundled into the back of the man's van to be gassed en route to the nearest rubbish tip.

On arrival the catcher threw Dumpy's lifeless body in front of the nearest bulldozer. But to his astonishment the tough little critter began hauling himself out of the sodden trench to escape the huge vehicle bearing down on him.

Immediately the dog catcher squeezed off four bullets, hitting the beagle once in the leg and chest. It wasn't enough to stop Dumpy, who somehow drew on enough strength to keep going.

By now the bulldozer operator, a man called James Gilbert, had halted and leaped down from his cab intent on stopping what he saw as outrageous cruelty. He pleaded with the warden to go after the dog and put him out of his misery but the man refused point-blank. He said he might get his clean boots dirty and Gilbert shouldn't worry – the animal was at death's door anyway.

Gilbert was so traumatized by what he'd witnessed that he ran to telephone a couple of friends, asking them if they could find the dog and ensure it didn't suffer. Jean Fluharty and Joyce Guiler answered the call and in the teeming rain began searching for Dumpy by torchlight. They at last found him sheltering in a shed, too terrified even to whimper.

Later Jean said: 'Every hair on that dog was on end. He was scared to death after all that had happened to him … his eyes were glazed … and he was nothing but mud and blood. He didn't try to bite us, he just didn't make a sound.'

The women took Dumpy – their choice of name – to a local vet who was astounded the animal was still breathing. He patched him up as best he could and amazingly the gallant dog made a full recovery.

Within days of the story getting out hundreds of requests had been fired off from the folk of Salem to give Dumpy a good, caring home. And that's exactly what he got, along with larger than usual amounts of comforting and spoiling.

But what of the dog catcher? Like all the best stories in life, this one ends on a note of justice.

His municipal employers suspended him pending an investigation. This, however, was not enough for the dog lovers of Salem. They began sending threatening letters advising that if they got hold of the man he could expect similar treatment to that Dumpy received. Police had no doubt the threats were serious and the hapless warden was given police protection and advised to be careful in all his movements.

Clearly his life in Salem was untenable. Within months he decided his job wasn't worth the candle and he packed his bags to begin a new life well out of town.

It was, as they say, the right result. And Dumpy remains one of the few hounds in history ever to have driven a dog warden out of business.

DOG-GONE!

Surviving against the odds was also a speciality of a long-haired dachshund called Maxi. He managed to keep himself going for six tortuous weeks in the world's driest place – Chile's Atacama Desert.

In 1977 he visited the area with his owner, a German press attaché called Raban von Mentzingen, who was touring the El Salvador copper mine with his wife and children. The mine was in the heart of the desert and among the country's wildest places.

The Von Mentzingens were paying a final sightseeing visit before their transfer back to Bonn and when Maxi strayed they couldn't wait for him to be found. So local police were given instructions to keep an eye out for him in the hope he could be re-united with the family later.

After a month, all hope faded. Police assured Mr von Mentzingen, by now back in Germany, that his pet could not have survived without food or water in temperatures which could fry bacon in the day and drop below freezing at night.

Then, in March of that year, a Chilean mineral prospector saw the unlikely sight of a long-haired dachshund half-crawling along a sun-parched hillside track 48 miles from the El Salvador mine. Maxi was rescued, flown to Santiago for veterinary treatment and from there was sent on to Germany for a rapturous welcome from his family.

To this day, no one has ever explained how a domestic animal with no experience of hunting (and indeed hardly any food to hunt) managed to survive.

Other fantastic feats to match Maxi's include that of a mongrel called Cindy from San Leandro, California. She was in her owner's car when it was stolen from Stateline, Nevada, on 28 September 1972. Owners Mr and Mrs Ernest Nechvatal sadly gave their pet up for lost. Yet in fact the thieves seem to have returned their car – with Cindy in it – to exactly the same spot after only a few days.

The poor animal was only discovered much later after snowploughs moved in to clear away heavy falls in the area. A workmen found Cindy looking painfully thin, but still alive, on the seat. Her usual weight of 30 lb had been cut by almost half but she had given herself a chance by licking snow that dropped through the slightly open window of the car.

Vets estimated that she had gone without food for up to 73 days.

On a similar note, spare a thought for an Italian wire-haired pointer called Reno. He was trapped under the rubble left by an earthquake in the south of the country for 43 days, finally getting rescued when his owner returned to her devastated home to hear him barking. He had kept alive by drinking rainwater.

A couple of Welsh Jack Russells went through similar ordeals. The first, Judy, spent 36 days trapped down a deep rabbit hole in Builth Wells. She was fortunate enough to have an 11-year-old owner who refused to give up hope and on one of his walks over the land where she was last seen he suddenly heard her bark coming from deep underground. Judy was dug out, emaciated but full of licks, and lived to tell the tale.

The second dog, Sam, got himself trapped inside a Gwent quarry for more than two weeks. He was finally reached by cavers but only after 100 tons of rock had been removed to create a 40 ft tunnel in an operation costing well over £1,000.

Then there was a Jack called Jane (if you follow), found by a poultry worker who'd sent his ferret down a hole to catch a rat. The ferret came back with a nasty bite on the nose that was clearly no rat bite – faint barks coming from below testified to that.

It took an hour to dig Jane out, putting an end to her 27 days without food or water in her deep, dark prison.

THE DOG HAD BEEN MISSING FOR **36** DAYS BUT HER YOUNG OWNER CONTINUED SEARCHING FOR HER.

Below: *Really, it's the only way to travel. This mutt in Redondo Beach, California, helps brighten the day for drivers stuck in jams. No other two species are as close as humankind and dogs.*

Above: *The memorial to Barry the St Bernard in Asnieres Cemetery, Paris. His skill and courage saved the lives of 40 people.*

In 1989 truck driver Ray Ashworth actually consulted a medium to discover the fate of his missing terrier Nipper. The little dog had been a passenger in Ray's parked car when it was snatched by joy riders. The car was found but Nipper was nowhere to be seen.

The psychic assured Ray he'd be reunited with his pet within 12 hours. It was a remarkable prediction ... for within three hours a 10-year-old girl rang him to say she'd picked up Nipper in a local park.

HAIRY HEROES

The cases of humans rescuing dogs and dogs rescuing humans seem to occur with roughly equal frequency. But perhaps the most famous and successful on the canine side are St Bernards, who over the years have been credited with saving the lives of more than 2,500 climbers and walkers stranded in the Alps.

They are particularly good at tracking and can scent out a live human being even if he or she is buried beneath 10 ft of snow. Their other mysterious talents include early warning of an avalanche, and of a blizzard approaching.

Among this much loved breed a dog called Barry, of the Hospice du Grand St Bernard in Switzerland, stands out as the most celebrated of all. In his career on the slopes he saved more than 40 lives, including that of a little boy stranded unconscious on an icy precipice after his mother was submerged by an avalanche.

Barry licked the youngster back to life, then persuaded him to climb up on his back for the treacherous journey back to the hospice.

When Barry at last became too old to perform his duties, the gallant hound was pensioned off to a good home in Berne, where he lived out his days in comfort until his death in 1814. His body was later stuffed and mounted and displayed in the Swiss Natural History Museum.

In Wales too, St Bernards have a reputation unmatched by any other breed. During one particularly cold winter, in 1981, a sheep farmer in the South Wales mountains discovered scores of his new-born lambs had been buried in deep snow. A dog called Bruno was brought in and promptly sniffed out 83 of them where the farm's Welsh collies had failed.

Yet there is an exception to every rule and in the case of the St Bernards the exception is a dog called George.

Where his breed made its name through efficiency, reliability and common sense, George excelled in being scatterbrained, stupid and generally clueless when out on a mission. His mountain rescue bosses finally lost patience when he was brought in to help track down two missing climbers and got himself detached from the main party.

Two hours later he still hadn't turned up and the rescuers had to locate the mountaineers on their own. They returned to base to find there was still no sign of the dog and a new search was mounted ... this time for George. It took them three hours to trace him and afterwards the rescuers were insistent: George would have to go. He'd got himself lost eight times in two years and in their neck of the woods they didn't need that kind of practice.

In Britain dogs served with great distinction during the last war and in 1943 Mrs Maria Dickin, founder of the People's Dispensary for Sick Animals, decided they should have their equivalent of the Victoria Cross, the nation's most prized medal.

First to be awarded the Dickin Medal was a cross-bred Labrador called Bob. His citation covered his immense skill and judgement in preventing an entire patrol of the Queen's Own Royal West Kent Regiment from being wiped out during a night operation in North Africa in January 1943.

Bob was leading the men near Green Hill but suddenly froze in his tracks, warning that the enemy was close by. The unit waited, but could hear nothing, and the commanding officer decided to move on. Bob refused to obey the order (an action that was technically a court martial offence) and the men again waited.

Then enemy movement was sighted and the patrol retreated safely without any casualties. Had they carried on they would have walked straight into enemy fire.

Strangely, Bob never returned to take the plaudits in Britain. In 1946 he was heading home through Milan airport but suddenly slipped his collar and went AWOL. He was never seen again, despite the best efforts of the War Office, who posted his description throughout Italy. In the end Bob's medal was collected by his owner, CQMS Cleggatt.

Of all the Dickin medallists none was better known than Judy, a pointer bitch born in Shanghai, who remains the only dog ever to be registered as an official prisoner of war.

Judy had served aboard a few Royal Navy gunboats in the Far East before being posted to HMS *Grasshopper* in 1942 as official mascot.

She saw action throughout the Malaya and Singapore campaigns and after the fall of Singapore found herself heading towards Java to await a supply ship rendezvous. However *Grasshopper* was bombed by the Japanese and forced to run aground, still blazing, on an uninhabited island. There she blew up, leaving the entire crew stranded.

From here on Judy's story reads like a script from some unlikely Hollywood war movie. She started by saving the lives of the sailors by discovering a fresh-water spring several miles up the seashore.

A few days later the castaways succeeded in commandeering a Chinese junk and a party set sail for Sumatra with the intention of organizing the rescue of their shipmates. Judy, of course, was on board.

But soon after landing they were caught by the Japanese and interned at a makeshift PoW camp at Medan. It was there that Judy was introduced to one Leading Aircraftsman Frank Williams, who shared his paltry rice rations with her. They quickly became the firmest of friends and Judy repaid the kindness she was shown

Above: Judy, the only official dog prisoner of war. Her war against the Japanese reads like a Hollywood script.

THE LABRADOR FROZE IN HIS TRACKS AND REFUSED TO BUDGE.

**THE SADISTIC COMMANDANT
ORDERED THE PRISONERS TO
KILL AND EAT THEIR PET.**

Right: *Sheila, the border
collie from England's wild
Northumbrian hills, remains
the only civilian dog to hold
the Dickin Medal. She
fought her way through a
blinding snow storm to
rescue the US crew of a
crashed Flying Fortress
plane.*

many times, alerting Allied prisoners to poisonous animals such as snakes and scorpions ... as well as any Japanese guards that just happened to be snooping about.

Perhaps it was because she boosted morale so much that she infuriated the camp commandant. He tried to have her destroyed but with a mixture of superb diplomacy and bare-faced cheek LAC Williams contrived to get her registered as an official PoW.

Not to be outdone, the commandant ordered that Judy should stay at his camp after receiving orders that the rest of her comrades were to be shipped from Sumatra to Singapore. But again his wishes were defied and the plucky little pointer was smuggled aboard the prisoners' ship in a rice sack.

The following day the ship was torpedoed by the Allies and Judy was separated from her new master. But a miraculous twist of fate ensured that within three days they were back together at another prison camp.

After a tumultuous week LAC Williams and Judy could have been forgiven for trying to take a breather and simply gather their senses.

It was not to be. Their new commandant turned out to be the self-same thug they'd encountered at Medan. And, sure enough, one of his first orders was that Judy should be killed and eaten by the British prisoners by way of some unspecified punishment.

More than likely, this command was thought up as a twisted brand of revenge for Japan's imminent humiliation at the hands of the Americans. Fortunately it was never carried out. Judy was taken into hiding and the Japanese guards were too petrified of what would happen to them come the liberation of PoWs even to mount a search.

After the war Judy was brought back to England to receive her Dickin Medal. Her master got the White Cross of St Giles, the highest honour bestowed by the PDSA, in recognition of his courage in standing by Judy in some of her darkest hours.

He later revealed one touching story of her time as a PoW. She found an elephant's shin bone, still meaty, and decided Christmas and her birthday must have come along together. According to one

witness it was bigger than her and weighed far too much for her to carry properly. Yet in the best hound dog tradition she did manage to bury it ... even though it took her two laborious hours.

Only one civilian dog ever won the Dickin Medal – a young collie called Sheila owned by Northumberland shepherd John Dagg. She ventured out with him in a blinding snowstorm to track down and rescue the four-man crew of an American Flying Fortress which crashed in December 1944.

But in fact civilian disasters have provided ample opportunities down the centuries for humble hounds to shine out suddenly as heroes.

In one case, in 1919, the coaster *Ethie* was cruising off the coast of Nova Scotia when she ran into rocks in heavy seas. The mountainous waves washed all the lifeboats overboard and prevented rescuers from getting anywhere close. One man, who fancied himself a powerful swimmer, had already died in a futile attempt to swim for the shore.

Then Tang, a Newfoundland dog who bellyflopped straight into the treacherous seas, stepped forward and boldly struck out for the shore carrying a light line.

Joyful hands pulled him to safety, a hawser was fixed to the line and minutes later the ship's hands were pulling it back and preparing a breeches buoy to take all 92 passengers and crew to safety. Even a baby was rescued, winched ashore in a mailbag.

Tang later received a medal for meritorious service from Lloyd's Insurance House of London, which he displayed proudly on his collar until the end of his days.

More than 100 years earlier a Newfoundland's swimming ability may actually have changed the course of history. In 1815 Napoleon was being smuggled out of exile on Elba to return to his beloved France. But he slipped on a rock as he prepared to board.

Panic set in (he was a hopeless swimmer) and as he splashed about helplessly his aides dashed hither and thither trying to spot him.

Eventually he was saved by a giant Newfoundland which plunged into the waters, grabbed the emperor by his shirt collar and towed him to waiting boatmen. Without that dog's actions there may well have been no return for Napoleon ... and no battle of Waterloo.

The undisputed Mark Spitz of the canine kingdom though must surely be the appropriately named Neptune, a Newfoundland which was one among hundreds then carried by vessels as ever-ready life-savers. Neptune's ship was being towed up the Mississippi en route to New Orleans when it lurched violently, toppling the dog ignominiously into the river.

The captain was distraught to see his faithful hound left in the river but had no way to stop his ship without the help and co-operation of the skipper up front. He tearfully watched Neptune attempting to keep up with the two boats but eventually he began to fall back and soon disappeared from sight altogether. The captain comforted himself with the knowledge that Neptune would surely swim ashore and be picked up by some other salty types in need of his services.

He was wrong. Far from swimming ashore, Neptune kept on course along the Mississippi. Three days later, to his old shipmates' total amazement, he waltzed onto deck as though nothing was amiss.

He'd tracked them an incredible 50 miles, swimming against the current to New Orleans, and then somehow climbed the supply ships berthed around his own.

Neptune's achievement lay as much in his sense of smell as in his strength. Dogs are thought to have an olfactory system more than a million times more sensitive than humans – hence the achievements of St Bernards in the snow.

ROVING ROVERS

This is one explanation for some of the extraordinary distances a pet will travel to find an owner who has gone missing. But it is not always enough. Some scientists

Below: *Doug Sampson and his amazing German shepherd bitch Nick. She crossed snowbound mountains and deserts to get back to him.*

THE COLLIE WAS DETERMINED TO HAVE A DAY OUT IN LONDON – AND HE PREFERRED TO TRAVEL BY COACH.

Right: *Yorkshire terrier Thumbelina was officially declared the world's smallest adult dog in 1993. What she lacks in size, she makes up for in beauty.*

believe animals may use some sort of navigation system based on the stars, though how they do it is a total mystery.

In 1923 a legendary collie called Bobbie was lost by his master during a holiday in Walcott, Indiana. Six months later Bobbie showed up at the family house in Silverton, Oregon, after travelling a distance of around 2,000 miles. When publicity on his journey leaked out many householders along the route stepped forward to say that they had seen Bobbie and offered him food and water. It was soon obvious that he had travelled through Illinois, Iowa, Nebraska and Colorado before negotiating the Rockies in the middle of winter and reaching home via Wyoming and Idaho.

Since then records show at least two German shepherd dogs have drawn on equally amazing homing instincts. The first, a bitch called Nick, was stolen while she and her master Doug Simpson were on a camping holiday in southern Arizona. After two weeks of looking for her a distraught Doug had to go home to Pennsylvania. By now heavy snow was blocking the mountain passes yet Nick had already disengaged herself from her captor and was homeward bound.

She eventually made it, successfully navigating both the Arizona Desert and the Grand Canyon, and turned up four months later at her master's car parked at his parents' house in Selah, Washington.

She'd sustained nasty wounds, and a poor diet had left her almost unrecognizable, but Nick later made a full recovery.

The second German shepherd to hit the headlines in a similar way managed a slight variation on the theme. Jessie decided she didn't want to move from her home in Rhode Island to Colorado. Hardly had her owner, Dexter Gardiner, finished arranging his furniture than Jessie pelted off and never looked back. She had apparently been pining for the rest of Dexter's family and the friendly dog next door.

The dog-homing phenomenon is also well documented in Australia. A little fox terrier called Whisky managed a 1,700-mile trek from Hayes Creek, south of Darwin, to Mambury Creek 150 miles north of Adelaide. And a labrador cross called Jimpa turned up at his old home in Pimpinio, Victoria, after a 2,000-mile hike across the nation's inhospitable central plains. It took him well over a year and how he ever survived remains a mystery.

Among the most sensible of all rovers was a British cross-bred collie called Spot who seemed to have an ambition to see the bright lights of London. In March 1983 he hopped on a National Express coach at Cardiff, refusing the driver's insistent

requests to leave, and curled up on a front seat to sleep out the journey.

On arrival at London's Victoria coach station he cleaned himself up and jumped off for a look round. That was the last the driver thought he'd see of Spot … until the canny animal turned up a few hours later, just as the coach was about to begin the return leg of its 150-mile trip. At Cardiff Spot was taken in by the RSPCA and later claimed by his speechless owners.

There is little doubt, though, of the most travelled dog, not counting of course the 40 or so animals zoomed into outer space aboard the first experimental rockets. The terrestrial accolade has to go to a scruffy mongrel called Owney, who was said to have travelled well over 200,000 miles, both on land and sea, in his much vaunted career.

The Chinese have a saying that every great journey must begin with a small step and so it was for Owney when he padded in to a post office in Albany, New York, in 1888.

He was quickly adopted by the employees, who indulged his favourite pastime of riding on top of mailbags as they were ferried to the local railway depot. One day Owney decided it was time he stretched himself a little more, so he boarded a mail train for New York City. That was just the start.

In the years that followed Owney was a regular sight on trains as they criss-crossed the country. His old friends at Albany couldn't help worrying about him, though, so they attached a tag to his collar asking clerks along the route to fix metallic baggage labels to his collar so that a full record could be kept of his travels.

Owney picked up so many tags that a special jacket was made for him to display them on. He received it from the Postmaster General during a visit to Washington and became so proud of his flashy coat that anyone who touched a tag got an ominous growl for his trouble.

As the years slipped by Owney notched up Canada and Mexico, but the unique highlight of his life was a round-the-world trip set up for him by postal workers at Tacoma, Washington.

From that city Owney called at Yohohama, Shanghai, Woosung, Foochow, Hong Kong, Singapore, Suez, Algiers and the Azores before making it back to New

York and the commuter train back to Tacoma.

Throughout this time he was welcomed everywhere he went. Railmen regarded him as a lucky omen for no train that carried him ever encountered a mishap.

But as with all travelling there is an element of danger and Owney's own luck ran out on 11 June 1897.

By then he was well into old age and able to eat only the softest of foods and water, but he still managed the occasional railcar ride and on that day had taken the

Above: *You've seen them scuba-diving and motorbiking. Now meet the original jet-skiing Alsatian!*

Above: *Billy the champion ratter. In 1825 he caused a sensation in the rat-pits of London, killing 4,000 vermin in 17 hours. In his heyday he was supposed to have despatched one rat every 3.24 seconds.*

train to Toledo. No one ever gave a clear account of exactly what happened but it appears Owney suddenly became 'ill-tempered' while being introduced to a local journalist. Perhaps the man touched one of his 1,017 tags and tokens. Or perhaps, like many stars before and since, Owney just didn't like the press.

Either way the much loved mongrel was shot and killed with a single bullet. His body was later stuffed and exhibited in Washington DC's Smithsonian Institute.

Britain's answer to Owney was a fox-terrier called Jack. And what he lacked in distance travelled, he made up for in social climbing.

Such was his fame that in 1883 he was presented to the then prince and princess of Wales, one of only a handful of mutts to be honoured by an official visit from royalty.

Jack's train-hopping life was centred on the Sussex town of Lewes in southern England. From here he would explore the whole south-eastern rail network, though

he was particularly partial to the now defunct Brighton and Horsham line.

In 1881 the *Illustrated Sporting and Dramatic News* reported a typical day in Jack's life: 'He arrived from Brighton by train, reaching Steyning at 10.50 where he got out for a minute but then went on by the same train to Henfield. Here he popped in to a public house not far from the station where a biscuit was given to him and after a little walk he took a later train to West Grinstead where he spent the afternoon, returning to Brighton in time for the last train to Lewes.'

Jack sported a silver-plated collar inscribed 'I am Jack, the London, Brighton and South Coast Railway Dog. Please give me a drink and I will then go home to Lewes.' He appears to have taken his semi-official status very seriously. On the day of the funeral of the Eastbourne station inspector Jack turned up by train and followed the hearse to the cemetery. He even walked to the graveside to pay his last respects.

The little dog's exploits brought him

close to death himself. On one occasion he wandered on to the line at Norwood Junction, south London, and was hit by a train which crushed one of his front legs. Railmen who saw the accident rushed him onto a fast train to Lewes where two vets were forced to amputate his useless leg. But it didn't stop his travelling and he got about on three legs just as well as on four.

Jack eventually retired at the same time as the Lewes stationmaster and joined him to live at Mayfield in Sussex. But the two of them would still make the occasional journey – first class of course.

Yet occasionally Jack would creep back to his favourite spot: nothing, it seemed, could match the comfort of the guard's van.

SHAGGY DOG STORIES

His fame among the dogs of 19th-century England was probably matched only by an animal of doubtful parentage who became the nation's champion ratter.

Billy, who weighed in at 26 lb, would compete in rat-killing matches and apparently won his first ten contests with such ease it became almost boring for the bloodthirsty spectators.

In 1825 he was reported to have despatched 4,000 rats in just 17 hours, an incredible achievement considering he was blind in one eye. Other claims made for him include the killing of 100 rats in 5½ minutes, although this particular exhibition was not covered by a later rule prohibiting dog handlers from touching either dog or rats.

Billy was even said to have notched up 1,000 rats in 54 minutes, though this was surely an exaggeration considering that he'd have had to kill an average of one every 3.24 seconds. In those days one kill every 5 seconds was considered champion form.

Even in his old age Billy could still draw a crowd to a rat pit. At 10 years old he outshone a younger rival by sending 100 rats to meet their maker in 8 minutes 54 seconds. The younger dog took 12 minutes to accomplish the same task.

Tales of dogs as killing machines are legion. In both Europe and the US much has been made of the ferocity of pit bull terriers, trained to savage each other.

Certainly one family from Devon, England, learned to their cost the savagery of a pit bull. It went berserk and wrecked their home after being stung by a wasp. The dog, Smudge, caused around £1,000 damage by tearing apart furniture, smashing windows and chewing through a door. One vet called to calm the dog said later: 'It looked like a hostage shootout, as if the SAS had been in there.'

Not all reputations stand up to the test, however. In 1990 a British Rottweiler called Rossita, on a diet because she was failing to impress show judges, tried to steal the family rabbit's carrot lunch.

The rabbit, aptly called Rambo, took exception and turned on the terrified hound, seeing her off with a lacerated nose, cuts and bruises ... and a severely damaged ego.

THE PIT BULL WENT BERSERK WHEN IT WAS STUNG BY A WASP.

Below: *Police super-dog Trep. Cadets at a training school were once told to hide ten packets of marijuana for him to track down. Trep found 11.*

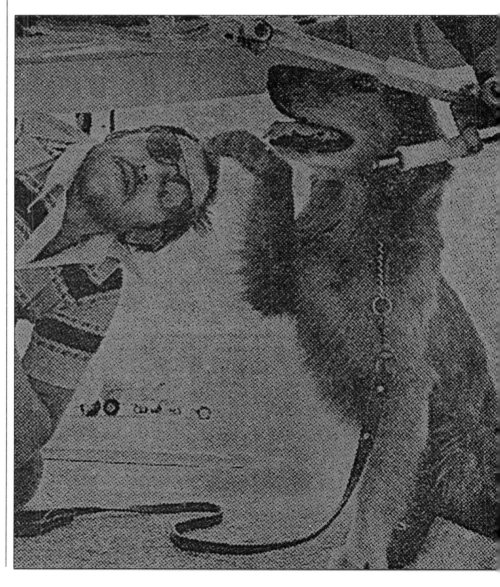

THE TRAIL WAS 8 YEARS OLD – BUT THE DOG SNIFFED OUT THE MURDERER WITH EASE.

Talking of doggie egos, a 15-year-old mongrel called Ari actually sued the American airline USAir for allegedly causing him to circle pointlessly around a baggage claim carousel while his owner had vanished into thin air.

Ari's owner was a lawyer, who immediately slapped in a $60,000 compensation demand for the temporary loss of his best friend. The writ was filed in the dog's name but kicked out on the orders of a judge who ruled that dogs were not American citizens.

Other legal firsts include the case of a poodle who sought registration, via her owner, for Abbey National plc shares. The bank turned the mutt down on the grounds she was only a trustee account holder.

Then there was the Surrey sheep farmer who bought a pedigree Welsh collie only to find it had been taught in Welsh and didn't understand his commands. He tried to persuade his local trading standards department to sue … but the case never got off the ground.

Some dogs, like humans, just seem to be born lucky. One Italian Alsatian, Gunther, was actually left £65 million by his owner and ended up getting begging letters from cash-strapped soccer clubs.

But others have to work for a living and what could be more satisfying than a job with the police?

Duke, the first guard dog to work for the Metropolitan Police in London, seemed set for a distinguished career – until he found himself fingered. For weeks there had been a series of thefts from handbags in the typing pool at Brixton nick and an insider was suspected. Then one typist noticed Duke nosing about in her bag and his dirty deeds were exposed.

Many mutts, though, do serve with flying colours. Some breeds with a particularly sensitive sense of smell are much sought after as crimefighters. For them, the trail of a crook can last weeks or even years.

A German shepherd delightfully named Harass II offers perfect proof of this. On 19 January 1974 the body of an unknown woman was found in scrubland close to the Kennedy Space Center near Titusville, Florida. For years dozens of leads were followed without success but on 22 July 1982 fresh information emerged and a suspect was pulled in.

Murder squad detectives tried to break him down without success. Believing they'd got their man, but unsure how to proceed, they called in Harass as a last-shot attempt to see if he could turn anything up. He was given some clothing owned by the suspect to sniff and about half a mile from where the woman's body was found, Harrass picked up a trail. He led police to a different spot and the officers concluded this must have been where the murder actually took place.

They returned to the suspect armed with this new information. Convinced they must have a strong case against him he admitted his crime and made a full confession.

The time between murder and tracking was an incredible eight years, six months and three days.

Among many other famous police dogs special credit must go to a drug sniffing specialist called Trep.

On his first assignment in Florida he was being taken to sniff around a boat at Fort Lauderdale when he suddenly made a break for it and headed for a racing sloop that had already been painstakingly hand searched four times by agents. Trep boarded the vessel and located $2.5 million worth of hashish (1973 prices) hidden in a false wall.

This animal later went on to break new legal ground when a judge issued him with a search warrant to check out a house where drugs had earlier been identified. The police found a massive hoard of marijuana inside.

But Trep's best-known – and best-loved coup – came when he visited a police academy to show off his skills. His handler gave cadets marijuana to hide anywhere they wished on the premises. Ten packets were handed out. Trep found eleven.